NORTH FROM THE BATTERY, UP THE EAST RIVER TO EAST 80s

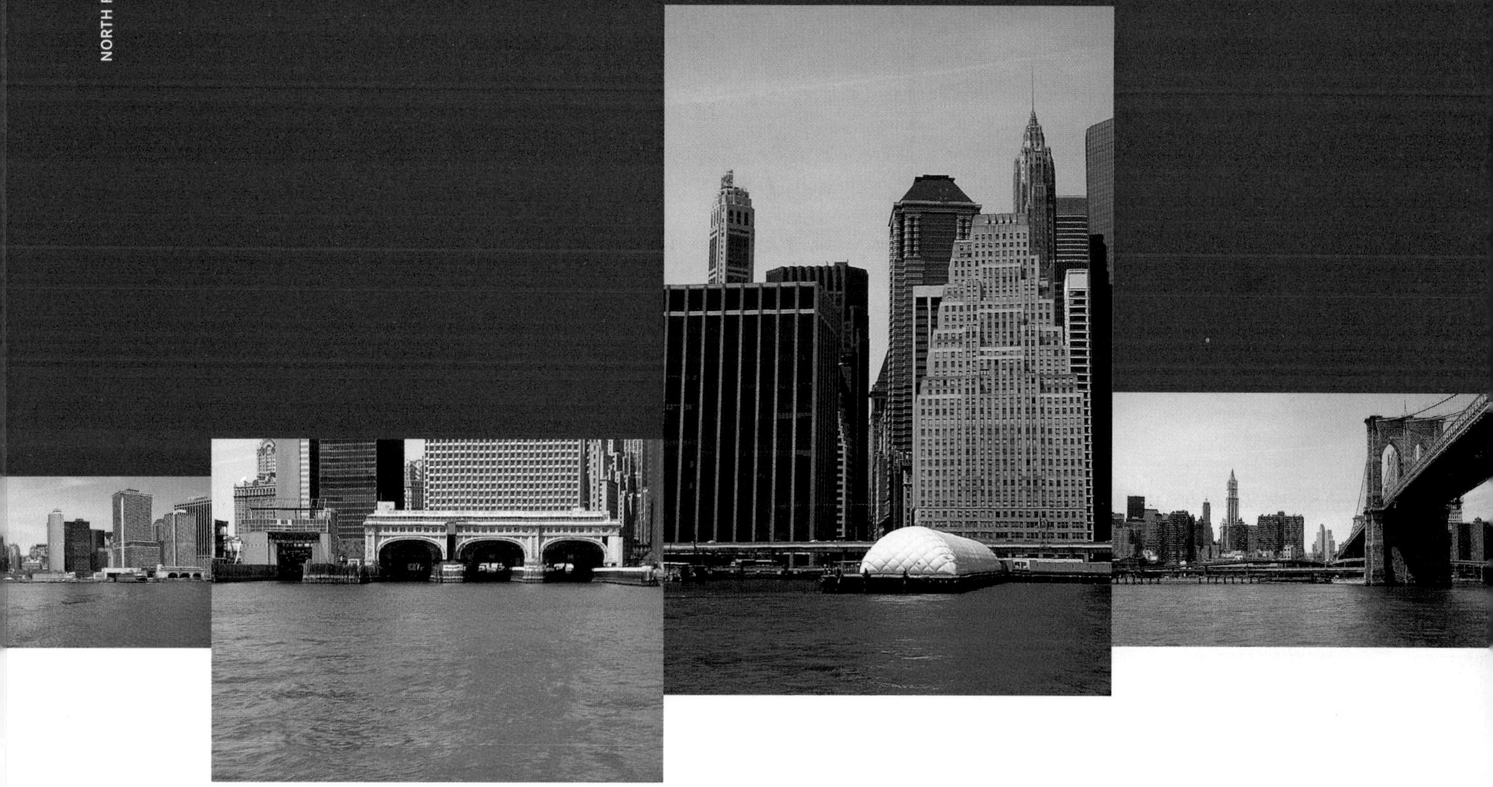

BEYOND THE EDGE

Published by

Princeton Architectural Press

37 East Seventh Street

New York, New York 10003

For a free catalog of books, call 1.800.722.6657.

Visit our Web site at www.papress.com.

Publication of this book has been supported by a grant from the Graham
Foundation for Advanced Studies in the Fine Arts.

Additional support was provided by a grant from the Stephen A. and Diana L.
Goldberg Foundation.

Editor: Nancy Eklund Later

Copy Editor: Elizabeth Nicholson

Designer: Jan Haux

Special thanks to: Nettie Aljian, Ann Alter, Nicola Bednarek, Janet Behning, Megan
Carey, Penny Chu, Russell Fernandez, Clare Jacobson, Mark Lamster, Linda Lee,
Katharine Smalley, Jane Sheinman, Scott Tennent, Jennifer Thompson, and Deb
Wood of Princeton Architectural Press—Kevin C. Lippert, publisher

Library of Congress Cataloging-in-Publication Data

Gastil, Raymond, 1958–

 Beyond the edge : New York's new waterfront / Raymond W. Gastil.—1st ed.

  p. cm.

Includes index.

 ISBN 1-56898-327-1 (alk. paper)

 1. Waterfronts—New York (State)—New York. 2. New York

(N.Y.)—Buildings, structures, etc. I. Title.

 NA9053.W38 G37 2002

 720'.9747'1—dc21

                      2002010314

BEYOND THE EDGE

NEW YORK'S NEW WATERFRONT RAYMOND W. GASTIL

VAN ALEN INSTITUTE | PRINCETON ARCHITECTURAL PRESS | NEW YORK

ACKNOWLEDGMENTS

My first debt, as for anyone who risks writing about it, is to the city of New York, to its buildings, its landscapes wet and dry, and its ineluctable culture. The trustees of Van Alen Institute made *Beyond the Edge* possible by their openness to a broad waterfront design program: they reckoned that for an institute dedicated to improving the design of the public realm, the future of the waterfront merited its energies and focus. This book reflects my own conclusions, not ones vetted by the institute, but the context for writing it has been thick with the trustees' ready support and expertise. Two grants specifically supported the book, the first from the Stephen A. and Diana L. Goldberg Foundation, and the second from the Graham Foundation for Advanced Studies in the Fine Arts. In addition, two sponsored programs were highly valuable, the highly valuable, the HGIS International Program of the Netherlands Architecture Institute/Consul of the Netherlands at the start, and the MacDowell Colony residency toward the finish.

The opportunity to teach a graduate seminar on urban waterfronts at the University of Pennsylvania's Department of Landscape Architecture and Regional Planning, then chaired by John Dixon Hunt, gave me the opportunity, and necessity, to focus on the dilemmas for waterfront design beyond New York, and I learned from both the faculty and students there. Alan Balfour's invitation to contribute an essay on New York's public space for his unassumingly polemical *World Cities: New York* (John Wiley & Sons, 2001) reinvigorated my desire to write about New York. Earlier, Richard Scherr at Pratt Institute invited me to coteach an urban design studio on the waterfront light rail line along New Jersey's Hudson riverfront, with the thoughtful urban designers Mark Strauss and Uwe Brandes, which also helped lay the ground for this project.

Many of the architects, landscape architects, planners, activists, developers, elected officials, public agency professionals, artists, scholars, critics, and journalists who have helped me to understand design and the waterfront are cited in the text. There are many more, and I can begin by describing the categories: designers who agreed to be interviewed for this book and those who supplied us with illustrations of their work, as well as those who participated in the hundreds of conversations and exchanges that the question of design on the waterfront engenders; the range of experts and advocates who served as cosponsors of institute projects and on competition juries and project reviews, spoke at institute forums and roundtables, contributed comments to reports, and offered their advice and knowledge in fields from hydrology to real estate development to waterborne swimming pools, which float somewhere between the other two. I have been moved by the sincerity and accomplishment both of planners and designers in private practice and of public servants committed to improving the waterfront. Whether or not all of us are always satisfied with every project and whether or not public agencies are all angels, let me attest to the presence of dedicated, intelligent planners, designers, and others, at work in the city, people who know New York in their bones.

It would take an encyclopedia to record the creativity and ardor of all of them, and hopefully the Van Alen Web site (vanalen.org) heralds their contributions to panels, conferences, boat tours, Web sites, competition juries, workshops, interviews, and exhibitions and identifies some of the literally thousands of entrants in the waterfront design competitions the institute sponsored.

The following have all contributed, for the most part by being directly part of an institute-related project, and a few by their time and generosity with information and access outside the parameters of a studio, lecture, or jury. This has been my graduate course in waterfronts; the teachers have been extraordinary, whatever the abilities of the student. Among the names that must be mentioned, at different levels and at different intensities, from the public, private, civic, and academic sectors: all of the institute's trustees, with those who participated directly in panels and juries cited by name: Vito Acconci, Stan Allen, Paola Antonelli, Thomas Balsley, Christopher Bardt, Crystal Barriscale, Andrew Bartle, Kent Barwick, Philippe Bauman, Laurie Beckelman, Tobi Bergman, Michelle Bertomen, Aaron Betsky, Alice Blank, Kevin Bone, Christine Boyer, Michael Bradley, Allison Brawne, Anne Breen and Dick Rigby, Hillary Brown, Maria Buhigas San-Jose, Amanda Burden, Ann Buttenwieser, Leroy N. Callendar, Dan Campo, Colin Cathcart, Elisa Charters, James Corner, Mario Coyula, Carter Craft, Eedie Cuminale, Elizabeth Diller and Ricardo Scofidio, Noreen Doyle, Cathy Drew, Winka Dubbeldam, Kate Dunham, Douglas Durst, John Edminster, Nancy Egan, Lucy Eichenwald, Peter Eisenman, Ron Evitts, Ann Ferebee, Jonathan Friedman, Martin Friedman and Mildred Friedman, Virginia Fields, Bruce Fowle, Tom Fox, Lawrence Frommer, Doreen Gallo, Jim Garrison, Alex Garvin, Frank Gehry, Stephanie Gelb, Rosalie Genevro, Alan Gerson (the force behind Community Board 2's decision to sponsor an ideas competition for Pier 40), Leslie Gill, David Gissen, Ken Greenberg, Miriam Gusevich, Kathryn Gustafson, Gary Hack, Laura Hansen (who got Cherry Jones to read Herman Melville for a boatload of rapt New Yorkers), Hugh Hardy, Laurie Hawkinson, Douglas Hecker, Judith Heintz, Barry Hersh, Maggie Hopp, Frances Huppert, Michael Jacobs, Georges Jacque-

mart, Shirley Jaffe, Karl Jensen, Carlos Jimenez, Wendy Evans Joseph, Andrea Kahn, Elizabeth Kennedy, Robert F. Kennedy, Jr., Sheila Kennedy, Fred King, Jeffrey Kipnis, Ed Kirkland, Jonathan Kirschenfeld, Patricia Kirschner, Robert Kloos, Sebastian Knorr, Rob Lane, Roger Lang, Michael Laviano, Sylvia Lavin, Penny Lee, Linda Lees, John Leonforte, Ralph Lerner, Kyna Leski, Brenda Levin, David Lewis, Paul Lewis and Marc Tsurumaki (curator/designers of the Institute's breakthrough *Architecture+ Water* exhibition), Frank Litgovet, Philip Lopate, Thomas Lueck, Michael Manfredi, Deborah Marton, Peter McCourt, Jon McMillan, Jayne Merkel, Sheila Metcalf, Elizabeth Meyer, Eve Michel, Enric Miralles, Mary Miss, Aaron Neubert, Guy Nordenson, Alan Olmsted, Tom Paino, Robert Perris, Thomas Phifer, Robert Pirani, Richard Plunz, Warrie Price, John Rahaim, Jeannette Rausch, Charles Reiss, Marcia Reiss, Shawn Rickenbacker, Dick Rigby, Mark Robbins, Keith Rodan, Chris Rogers, Elizabeth Barlow Rogers, Joseph Rose, Heather Roslun, Peter Rothschild, Karla Rothstein, Margie Ruddick, James Russell, Tony Schnachkus, Michael Schwarting, Tom Scerbo, Fred Schwartz, Brendan Sexton, Ron Shiffman, Joshua Sirefman, Susanna Sirefman, Martha Skinner, Adrian Smith, Glenn Smith, Michael Sorkin, Marcelo Spina, Robert A. M. Stern, Jeffrey Sugarman, Allen Swerdloe, Marilyn Jordan Taylor, Susana Torre, Steven Tupu, Ben van Berkel, Anne Van Ingen, Karen Van Lengen, Ian Van Praagh, Michael Van Valkenburgh, Christian Volkman and Lynette Widder, Rosemary Wakeman, Donna Walcavage, Charles Waldheim,

Chris Ward, Roberta Weisbrod, Marion Weiss, Peter Wheelwright, Barbara Wilks, Paul Willen, Tod Williams, Bill Woods, Robert Yaro, Alejandro Zaera-Polo.

My colleagues at Van Alen Institute contributed beyond the call of duty. Nathaniel H. Brooks is credited for his admirable photographs taken for this project, and he also contributed with research and coordination on the images so vital to this book, as did Zoe Ryan, editor of the *Van Alen Report*. Claire Nelson, Marcus Woolen, and Barrett Feldman provided additional, valuable support. Before this book began, Casey L. Jones and Bay Brown contributed enormously to the Institute's slew of waterfront design studies, competitions, and research, and that work informs this volume. The partners of Engine Books were also instrumental, at an early stage, in working with me to envision what a book on this topic might be. Time and consequences yielded a very different project, yet their thoughtfulness and professionalism are much appreciated. At the end of the process, Abby Bussel, one of those partners, came back independently and gave tirelessly in an effort to ensure the text's evenness, coherence, and accuracy.

Friends and family gave grants in the currency of the heart and mind. Their support ranged from the professional to the personal, including key moments of moral and intellectual support for the endeavor from Steve Chivers, Michael Dodson, John Dutton, Keller Easterling, Jane Hollister, Melody Lawrence, Pat Morton, Liz Newman, John Oddy, Stuart Parks, James Reginato, Bill Ryall, and Natalie Shivers, as well as Jeannette C., Raymond D., and Leila Gastil. Without Mike Cannon, I would never have found an apartment overlooking piers and parks and barges—so I don't have to move back to Seattle to live by the water—the same week this manuscript met its penultimate deadline.

The conviction at Princeton Architectural Press that there was a valuable, timely book here, and the support of the publisher, Kevin Lippert, and the committed editor, Nancy Eklund Later, gave the editorial process a literally unforgettable rhythm and verve, especially in the difficult process of revising a manuscript after September 11, 2001, which involved extensive rewriting and editing. Finally, for all I have had to take from the world in order to write this book in the time and energy of others, I sincerely hope that the book will also give back. It is an attempt to participate in the culture of exchange that exemplifies what New York, the waterfront, and design are about at their most meaningful, and to be part of that exchange is one of the unstinting rewards of being there, being here, in this public realm.

Raymond W. Gastil
May 2002

NORTH FROM EAST 80s, UP THE HARLEM RIVER TO THE HENRY HUDSON BRIDGE

ICONS, INFRASTRUCTURE AND

THE PUBLIC LIFE

I. AERIAL VIEW OF BATTERY PARK CITY AND NEW JERSEY
WATERFRONT FROM 2 WORLD TRADE CENTER

The waterfront calls for an open mind. In major cities that were once or are still world ports, from Rotterdam to Yokohama to New York, the call is especially intense. Still flowing with the give-and-take of goods, people, and cultures, today's most successful waterfronts offer the experiences and articulate the values of an open society, in which ideas are exchanged freely, transparent transactions are valued, and people are free to come and go.[1]

For a dense metropolis, today as much as centuries ago, the waterfront is where a city opens up beyond the topography of daily life. In 1851, Herman Melville wrote in *Moby-Dick* of the "crowds of water-gazers" at New York's Battery, daydreaming of escaping their urban confines: "Nothing will content them but the extremest limit of the land; loitering under the shady lee of yonder warehouses will not suffice....Inlanders all, they come from lanes and alleys, streets and avenues—north, east, south, and west. Yet here they all unite."[2] One hundred and fifty years later desire and reality run both ways. New York's shore and skyline speak to the freedom of life in the city, as much as the harbor heralds the opportunities of the open sea.

Cities accommodate this exchange by designing and building docks, parks, memorials, and plants for power and waste, as well as transportation networks and infrastructure. Open-minded societies design waterfronts that accept change, recognizing, in a deeply pragmatic way, that all cities and all societies can be improved and thrive on continuous reinvention in their physical and cultural expression. The stakes for designing a waterfront interface are very high, and the task is inordinately complex, because in today's New York and in port cities around the world, the waterfront has to serve as front yard and service alley, cultural stage and civic space, playground and profit center. In short, it is the paradigmatic site for the future of public life.

Before two hijacked airplanes leveled the World Trade Center, taking almost three thousand lives, on September 11, 2001, millions of New Yorkers and visitors went to the Battery every year. Unlike in 1851, by any means but hot air balloon, they could also choose to take in a far more vast view, from which they could see how much the harbor had changed since Melville's time. They could take an elevator a quarter mile into the sky and climb out onto the roof of 2 World Trade Center, the south tower, where a vista of far more scope opened up to both the Upper Bay and out past the Verrazano Narrows to the Atlantic. In the 1990s, on the rising tide of talk about the information revolution and its consequences, discussants often forgot the extraordinary amount of information afforded by an open view from a great height. On the north tower, 1 World Trade Center, which like its twin was a design by Minoru Yamasaki & Associates completed in the early 1970s, contemporary technology was in evidence with a 365-foot television mast transmitting information across the region.[3] Yet from the top of the south tower there was a great deal of directly legible visual information, not only about buildings and parks but also about the natural systems and infrastructures that integrate them.

From the observation deck of the trade center tower in 2001, high-rise "water-gazers" saw not only a very different waterfront from Melville's but one radically changed from the 1960s, when the World Trade Center was conceived (fig. 1). The transformation of New York's waterfront was laid out in detail, including the plan of Battery Park City directly below, where fill from the twin towers' excavation had long since covered over the piers and berths of the outmoded shipping industry to serve as the ground of a ninety-two-acre "city" of apartments, offices, and open space. Looking

west across the Hudson River, visitors on the observation deck could see the rising slabs of offices and apartments, fronted by new parks and backed by a new light rail line, along what had been the docks of Jersey City and Hoboken. They could look north across Manhattan to the East River, long the city's backyard and bad conscience, still haunted by ruined relics of nineteenth-century psychiatric institutions on Roosevelt Island and obsolete industry along its Queens and Brooklyn waterfronts. The United Nations' glazed slab of mid-twentieth-century optimism on the Manhattan side of the river was still waiting for the city to catch up to it, although the 1998 opening of the first high-rise building of Queens West on the opposite bank showed that change was under way.

Observation deck visitors could look southeast of Battery Park City to Battery Park, where the walls of a round fort first completed in 1811 still stand. Once a fortified island off the tip of Manhattan, Castle Clinton was ensconced by landfill in the nineteenth century. The Battery adjacent to the fort has always been a place for recreation, always a place for the view out, not only for defense but also for pleasure.

From the middle of the nineteenth to the middle of the twentieth century, almost every other foot of shoreline on the southern half of Manhattan and the nearer shores of New Jersey and Brooklyn was dedicated to the industry of shipping—thick with docks, pier sheds, ferries, and freighters. The general public enjoyed at

2. AERIAL VIEW FROM DIRECTLY ABOVE WORLD TRADE CENTER SITE, SEPTEMBER 2001

least some visual and physical access to the less industrialized harbor at the South Street Seaport on Manhattan's East Side. By contrast, the more active, post–Civil War industrial waterfront on the West Side was for a century walled off behind warehouses and piers. Much of the property was private and reserved for the exclusive world of work. Yet its use was governed by public bodies for the public good of trade with enormous public subsidies, including the control and support of the New York City Department of Docks, established in 1871, and the Port Authority founded by the states of New York and New Jersey in 1921. Rail lines to service the shipping industry raised another barrier between the general public and the water, and when these lines were razed in the twentieth century, highways and parkways took their place, keeping apart the city and the waterfront.

The industrial barrier between the public and the water remained even after its function ended, when in Manhattan, Brooklyn, Hoboken, and Jersey City the "break bulk" docks, where longshoremen handled freight directly, were replaced by a containerized system in the 1960s. In the new method, freighters were loaded with sealed, truck-sized steel containers and off-loaded by huge cranes. Shipping moved to new docks with the new technology and new storage requirements (large yards for the containers) at what became the Port Newark/Elizabeth Marine Terminal on Newark Bay. There shippers had easy access to the national network of rail, truck, and air freight (smaller container ports were built in Brooklyn and Staten Island at the same time). Both in New York and New Jersey, the infrastructure of sheds and rail lines left behind by the rapid industrial change blocked access to the waterfront.

By September 10, 2001, as anyone on the World Trade Center's observation deck could see, the city had opened up to the water. The inward-looking city that a visitor saw in 1973 was gone. The harbor was active in a new way: the freighters were kept at a distance, waiting to be piloted through the Arthur Kill to the New Jersey docks, but closer in there were hundreds of pleasure craft, from kayaks to catamarans. The 1972 federal mandate to clean the nation's waterways had taken effect and the water was clean enough for recreation, even in New York. Dozens of ferries plied the waters with thousands of passengers, an extraordinary revival for a means of transportation that had reached its nadir in 1967 when the last New Jersey-to-Manhattan line shut down, leaving only the Staten Island Ferry in service for the next two decades.[4] The waterfront embraced this renewed public activity, from new marinas like North Cove at Battery Park City and those lining the New Jersey developments to the new Staten Island Ferry terminal under construction at South Ferry, just east of the Battery, due to open in 2004. Along the water, there were walkways and a range of activities and built environments, from art installations and museums to restaurants, offices, hotels, and apartments.

By noon on September 11, 2001, the waterfront's program of leisure had reverted to a program of work. The second most popular tourist attraction in New York City, the top of the World Trade Center and its view, no longer existed (fig. 2). The most popular attraction, the boat ride from the Battery to the Statue of Liberty, suspended operation.[5] Battery Park City, the prime emblem of New York's rediscovery of its waterfront since the 1980s, was covered in debris, sealed from public access. In New York Harbor, Governors Island, a decommissioned military installation that was on its way to becoming a post–cold war "peace dividend" for the city, was commandeered for military use, housing National Guard troops. It appeared, for a moment at least, that the great opening up of the waterfront would be shut down by security concerns. Most of the city's defense infrastructure had been long out of service, but now the forts, fleets, and batteries regained their symbolic and military roles.

Security at the waterfront had been a twentieth-century concern, but at a much different level. In the long push to open waterfront esplanades around Manhattan, planners and activists determined to see a ring of public walkways and bikeways around the island were always flummoxed by the United Nations headquarters on the East River between 42nd and 48th Streets. Long stretches of Manhattan's East River waterfront are now lined with public walkways, but despite efforts in the early 1990s, security concerns about terrorist attacks trumped any effort to cantilever an esplanade off the

UN complex. At the time of its development between 1947 and 1953, the UN, designed by the International Committee of Architects and its chairman Wallace K. Harrison, had tolerated the construction of a roadway underneath its waterside plinth. After September 11, no such tolerance has endured. Assemblies like the UN, which represent the highest ideals of the open society and are intentionally located at prominent waterfront sites to symbolize those values, are forced to keep the public at bay, using the water as a security barrier.

This contradiction between symbol and experience will be high on the list of challenges facing reconstruction at the World Trade Center site and other prominent sites around the world. Recent experience has not resolved it but brought it into greater relief, as in Genoa, Italy. Only months before September 11, in a city that had opened up its old port through a series of impressive plans and designs implemented in the 1980s and 1990s, the G-8 leaders held a summit. Fear of violent protest obliged the Italian government to hold the meeting on boats in the harbor. The remade port district was an off-limits "red zone" secured by a twenty-foot-high wall of double-stacked shipping containers dubbed the "ring of steel."[6] Postindustrial Genoa used the ubiquitous artifact of the contemporary industrial port, the container, to fend off activists rallying against globalization and world trade. In the middle of the harbor, those attending the summit remained secure; on the other side of the container wall, one protester died.

3. THE WALL STREET GUGGENHEIM MUSEUM PROPOSAL, MODEL, EAST RIVER, MANHATTAN, 2000, FRANK GEHRY

Designing the waterfront to embody and represent the open society was never an easy or unqualified task. When symbolic forms and activities dedicated to that ideal have to be insulated from the public, their meaning implodes. After September 11, finding a way to overcome this contradiction is inestimably more difficult, yet also more important than before. In New York, there are signs that it is possible. The city's third most popular tourist attraction, the Staten Island Ferry, came back into service six days after the terrorist attacks. Within weeks of the disaster, the Battery Park City waterfront to the west of the World Trade Center reopened to the public. Scenes of the harrowing exodus in which people ran to the esplanade as the towers collapsed were still vivid in collective memory, yet visitors and residents coming from the north could once again have that great moment of release when the view of the harbor opens up at North Cove, an experience intensified by the now empty view to the east, where the twin towers once stood. By the end of 2001, the special experience of the waterfront remained, but the context for rebuilding and renewing New York, and waterfronts around the world, had irrevocably changed.

Prospects for redevelopment at the water's edge were far different before the attacks. On September 10, the driving question for the future of New York's waterfront seemed to be whether the Frank Gehry-designed Guggenheim Museum on the East River would, or should, ever happen. The creeping recession had already put a chill on its prospects, but the design for a shimmering titanium cloud, up on stilts to preserve the view down Wall Street, thrilled museumgoers who had seen a large model and full exhibit at the Guggenheim's uptown galleries shortly after Gehry's design was unveiled in April 2000 (fig. 3). With sloping towers shooting up forty-five stories to accommodate both offices and an art museum's version of stadium skyboxes, it was unlike any museum proposal or waterfront proposal New York had ever seen. Slated to replace a set of declining piers at the east end of Wall Street, the project had $65 million in public money committed to it, and by the Guggenheim's own estimates, hundreds of millions more had been committed by the private sector. The projected final price tag: $678 million.[7]

It seemed that every issue that faced New York's waterfront was on trial with the Guggenheim proposal. Not that such issues do not abound in proposals like the citywide Olympics 2012 campaign, which relies on the waterfront to stage the Games without crippling traffic. Yet the Guggenheim appeared paradigmatic. A major cultural program, with a series of intelligent moves to connect it to the waterfront and the specifics of its site, the proposal engaged and enraged New Yorkers well beyond the limited audience typically focused on architecture and planning. The contradictory perspectives were bracing. The new museum offered a citywide,

4. LOWER MANHATTAN SKYLINE FROM EXCHANGE PLACE, HOBOKEN, NEW JERSEY, SEPTEMBER 12, 2001

even international program, yet it would have a huge, inevitably disruptive local impact. Like the waterfront Tate Modern in London, it was a program that could regenerate a district, but it was in a district that didn't seem to need regenerating, at least not before September 11, while other New York waterfront areas such as Williamsburg, Brooklyn, lay fallow. It would dedicate itself to environmentally sustainable architecture, yet it was a major building out over the East River, casting that natural system into unnatural shade. It would be tied into an emerging infrastructure of ferries and water taxis, yet it would generate volumes of passenger and freight traffic that could arrive only by car and truck. It would be a symbol that New York was finally ready to step up to the challenge of building architecture of world caliber, yet it felt as though the waterfront metropolis with the richest human talent and one of the handful of great natural harbors in the world was borrowing an idea from a small industrial river city in the Basque region of Spain.

On September 11, these contradictions, and their potential resolutions, became less important. In local terms, New York's downtown now has to focus on its west side, not its east. The public money promised the Guggenheim project has been put on indefinite hold, and the private money may be moving to more pressing needs as the museum faces declining revenues throughout its operations.[8] The nexus between the financial and cultural worlds, which the Guggenheim at the end of Wall Street made local, is no longer certain in a district that has thirteen million square feet of empty office space in addition to the twenty-nine million lost and damaged in the disaster.[9] The forces moving much of the financial industry out of Lower Manhattan were there already, but no one anticipated the combined effects of a recession and a disaster.

More fundamentally, there is a shift in the way the city and its citizens see themselves. With the destruction of the World Trade Center, New York has literally lost its view, both from above and below. New York must reconstruct the view, both of its skyline and harbor and from its towers and waterways, and in the process reevaluate and reconstruct its identity as a waterfront city. The first fundamental change generated by tragedy is that the waterfront has been reanimated as a place of work. Recognizing and respecting this is a core challenge for the architecture of the waterfront in New York, and perhaps, now, for major cities throughout the world.

The New York waterfront's role as a place of work was recast when thousands of workers and residents escaping the collapsing towers mobbed the shore of Battery Park City. Scores of ferries brought in to evacuate them brought to life the harbor's fundamental purpose, not as a decorative blue fringe for a green park but as a vital escape route for a working city (fig. 4). The shipping and trade of the piers and warehouses on the East River and the Hudson that so fascinated Melville's generation are gone for good, but

5. LOWER MANHATTAN FROM EXCHANGE PLACE, HOBOKEN, NEW JERSEY, 1977

tragedy put the waterfront back to work. There are new ferry routes for commuters, many of which may last beyond the scheduled reopening in 2003 of the attack-damaged Port Authority Trans-Hudson Corporation (PATH) commuter rail service that linked New Jersey to the World Trade Center.[10] By the summer of 2002 the grim work of removing World Trade Center debris by barge to the waterfront landfill at Fresh Kills, Staten Island, was done. The Coast Guard reduced its harbor patrols.[11] Yet even with the debris gone, the image of the harbor and its waterfront as purely a playground for pleasure craft and in-line skating has been tempered by experience. After 2001, it is apparent that the waterfront will remain a site for the infrastructure that moves services, goods, and people. The twenty-first-century waterfront cannot afford to exclude work in the pursuit of leisure.

The second fundamental change in the perception of the waterfront was a tragic reaffirmation of the waterfront's role as the symbolic front yard of a city and a civilization. The waterfront's role as the place of unparalleled iconic value for the modern city has been ripped from nostalgia's grasp. People from every walk of life have told of their misery and disbelief that the two towers are gone, recognizing, in their loss, how powerful they were as symbols of New York's aspirations. While they had a great presence on the skyline from every direction, their most powerful iconic impact was from the water, where the blue horizontal foreground meets the vertical city. With the twin towers' completion in 1973, the towers had, with two monumental strokes, revived New York's image as a waterfront metropolis.

Like most icons, the twin towers had many detractors. The history of their iconic status is uneven: when first built, they were viewed by many as overscaled monsters that would kill the beauty of the waterfront skyline. Gradually, people realized that the towers' sheer rise, 1,350 feet into the sky from the seawall, served as a near-geographic feature that brought the rest of Lower Manhattan into scale. By the 1990s, the towers of the World Financial Center and the waterfront landscape of Battery Park City had modulated that colossal character.

The World Trade Center's towers were waterfront buildings, not only in their role on the skyline but also in their physical and programmatic origins (fig. 5). They were built on a site cut off from direct access to the water by the fill of Battery Park City but not cut off from the pressure of the Hudson River, against which the trade center's engineers built the concrete "bathtub" whose structural integrity is key to the site's reconstruction.[12] In program, the World Trade Center was built by the Port Authority of New York and New Jersey, in part, to accommodate all the offices engaged in shipping.

The physical work of the port would move to Newark Bay, but its office work would continue where it had always been: at the waterfront in downtown New York. While not infrastructure in and of themselves, the twin towers, in their immense scale and scope, matched the fiscal and physical scope of the port's massive engineering projects. They were the first waterfront towers to equal the iconic power and heroic scale of New York's first waterfront "skyscrapers," the granite twin towers of the Brooklyn Bridge, raised in 1883.

How can New York rebuild its waterfront in a way that recognizes these two fundamental functions: the first, to accommodate a working waterfront, both for emergencies and the everyday; and the second, to serve as the iconic front yard of the city? The requirements for a reemerging urban fabric make for a complicated weave, one that includes tourism, culture, and leisure as well as transport and security. The waterfront's sites, structures, and forms need to work together to both embody and symbolize the open society. Not an easy agenda in the best of times, and in a city facing billions of dollars in budget deficits over the next decade, it is even harder.

More money, more planning, and better politics are all part of the answer. But it is not possible to rebuild a thriving waterfront metropolis without a design approach that, while committed to solving problems, recognizes the role of cultural ambition and imagination in its resolution. It is a cultural decision whether the city's waterfront infrastructure is expressive and functional. Design that establishes legible and necessary relationships between functions and places in the city is as important as the placement of thousands of miles of cable for information technologies.

The light rail line on the New Jersey side of New York Harbor is beginning to define a new waterfront district that is emerging between the line, which runs a few blocks inland, and the waterfront esplanade that sits directly on the Hudson and the Upper Bay. The line's stops and the waterfront's ferry terminals are beginning to express as well as service their functions. The street patterns brought to the water for major projects like Battery Park City and Queens West can, like the Manhattan grid itself, offer a powerful diagram for reimagining and rebuilding, though they are by no means the only or even the most useful models. A permanent system of ferry routes can help to renew the meaning of what a waterfront metropolis is. An esplanade ringing the waterfront can organize not only the edge but also the urban relationships inland and across the water. To give these networks presence, there is also the need for icons. Ferry terminals, ventilation shafts, water treatment plants, and stacked roadways are all visible infrastructure that needs to be "romanced," not "disappeared" by design.

The front yard of the city requires icons that are more than infrastructure, projects from museums to parks to towers. The city has to make use of the water for the flows of energy and waste, and, yes, the waterfront has to reflect this, yet it does not mean that the waterfront has to be a sealed-off work yard once again. As a front yard, it cannot be. The waterfront has to be open to

public assemblies of many kinds. It can even tolerate protest: as a civic staging ground, it has to manage protest without the bristling insecurity of Genoa during the summer of 2001. To design and build

6. BLACKFRIARS BRIDGE STATION PLATFORM, RENDERING, LONDON, ENGLAND, 2000, ALSOP ARCHITECTS

an environment of interdependent networks and icons also requires a commitment to the idea of major projects. The industrial development of the waterfront in the nineteenth and twentieth centuries was a huge public endeavor, and today's redevelopment requires vision and action at the same scale. An unerring concentration on the product—the built artifact, at both the scale of the building and the district—will advance what should be New York's greatest achievement: the renewal of its public life. From Barcelona to Seattle, there is increasing evidence that spectacularly creative talents can join with a city's communities and leadership to redesign and renew its public realm, from the scale of the sidewalk to the scale of the region. Architecture and design, in these cities, is seen as a valid cultural expression, integral to a city's experience and growth—not marginalized as a bit of necessary decorating after the planners, finance committees, and political actors have made all the decisions.

New York can aspire to this role for design. Roberta Gratz, a New Yorker who has written insightfully and extensively on urban life since the 1970s, represents a broadly held conviction among advocates of community-led planning processes that there is a dichotomy made up of the good guys—those who practice "urban husbandry"—and the bad guys—the "project planners."[13] For the future of design,

this can be a poisonous analysis. Such views cast doubt on any project not initiated by community groups, which precludes the possibility of major initiatives whose programs may serve a larger group and whose completion may require investments beyond local resources. Even in mature cities, there is a time and place for projects of this scope. Large-scale initiatives do not have to be destructive: the cultures of design, planning, commercial development, and community activism can find common ground.

Will Alsop, an English architect who has designed a remarkable train station platform on a bridge across the River Thames as well as an impressive roster of inventive waterfront projects in Europe, is able to both engage in intense public interaction and sustain a focused design process (fig. 6). "People are mad," he says, arguing that the public is often more open to bold designs than the planners and organizers speaking for it. He adds that the exchange between the architects and the community generates some of the strongest design ideas in any project.[14]

Since the World Trade Center's towers were completed in 1973, there have been many inspiring waterfront projects in New York, from temporary art installations to hundred-acre planning and design proposals. The modestly scaled Wall Street Ferry terminal by Smith-Miller+Hawkinson, opened in 2001, wears its refreshingly

7. WALL STREET PIER FERRY TERMINAL, LOWER MANHATTAN, 2001, SMITH-MILLER+ HAWKINSON

8. BUTTERFLY PIER, "EAST RIVER CORRIDOR" PROJECT, RENDERING, MANHATTAN, VAN ALEN FELLOWSHIP IN PUBLIC ARCHITECTURE, 1999, REISER+UMEMOTO RUR ARCHITECTURE

ambitious architectural agenda on its sleeve on an East River pier designed by Judith Heintz Landscape Architecture. The south-facing wall of its waiting room is an airplane hangar door, which serves as a reference to the industrial scale and character of waterfront structures and also frames the view to the south (fig. 7).

In New York, it is important to take inspiration from visionary projects. Van Alen Institute, among other civic groups, community organizations, and universities, has supported such projects as demonstrations of an alternative process and a refusal to accept that the city cannot build an engaging waterfront. Literally thousands of design visions have been created by architects, landscape architects, environmental activists, preservationists, and others throughout the 1990s. These proposals have ranged from the most aggressive build-outs, covering vast stretches of the Hudson and the East River with new structures, to the most reverently "natural," planting salt marsh and oyster beds to match those that existed before Henry Hudson's arrival. One notable proposal, supported by Van Alen Institute, was "East River Corridor" by Reiser+Umemoto RUR Architecture developed between 1998 and 1999 (fig. 8). The designers created an "interwoven system of public and private infrastructure" along the FDR Drive that reaches its most poetic moment of architectural form in the long, graceful arcs of the but-

terfly pier at the end of Wall Street, at the same site proposed for Gehry's Guggenheim.[15]

After September 11, there is a need for both powerful speculation—like the five-block-long butterfly pier—and bold action on the waterfront: the two do not cancel each other out. Even before the attacks, there were many promising proposals, from the redevelopment of the Con Edison site south of the UN to a community park combined with a university playing field on the East River waterfront in Williamsburg, Brooklyn. There are new minor league baseball stadiums on the water in St. George, Staten Island, and Coney Island, Brooklyn, and controversial talk of a major league football stadium adjacent to the Hudson on Manhattan's West Side. There are huge public parks on the old piers below Brooklyn Heights, and there is the vast riparian acreage of what was Hunters Point in Queens, where there appears to be a new openness to innovative design and more inventive programming. And at the Battery, there is funding and a design to raise the roof at Castle Clinton, reengaging it in the city's cultural program—a sign of resurgence for New York's waterfront.

Architects and planners, policymakers and the public need to seek inspiration in regenerated waterfronts worldwide. They

9. STORM OVER MANHATTAN, LITHOGRAPH, 1935, LOUIS LOZOWICK

can also look for inspiration to the city's experience of the waterfront in the decades since the World Trade Center rose. The relatively slow redevelopment of the past thirty years has yielded the opportunity to understand the challenges and possibilities presented by the waterfront. Artists, environmentalists, filmmakers, fishers, and rowers went down to the waterfront and learned how to look at it and the city in a new way. Calling for major projects, bold programs, and adventurous design does not shut out this history, but it does call for interpreting it. Louis Lozowick's 1935 lithograph *Storm over Manhattan*, printed during the Great Depression, saw the passion and potential of the waterfront skyline even when New York was in dire condition (fig. 9). Seventy years later, New York has to learn to see itself again, and the waterfront is the place for that passionate endeavor to begin.

NOTES

1. The term "open society" is used here as a general term, as in "if the terrorists are just going to keep using technology to become better and better, how do we protect against that, while maintaining an open society?" Thomas L. Friedman, "Naked Air," *New York Times*, 26 December 2001, A29. This usage is certainly related to, but not defined by, the explanation of the term offered by Karl Popper in *The Open Society and Its Enemies* (1943; reprint, Princeton: Princeton University Press, 1971), or more recently, by the investment manager and philanthropist George Soros, who has articulated his vision of the term through the Open Society Institute and articles such as "Toward a Global Open Society," in *The Atlantic* 281/1 (January 1998).

2. Herman Melville, *Moby-Dick, or The Whale* (1851; reprint, New York: Penguin Books, 2001), 3.

3. 1 World Trade Center completed 1973, 2 World Trade Center completed

1972, Minoru Yamasaki & Associates, design architects; Emery Roth and Sons, architects; John Skilling and Leslie Robertson, consulting engineers. The Observation Deck, 2 World Trade Center, opened in 1975.

4. Arthur G. Adams, "Ferries," *The Encyclopedia of New York City*, ed. Kenneth T. Jackson (New Haven: Yale University Press, 1995), 397–401.

5. The boat ride, but not the tour of the statue, was restored by the end of December 2001.

6. John Tagliabue, "Genoa's Protestors March Peacefully, but Vow Stronger Action," *New York Times,* 20 July 2001, A10.

7. Eric Lipton and Robin Pogrebin, "Guggenheim Gets Backing for New Museum," *New York Times*, 28 November 2000, B1.

8. Celestine Bohlen, "The Guggenheim's Scaled-Back Ambition," *New York Times*, 20 November 2001, E1.

9. New York City Partnership and Chamber of Commerce, "Economic Impact Analysis of the September 11 Attack on New York City" (November 2001).

10. Regarding ferries, see Denny Lee, "They Don't Just Go to Staten Island," *New York Times*, 2 December 2001, City 4; Linda Richardson, "Public Lives: On the Busy Ferries, It's Steady as He Goes: Arthur E. Imperatore, Jr.," *New York Times*, 19 December 2001, D2; Josh Rogers, "Planners Agree Ferries Can Help Save Downtown," *Downtown Express*, 20–26 November 2001, 13. Rogers's article notes that New York Waterway, the private ferry operator, evacuated or took 160,000 people off of Manhattan on September 11 and as of November 2001 had seen its World Financial Center passenger trips, temporarily moved to Pier A at the Battery, increase from 12,000 to 36,000. Regarding the PATH, see "P.A. Plans to Put PATH Back on Track," *Crain's New York Business, 5* November 2001, 12.

11. Thomas Zambito, "On the Alert Against Terror: Coast Guard Has Critical New Mission Since September 11," *Daily News*, 16 December 2001, 30.

12. Angus Kress Gillespie, *Twin Towers: The Life of New York City's World Trade Center* (New Brunswick: Rutgers University Press, 1999), 61–68.

13. Roberta Brandes Gratz with Norman Mintz, *Cities Back from the Edge: New Life for Downtown* (New York: John Wiley & Sons, 1998), 59–83.

14. Will Alsop, interview by author, 4 June 2001.

15. Reiser+Umemoto, "East River Corridor: Manhattan Segment—An Interwoven System of Public and Private Infrastructure along the FDR Right-of-Way," project description (January 1999).

LEARNING TO LOVE THE NEW
IN THREE DECADES

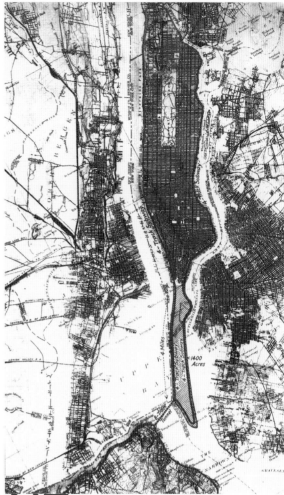

I. EXTENSION TO MANHATTAN PROPOSAL, 1913 PARIS PRIZE

YORK WATERFRONT,

1

In 1972, the same year that the World Trade Center's south tower opened, the United States Congress passed the Clean Water Act, which mandated compliance and provided federal funds for states to clean up their lakes, rivers, and streams. For a municipality like the City of New York, the greatest technical and financial challenges were to build water treatment facilities, less euphemistically called sewage plants, for the waste generated by the millions who lived and worked there, and to clean up the legacy of more than a century of intense industrial use.

Conceived by General George McClellan, the Civil War leader who became the engineer in chief of the Department of Docks, the master plan for New York's industrialized waterfront called for building miles of seawall. The plan was adopted in 1871 and completed

through public and private efforts by 1916.[1] Fifty-six years later, the Clean Water Act promised to drive an equally long and arduous deindustrialization project, one that would require as much engineering, albeit less building, than the earlier effort. This new environmental approach was aimed at improving ecological, rather than industrial, performance. It initiated a reconceptualization of the harbor as not primarily a port but a living estuary. By cleaning the water, it would not only dramatically improve conditions for flora and fauna but also for the locals, commuters, and tourists who would be drawn to the edge of a clean harbor far more easily than they had been to a famously foul one.

At the same time, the waterfront would have to be cleared of its industrial wall, or at least see it punctured and transformed, if New Yorkers were to be connected to their estuary as they were in earlier generations. In 1973, the same year that the north tower of the World Trade Center opened, the opportunity for transformation came with an accident: a loaded dump truck fell through a section of Manhattan's West Side Highway. For decades, the roadway, more formally known as the Miller Elevated Highway and completed between 1931 and 1948, had separated the Hudson River from Lower Manhattan and much of the west side of the city, from the Battery to Riverside Park. The logic for the siting of the elevated highway had been that vehicle traffic needed to be lifted up above the busy streets servicing the piers. By the late 1970s, with most of the passenger ships and all of the freighters gone, that logic no longer stood. The truck's plunge gave new impetus to plans to tear down the elevated road. A year before the road's partial collapse, the Regional Plan Association (RPA) had led an effort to plan a six-lane highway running underground north of the Battery to 42nd Street, with commercial projects and parks sited on what had been the Miller Highway's right-of-way. Westway, when formally launched by the federal, state, and city governments in 1974, called for mixed-use development across 181 acres, much of it new land from fill out to the pierhead line of the disused West Side piers.

In the end, Westway would not prevail; among other challenges it faced were both the law and the spirit of the Clean Water Act, which made it essentially impossible to push landfill projects through environmental review. The combination of New York's financial crisis, environmental legislation, and the rising power of community advocates to block unwanted projects stalled and killed the project. Waterfront initiatives that proposed major residential and commercial development found little support in those days. Instead, there were pioneering efforts to reconnect to the waterfront through events, art, and recreation. Yet there were still major projects, slow though they were to evolve, like the ninety-two acres of Battery Park City. There the public learned to love the landscaped, multitiered esplanade, a far finer perimeter walk than the ribbons

of asphalt that New York's master builder Robert Moses had allowed along his waterfront highways in the 1950s and 1960s. With Battery Park City, New Yorkers came to expect esplanades, with or without the residential and commercial development to bankroll them. To understand the city's decades-long struggle to change its waterfront, it is essential to understand the impact of the esplanade, an overarching design idea, and the range of waterfront designs and programs—some challenging it, some embracing its logic—that are its legacy.

2. EAST RIVER PARK AND FDR DRIVE, MANHATTAN, OPENED 1941

ENGINEERING AN EXPANDING WATERFRONT

Plans for the World Trade Center and Battery Park City, both projects conceived in the 1960s, marked the end of the era when the water was perceived as a temporary condition, a condition that could be filled in as New York's industrial needs expanded, with no conceptual limits except keeping the shipping lanes open. An extraordinary example of this attitude comes from the early twentieth century, when New York experienced explosive growth. In 1913, the original charter organization of Van Alen Institute sponsored its annual Paris Prize competition, calling for the design of a monument at the end of a visionary proposal for a southern extension to Manhattan, right into the Verrazano Narrows, fifty-nine years before the opening of the bridge (fig. 1). The extension would afford the acreage that the finance and shipping industries needed to expand. In the words of the competition program, "This extension of the island will have wide boulevards in two levels along the waterfronts and its central axis will be developed as a broad parkway." The competition sponsors envisioned a total of eight more miles of working waterfront, which they were confident the port could absorb, and a grand public monument, yet they did not see a contradiction between the two functions: extending the island of Manhattan for private enterprise while building a monument to honor New York's "international commercial supremacy, and its surpassing in population all the cities of the world." In outlining the parameters for the monument itself, which was the subject of the competition, the sponsors wrote a program focused on the city's iconic waterfront identity, well beyond the 1886 Statue of Liberty: "The competitor must bear in mind that his composition should be considered in relation to the irregular sky-line [sic] of tall buildings behind as one enters the harbor."[2]

The ambition of the Paris Prize sponsors was matched a short time later by New York's great city builder (and city destroyer), Robert Moses, who held a range of state and city positions including New York City Parks Commissioner and head of the toll-rich Triborough Bridge and Tunnel Authority. He never built a four-mile extension to Manhattan, but he had no qualms about creating thousands of acres of landfill to achieve his waterfront aims for highways,

3. UNTITLED, BATTERY PARK CITY LANDFILL, LOWER MANHATTAN, 1973, MARY MISS

4. *DAY'S END/PIER 52*, HUDSON RIVER, MANHATTAN, 1975, GORDON MATTA-CLARK

parks, and housing.[3] In his years in power, from 1924 through 1968, Moses built the parkways and highways that turned the dense city into a vast sprawling suburban metropolis, with the main form of transportation for people and freight shifting from rail to highways, often highways along the waterfront. Projects like the East River Drive running from the Battery to 125th Street, opened in 1941 and eventually renamed Franklin Delano Roosevelt (FDR) Drive, demonstrated the best and worst of his agenda and accomplishments (fig. 2). The new roadway, which rose and fell to accommodate ongoing industry, nonetheless was part of a postindustrial vision, taking the ragged edge of the Lower East Side and, with landfill, remaking it as the sports field and auditorium-filled fifty-one-acre East River Park (renamed John V. Lindsay Park in 2001).

In dedicating the water's edge to highways, Moses acknowledged the declining importance of the shipping industry for Manhattan. The city as a whole came to this realization more slowly. In 1961, when the future of break-bulk freight was fading into obscurity, New York City passed a zoning resolution that designated a third of the city's 578 miles of shoreline for manufacturing and shipping.[4] In 1963, when the dominant role of containerized shipping was ever more of the present and not just the future, New York issued a plan for the Hudson River waterfront that, while it called for a

convention center and adumbrated what would become Battery Park City, still envisioned active maritime industries along most of the river's edge. At the same time, the Port Authority of New York and New Jersey chose to build the World Trade Center, a potent symbol for the postindustrial waterfront, and had already hired Minoru Yamasaki to be lead design architect for the project in 1962. Accessed by PATH train from New Jersey and by subway from points north and east, the trade center was a white-collar vision for the harbor, in which all the companies involved in shipping, freight, and international commerce would house themselves in glass and steel towers, not on the waterfront but overlooking it. The actual port might have moved to New Jersey, but New York's role as an engine of trade would continue, housed in two four-million-square-foot office towers.[5]

5. *EINSTEIN ON THE BEACH*, SET SHOWING IMAGE OF HOLLAND TUNNEL VENTILATION TOWER, MANHATTAN, ORIGINAL PRODUCTION 1976, ROBERT WILSON

THE WAITING YEARS: ART AND SCIENCE PIONEER THE WATER-FRONT

With a fiscal crisis both local and national, the revamping of New York's edges stayed on hold through much of the 1970s and into the early 1980s. It left the waterfront to the more adventurous, including artists who saw an opportunity to comment on urban life in analyzing the physical fabric of industry left behind by shipping and manufacturing. In 1973, on the Battery Park City landfill created by the excavation of the World Trade Center site, artist Mary Miss completed a series of wood barriers, an untitled piece with a descending cut-out circle in a perspectival alignment, marching west at fifty-foot intervals (fig. 3). In its rich connection and confrontation among viewer, barriers, and site, Miss's project, even now in photographs, regenerates a sense of wonder at the situation of a blank sand fill at the edge of a huge river and the phenome-

nology of experiencing the shifting perspectives on the city, nature, and time offered by the piece. With the 1,350-foot-tall glass-and-metal walls of the trade center as her backdrop and the harbor as her foreground, Miss found a potent way to represent the potential for the individual to examine his or her relationship to the built environment and to demonstrate, as she puts it, "the experience of interior life in the public realm."[6]

Other artists worked with denser, if equally public, environments left by the waterfront's years as a port. This work sometimes took on the experience of a revelatory hangover; after the long drunk of industrialization the viewer could see the formal attributes of the working waterfront for what they really were. Artists' interventions revealed the power of these sites, whether in a photograph or in a direct action such as Gordon Matta-Clark's 1975 *Day's End/Pier 52*, a crescent cut into the shed wall on the pier at Gansevoort Street, at the western edge of Manhattan's meatpacking district (fig. 4). It is now almost impossible to recall the New York of the time, where grittiness and menace were a constant reality and where Matta-Clark, who died three years later, would carry out an illegal cut, call his friends, and declare an art event until the police closed him down. In his eight years in New York, Matta-Clark was drawn again and again to the piers, whether dangling inside one

6. FREEDOM OF EXPRESSION NATIONAL MONUMENT, *ART ON THE BEACH*, BATTERY PARK CITY LANDFILL, 1984, LAURIE HAWKIN-SON, ERIKA ROTHENBERG, JOHN MALPEDE

7. SCULPTORS WORKING, EXHIBITION POSTCARD, SOCRATES SCULPTURE PARK, ASTORIA, QUEENS, 1986

above a pile of trees, or drawing up the *Parked Island Barges on the Hudson* series. He always looked to this edge to test his ideas about openings, circulation, the body, freedom, and exchange.

Artists also began to see the expressive richness inherent in an earlier generation of infrastructure. Robert Wilson, for one, recognized what a generation of designers and engineers had forgotten: before World War II, New York built an infrastructure with a great architectural integrity, one that it could later draw on for an expression of its culture as much as its function. For *Einstein on the Beach*, the 1976 opera he created with musician Philip Glass, Wilson used the view from his loft window of the 1927 Holland Tunnel ventilation tower as a key image for the production. Following the design of its chief engineer, Clifford M. Holland, the tower was a testament to infrastructure as architecture, rising from the Hudson as an elegant, brick-clad monument (fig. 5).

By 1984, with an improving economy, Battery Park City had moved ahead in its first phase of residential construction. But most of its acreage remained vacant, including ten acres of fertile ground for the artists and architects who participated in Creative Time's *Art on the Beach* beginning in the late 1970s.[7] These artists, and their

audience, embodied a resurging New York, yet as their work sometimes expressed, the rising economy threatened to erase the types of waterfront experiences that Gordon Matta-Clark among others had celebrated. The "majestic, towering megaphone, bright red and aimed like a smoking gun toward the base of the World Trade Center" by artist Erika Rothenberg and architect Laurie Hawkinson with performance artist John Malpede, as critic Kay Larson wrote, stood on the sand of what would become the northern part of Battery Park City. (The metaphor of violence against buildings was, at the time, just that, a metaphor.) The piece included a statement inviting "all those who feel silenced by the electronic media to shout their opinions into the wind" and holler up to the indifferent television mast atop the twin towers (fig. 6).[8]

As the Hudson waterfront began its reinvention, thanks to the slow but sure advancement of the mixed-use Battery Park City, the East River too was ready for its round of artist-led reawakenings. A sculptor who had earned a major international reputation, Mark di Suvero, decided to more actively and permanently engage the deindustrializing waterfront. Di Suvero installed his own sculpture studios in two huge sheds on the north Astoria waterfront, and then in 1986 he and a group of community members and artists founded Socrates Sculpture Park, 4.5 acres where artists could create and install large-scale works, directly across the river from Gracie Mansion, the mayoral residence on Manhattan's Upper East Side. For di Suvero, the project was less about sustaining a romantic, gritty environ-

8. *AQUA LUMINA*, HALLETT'S COVE, SOCRATES SCULPTURE PARK, ASTORIA, QUEENS, 1996, SUZY SUREK. POEM BY FIIFI ANNOBIL

9. CATHY DREW, DIRECTOR, THE RIVER PROJECT, IN THE HUDSON OFF PIER 26, MANHATTAN, 1999

ment than about maintaining a working character to the place, about giving artists opportunities that were relatively informal (fig. 7). It was also about engaging the local community in the process. Di Suvero, who works in steel and needs huge sheds to fabricate large-scale pieces, recognized that the waterfront is one place where his work can not only be produced but exhibited, effectively keeping the waterfront a place of work even as it serves as a site for cultural expression. A boon to the city and its arts community, but even more, a demonstration of the visual and physical relationship between the city and the water and how that complexity could be sustained, Socrates became a city park in 1998 (fig. 8).

Artists were not the only New Yorkers to find something potent in the waterfront in the years when New York did little to alter its edges. Like artists, environmentalists had the vision to take local actions that responded to citywide issues. By the early 1970s, environmentalists had recognized that the first and primary point for the waterfront was to understand it ecologically. They acknowledged that the harbor did not belong solely to New York. It was not just the mouth of the Hudson River, it could not be defined primarily by political or cultural boundaries. It was first and foremost the Hudson-Raritan Estuary. It encompasseda rich if damaged ecology, abundant in salt marshes and shellfish beds, that could be

regained.[9] The working map of the region's habitat restoration and preservation sites extends from south of Sandy Hook west to Morris County (both in New Jersey), north to the Tappan Zee on the Hudson, and at the east from Long Island Sound to Jamaica Bay and the Rockaways (all in New York).

Some adopted a far from technocratic approach, as in the work of marine biologist and educator Cathy Drew. Her research had focused on coral reefs around the world, but in the mid-1980s she found a project much closer to home. From the window of her Tribeca loft she saw an abandoned pier given over to parking, where she could continue her hands-on work on marine environments. Snorkeling in the Hudson River was an unhealthy prospect when she began, but Drew got in the water anyway (fig. 9). She founded the River Project in 1986, the same year that di Suvero founded Socrates Park in Queens. The program, a nonprofit center for the study of urban estuaries, included a water-quality monitoring station tracking the health of the marine life below the pier and an educational program about the river and its ecology. She housed the center in an existing industrial shed on Pier 26. The project is ongoing, and its program is incorporated into the plans of the Hudson River Park, the public space from the Battery to 59th Street that succeeded the Westway proposal.

THWARTED AMBITIONS: WESTWAY AND BEYOND

While artists and environmentalists worked at relatively small-scale endeavors to reimagine what a waterfront city might be, large-scale projects were on the boards, if not on site, at the same time. Before the 1980s, the economic slowdown, not to mention the financial collapse of its public developer, New York State's Urban Development Corporation, shut down the growth of the semiutopian community of Roosevelt Island. The 1969 master plan by Johnson/Burgee illustrated a vivid waterfront. This sliver of land in the East River between the Upper East Side in Manhattan and Astoria, Queens, had been called Welfare Island, reflecting its heritage of hospitals, insane asylums, and prisons, and had much to overcome in its new identity. In its realization in the 1970s the project focused, miserably, not on the waterfront as proposed by Johnson, but on its main

street, lined by gloomy arcades below twenty-story residential buildings designed by Sert, Jackson & Associates. Between the troubled economy and the imperfect design, the project failed to arrive at either the critical mass or critical connections between the center and edge of the island that could have established a new paradigm of life in New York, long before Battery Park City. The one moment of inspired waterfront experience is on the Roosevelt Island Tramway, opened in 1976, which runs from just north of the 59th Street Bridge approach in Manhattan, 250 feet above the East River, and down to the island. The view offers dramatic evidence of the still-unrealized opportunities for the East River's waterfronts.

The boldest move that never happened was Westway, which in its definitive 1974 proposal called for a thick edge of superblocks, much of it landfill to be added to Manhattan's West Side. The elevated Miller Highway would be replaced by one running below grade. The most gifted politicians, developers, planners, and designers, including Robert Venturi and Denise Scott Brown, participated in Westway's development process, but in the end, community action and federal law stopped it (fig. 10). After more than a decade of design, politics, and protest, Westway died for the first time with a 1985 court ruling revoking the environmental permit, based on the grounds that the fill around the extant piers' aging pilings would destroy an excellent breeding ground for the striped bass. Five years later, Westway formally ended when the federal government withdrew its support.

10. WESTWAY, MODEL, WEST SIDE OF MANHATTAN, 1974,
VENTURI, RAUCH, AND SCOTT BROWN

11. WHITEHALL FERRY TERMINAL, RENDERING, WINNING COMPETITION ENTRY, LOWER
MANHATTAN, 1992, VENTURI, SCOTT BROWN AND ASSOCIATES, ANDERSON/SCHWARTZ
ARCHITECTS

The court's ruling may have been a very good thing for the bass, for the estuary, and for SoHo and the West Village, but it delayed the transformation of the waterfront for another fifteen years. The demise of Westway heralded the growing power of community and environmental activists to stop projects, setting up a dichotomy that, at its best, saves important landmarks, preserves neighborhoods, and sustains ecosystems, and at its worst, paralyzes planning and design processes and establishes an ideal of an underprogrammed, underused waterfront. Yet one large-scale project was completed: by 1989 the Miller Highway had been razed from Rector Street to 59th Street. The city was ready to engage its waterfront.

Between 1980 and 2000, public and private entities pushed for more than a dozen major projects, proposing to remake vast stretches of the cityscape and its waterfront. Most, like Westway, never made it off the drawing boards. South Ferry Plaza (1984–1991), Manhattan Landing (1966–1991), and Harlem on the Hudson (1981–1993) are among the most prominent projects destined to be built only in cardboard, although the latter may be back in a new guise. And a few, such as Harlem Beach Esplanade, first proposed in 1991, have yet to give up hope.[10] Much of the past thirty years has been about projects not happening, because, among other reasons,

environmental regulations invalidated proposals that relied on New York's past practices of extending the island's rim with decking and fill, squelching, among other plans, Manhattan Landing, a mile-long mixed-use development on a landfill extension into the East River at Broad Street. In Brooklyn, community protests put an end to the proposals by the Port Authority and its partners in the 1980s for Piers 1 through 5, a stretch of outmoded docks just south of the Brooklyn Bridge. Their plan called for residential towers that would have blocked the treasured view from the Brooklyn Heights promenade. After years of acrimony, the state and city, the port, and most of the community came together in 2001 to support the creation of what is primarily a park: one that incorporates some commercial activities but has no high-rises.

Equal in prominence if not in scale to the projects for urban districts is the shelved original design for the Manhattan-side terminal that serves the Staten Island Ferry. A potential icon that never happened, the 1992 competition-winning design by Venturi, Scott Brown and Associates (VSBA) and Anderson/Schwartz Architects to replace the Whitehall Ferry Terminal for the Staten Island Ferry provoked controversy from the start (fig. 11). An earlier competition, held in 1985 for a site just east of the terminal,

12. BATTERY PARK CITY PROPOSAL, PERSPECTIVE, MANHATTAN, 1969, CONKLIN
AND ROSSANT

came to a dead end.[11] A 1991 fire damaged the 1954 terminal structure, and New York had the opportunity, but perhaps not the will, to build a piece of urban infrastructure that matched the other landmarks of the harbor. The sponsors of the proposed new terminal did not count on the shifting political winds. The competition, initiated by the Dinkins administration, yielded a result to be built in the Giuliani one, and the new mayor's greatest ally, Staten Island Borough President Guy Molinari, was not amused by the winning scheme. The design by the VSBA-Anderson/Schwartz team drew on the historic forms of the nearby Battery Maritime Building's heroically scaled portals, with a 120-foot-diameter clock emblazoned with the seal of the City of New York above three arched ferry berths. The design of the clock, which won a juried competition, employed humor, precedent, and iconic imagery—an approach that Venturi had been promoting since his liberating manifesto on complexity and contradiction in the 1960s—and, as is almost always the case with his firm's work, it was also a remarkably intelligent piece of architecture in its functionality.

In response to the borough president's complaint that once again Manhattan was mocking Staten Island, Venturi's team drew up a second scheme, one that eliminated the analog timepiece and replaced it with a digital array of images exemplifying ideas about communication and contemporary life, which his firm had been working on since their groundbreaking Football Hall of Fame proposal of 1967. Molinari suspected mockery in the second scheme, too, and it was rejected. Nearly a decade after the unveiling of the "clock proposal," Frederic Schwartz Architects, a successor firm to Anderson/Schwartz, led a team that completed the design of a revised scheme for the ferry terminal: a glass box with a bracing view of the harbor and a deliberate paucity of humor.

13. ESPLANADE PLAN, BATTERY PARK CITY,
MANHATTAN, 1979, COOPER, ECKSTUT ASSO-
CIATES

REALIZED AMBITIONS:
BATTERY PARK CITY
AND BEYOND

Battery Park City, at the southern tip of Manhattan on the West Side, has become a model—and an antimodel, for some—of waterfront design. Whatever its merits, in design terms it began as something very different. The original master plan, presented jointly by the city and the state in 1969, was based on a system of multilevel pods connected by a spine. Developed by Conklin Rossant Architects, Harrison & Abramovitz, and Philip Johnson, the megastructural conceit, typical of projects initiated by Governor Nelson Rockefeller during the era, required an enormous up-front investment and a faith in a campus concept of urban space that had rarely succeeded, however modulated by the urban design talents of James Rossant (fig. 12).

For ten years, first political struggles and then the city's fiscal crisis and the collapse of the real estate market left the proposed Battery Park City site vacant. By 1978, Battery Park City was close to defaulting on its bonds, and the entire project, beyond construction plans for the residential towers of the first pod, which were completed in 1982, was in doubt.[12] Yet with architects Alex Cooper and Stanton Eckstut, Battery Park City Authority director Richard Kahan explored a possible building scenario and moved rapidly to develop a physical design plan that interpreted the traditional street and block patterns of the city with flexible urban design guidelines, as opposed to the earlier spine-and-pod superblock organization. Cooper, Eckstut Associates developed the esplanade further with landscape architects Hanna/Olin, first opening in 1983. Intentionally recognizable as "park" and "street" to New Yorkers, the first stretch of the esplanade used expensive materials and plantings at a time when most of Battery Park City was a barren site. On the one hand, it was simply good marketing sense—building the roads and the clubhouse at the resort community to convince people to go ahead and buy their lots. On the other, it was a formidable demonstration of the power of design to shape successful public space in response to its site and program (fig. 13). For decades, almost no patron, and no architect, had treated a New York waterfront public

14. SOUTH COVE, BATTERY PARK CITY, MANHATTAN, 1988, MARY MISS
IN COLLABORATION WITH STANTON ECKSTUT, ARCHITECT, AND SUSAN
CHILD, LANDSCAPE ARCHITECT

walkway as a site for much care or attention, where the experience could be modulated from a shaded upper walkway—for the slow-moving and the still—to the lower one—for the busy (and ultimately very fast-moving)—to the edge itself. At the time, the public park just to the east at the Battery was beaten up and tired. The walkways along the Hudson and the East River were in disrepair. The legendary boardwalks of Coney Island had become more legend than fact. The esplanade restated the possibility of pleasure without menace or desuetude for the city's waterfront.

However, the design, perhaps because of its prominence and influence, has generated more bile from the design community than any project in New York. Ever since Battery Park City began to build out in the second half of the 1980s, academic studios, from planning to architecture, have felt compelled to discover its faults, sending out teams of students to investigate and return to solemnly report to design and planning reviews that this development is not urban, not part of New York, that it is exclusive, a gated community for the wealthy financiers who work nearby, tricked out as public space.[13] Some critics condemn it for not being a public street, arguing that in America walkways are too open to privatization and too open to being perceived as backyards rather than front yards.[14] Yet before

September 11 there were, and after September 11 there will be, untold thousands of bikers, walkers, children, rich kids, tough kids, museumgoers, body cultists, boaters, locals, and people from every culture of the world moving along the esplanade.

What's not to like? Focusing on the urban design of the Battery Park City esplanade itself and not on the individual buildings—where indeed the first decade of residential architecture could have been less ham-fisted as it strove to recall the gracious brick and limestone apartment blocks uptown—it is fair to say that after almost two decades, the eyes and minds (and knees, for in-line skaters) of many New Yorkers have tired of hexagonal pavers and "traditional" street lamps. Yet it performs, and it also provided a framework for remarkable artist-architect-landscape architect partnerings. The small jetty at South Cove with artist Mary Miss, architect Stanton Eckstut, and landscape architect Susan Child opened in 1988. The rawness of the Battery Park City landfill, the blank slate where Miss had installed her temporary work fifteen years before, was gone, but even in the midst of a huge urban development, Miss made her viewer confront the site, whether by cutting open the deck of the arcing jetty to the piles below, or in the framing devices of South Cove's elevated platforms (fig. 14). The elements of the piece, like much of Miss's work, grappled with the "radical center," not by emphasizing dream or myth but by insisting on a dialogue in real time and space among the viewer, the work, and the site.

Not all the collaborations were easy or successful. In 1988,

15. CAFÉ AND VIEWING PLATFORM, ROBERT F. WAGNER JR. PARK, BATTERY PARK CITY, MANHATTAN, 1996, MACHADO AND SILVETTI ASSOCIATES

EMBLEM OF THE NEW ATTITUDE: THE UNWANTED PRISON BARGES

artist Jennifer Bartlett and architect Alex Cooper submitted a proposal for a walled garden at the southern end of the development, which the community roundly knocked down. Eventually, the walled garden was replaced with the 1996 Robert F. Wagner Jr. Park, designed by architects Machado and Silvetti, landscape architects Hanna/Olin, and garden designer Lynden Miller, with the café and viewing platform designed by the architects (fig. 15). In a debate that echoes for all waterfront design choices in a densely populated city like New York, Machado and Silvetti proposed a paved plaza opening to the harbor in front of their impressionistic brick arch gateway. The community board, who had fought the wall, insisted this time that the ground be grass, not paving. For advocates of the primacy of design and the necessity of an urban rather than suburban identity for the city, this is a testing ground with ambiguous results. The community review process yielded the right result: the perfect orthogonal green, ground for the slate blue water beyond, is one of the most unforgettable visual and experiential moments on the waterfront.

The popularity of Battery Park City's esplanade put the city on notice that at least as far as the West Side of Manhattan was concerned, the waterfront was no longer a rotting jumble for the tow pounds and vagrants. Yet the days when the city sent its undesirable constituents—the sick, the mad, and the criminal—to the waterfront were not quite over. In the 1980s, with its prisons overflowing, New York City purchased two troop barges, *Bibby Venture* and *Bibby Resolution*, used by the United Kingdom in the 1982 Falklands War. Retrofitted as prisons, the ships were docked at Pier 40 in the West Village and at Pier 36 at Montgomery Street on the Lower East Side. The floating prisons hulked over the waterfront as a symbol of a city whose economy and culture had gone terribly wrong. If the shipping industry had been

16. THE *BIBBY VENTURE* PRISON BARGE, PIER 40, MANHATTAN, 1994

replaced by the corrections industry, New York's future was in doubt.

As an urban intervention, the prison ships, stacked with cells of human cargo like a freighter loaded with containers, were both an eyesore and a fascinating curiosity, serving as a reminder, if not a pleasing one, that the waterfront could still accommodate industrial programs (fig. 16). The city still saw the docks as part of a working waterfront, as a leftover system that they could use for emergency needs. The neighborhoods, on the other hand, were ready for an esplanade. By 1992, the prisons were shut, and by 1994, the barges, which had been greeted by protest marches and lawsuits, were quietly towed away. On the one hand, this was a triumphant moment for the public, establishing access to the waterfront as one of their fundamental rights as New Yorkers. On the other hand, it began to limit the alternative programs for the city's edge, in which ultimately there would be no room for industry, garbage, or even a boat launch.

NEW ATTITUDES TOWARD THE HARBOR'S HERITAGE

Battery Park City was new land; it could only reference the waterfront's heritage (or invent it). But one of the great changes of the last thirty years has been a new attitude toward the artifacts of the harbor's heritage. Few New Yorkers saw much merit in reveling in the waterfront's heritage of hospitals and prisons, but they did respond to other histories. The slow-moving transformation of New York's waterfront in the 1960s and 1970s not only let artists and environmentalists rediscover it but also historic preservationists and others committed to preserving the history of the port, even as its shipping activities moved to Newark Bay. In 1967, on the east side of Lower Manhattan, the South Street Seaport Museum opened, the work of ardent believers in preserving the physical evidence of Lower Manhattan's heritage as a port. Through various starts and stops, they saved blocks of early nineteenth-century buildings and brought high-masted ships to its piers. In 1979, the Rouse Company, creator of festival marketplaces in Boston and Baltimore, began to develop the historic district, including the Seaport's Fulton Market Building, a food hall designed by Benjamin Thompson & Associates that opened in 1983, the same year as the Battery Park City esplanade. South Street Seaport had been in decline for a century, so, as often happens in preservation, the effort was less to conserve the immediate past than to recapture a much earlier one. The Fulton Fish Market, a fishmongers' market since 1822 and a wholesale operation still supplied by fishing boats into the 1970s, was the last historic connection to the area's pretouristic past. (The groundbreaking for a new facility in the Hunts Point section of the Bronx was in November 2001).

At Ellis Island, New York found that adaptive reuse was a viable option for redevelopment of the waterfront, given a site of unlimited sentimental and historical value and national significance. Beyer Blinder Belle led the redesign of the main building at Ellis Island, which opened in 1985, and it is fair to say that it revolutionized the sense of the harbor by memorializing one of the most important sites of human exchange in United States history. Together with the Statue of Liberty, whose renovation was completed the next year, New York's harbor gained a renewed stature in the minds of natives and visitors, one tightly connected to its heritage as the country's historic gateway for generations of immigrants. The harbor's poten-

tial role in the city, both for tourists and residents, increased exponentially. This promise of a harbor-oriented city was anticipated by the restoration of the Battery's Castle Clinton in 1976 and echoed in the state's inauguration of Harbor Park, a New York State Heritage Area established in 1987 that incorporated not only well-known monuments but also the Civil War–era Empire Stores adjacent to the small state park in Brooklyn. In the shadow of the Manhattan Bridge, the Empire Stores warehouses have been vacant for decades; all that is left is a slight smell of the coffee and peppers they once stored. On Governors Island, the forts and officers' housing of the northern half hang on to the national monument status assigned in early 2001. There is still no secure future or reuse for the island, despite inspired planning and design proposals, from the studies initiated by the General Services Administration to the hundreds of proposals for new uses by civic groups and government agencies.

Harbor Park envisioned a group of sites, not all owned by the state, that would be linked physically and thematically "in their historic contexts as related to maritime trade and immigration."[15] This was a new idea for the harbor, one that, while proceeding at a slow pace, could link Manhattan's Battery Park and Pier A, the Statue of Liberty, Ellis Island, Sailors' Snug Harbor on Staten Island, South Street Seaport, the Empire Stores/Fulton Ferry State Park, and the broad harbor itself. Like most design and planning efforts focused on the heritage of a place, it chose which heritage it valued most.

17. RIVERBANK STATE PARK, HARLEM, 1993, RICHARD
DATTNER & PARTNERS ARCHITECTS

RECREATION AND CLEAN WATER: THE STATE PARK–WATER TREATMENT PLANT

New York's relatively slow transformation of its waterfront did not mean that the city's edge was stable. By the end of the 1980s, marine borers, worms too big to contemplate on dry land, were flourishing again, eating away at the piles of New York's piers. Preservationists, park advocates, and developers faced enormous expenses to remedy the problem by razing the piers before they were destroyed by the borers, wrapping the pilings in plastic, or rebuilding them in concrete. The worms' return was the downside of a harbor that had, in fact, been too polluted for them to survive in earlier decades. The city's federally mandated program of new sewage treatment plants had cleaned the water enough for the worms' revival—and they were hungry. When the city began planning new sewage treatment plants, the threat to wood pilings was remote from their concerns. The first of a

new breed of waste treatment plant, a hybrid of functions and political exchange, was built on the Harlem waterfront, the result of a process that began in the late 1960s. The Riverbank State Park, designed by Richard Dattner & Partners Architects and opened in 1993, sits atop the North River Water Pollution Control Plant, which became operational in 1990 (fig. 17). The project was mired in controversy from its conception, when, seemingly as with all waterfront projects, Philip Johnson took a hand in designing amenities to mitigate the community's anger at being the sewage site after the Upper West Side successfully pushed the treatment plant north. After it opened, community activists led by Peggy Shepard, executive director and cofounder of West Harlem Environmental Action, forced the city and state to better contain the facility's odors and also set a new standard for environmental sensitivity in Harlem waterfront projects. Despite its malodorous beginnings, the state park, set above a handsome range of arches, completed an energetic design incorporating avariety of sports. Engaging views north to the Palisades and south to the harbor, the park has been embraced as a lively amenity by the community. It also meets one of the great urban design ideals of managing to combine necessary industrial functions of urban waterfronts—

if not for shipping, for sewage—with the recreational waterfront that both developers and activists have come to demand.

18. DRIVING RANGE, CHELSEA PIERS, MANHATTAN, 1995

RECREATION AND ADAPTIVE REUSE: CHELSEA PIERS

Waterfront recreation as a source of profit, rather than as a state-provided amenity designed to offset the quality-of-life implications of a sewage plant, came about in the first half of the 1990s at Chelsea Piers. In 1992, developer Roland Betts's envisioned an aggressive adaptive reuse program for the Chelsea Piers, a group of four docks, pier sheds, and a headhouse dating back to 1910, a site that had seen great luxury liners in their heyday, immigrant ships from Europe, troop ships during World War II, and, in the waning days of the city's shipping industry, sanitation department repair workers. Unlike most waterfront projects, the planning and construction of Betts' recreation and entertainment complex proceeded swiftly, with its thirty acres incorporating Piers 59 through 62 opening in 1995. The golf driving range, with its netted two-

hundred-yard fairway, is a brilliant reuse for a pier (fig. 18). "Form follows function" is hardly the only directive for meaningful design, yet it is one of the most compelling ones: the golf range, with its stacked teeing platforms and its trusses designed like construction cranes for enormous strength and lightness with fine netting hanging between them, is one of the most arresting pieces of contemporary industrial architecture in the city. It is memorable waterfront architecture, huge but light, sheltered but open, with all the function and metaphor of exchange that a waterfront design can assemble.

Overall, Chelsea Piers, while no design triumph in its recladding or in the continuous wall of the headhouse, is arguably (and it has been argued) a programming success for the waterfront. Critics of the project focus on its indifference to the local community's demands for more open space on the piers and fewer commercial activities. An important concern, but one that prompts the question of the importance of waterfront resources for the broader community. The waterfront is one of the places in a densely built city where large programs can and—when the city needs them—should be realized. The waterfront can be a place where activities that do not fit on city blocks but that fit the desires of city people, whether for television studios, gyms, field houses, extreme sports, cruise ships, or a dock for kayaking up and down the Hudson, as at Chelsea Piers, can happen.

THE COMPREHENSIVE PLAN: MAKING ROOM FOR THE FUTURE

Astounding as it may be with so many waterfront redevelopment projects on the boards between the 1960s and the 1990s, New York City had no overarching physical plan for the waterfront until 1992. Prepared by Wilbur T. Woods, director of waterfront planning, and his colleagues in the Department of City Planning, the Comprehensive Plan draft was adopted as law as part of the Waterfront Zoning Reform Act, approved by the City Council the following year. One of the plan's primary goals was to identify where industry could and should stay, where it should be replaced by new development, and where the waterfront should be open space. Against this background, New York has undertaken an array of planning and development projects, including Hudson River Park, a massive strip of green from Battery Park to 59th Street now well under way,

as well as community-based plans for Greenpoint, Williamsburg, Red Hook, and Sunset Park in Brooklyn, and the overall community plan for Manhattan's waterfront, which was approved by the City Council in 1997.

The waterfront has been planned, and it has been thought about, and while New York needs the will (and the capital) to turn many of the aspirations of the plan into actual projects, it does not need to call for a new Robert Moses. The era of autocrats who could turn plans into a building program through sheer political force has passed. It takes analysis and negotiation, and the Department of City Planning's analyses of "The Natural Waterfront," "The Public Waterfront," "The Working Waterfront," and "The Redeveloping Waterfront" documented in the Comprehensive Plan started that process. The department took the plan through an exhaustive review and refinement, holding up public access as an overarching value system. For New York it is an eminently sensible humanist position. Woods and his colleagues identified a hundred sites for new public spaces, including large parks and esplanades as well as street ends. The Comprehensive Plan looked at every square foot of New York's waterfront, dividing it into "reaches" and documenting the waterfront wish list of every community board. It agreed to the overall policy that the waterfront was becoming increasingly less industrial, although it designated areas for "maritime industrial" uses. It required developers to put in a waterfront walkway—an esplanade—yet allowed them to provide alternative waterfront access plans.

19. KAYAKERS ON THE HUDSON RIVER ADJACENT TO INTREPID SEA-AIR-SPACE MUSEUM

SIGNS OF CHANGE

There were concerns that the Comprehensive Plan was giving away the store—not focusing enough on sustaining and restoring ecosystems and turning over too much land from manufacturing to redevelopment that would replace industry with luxury housing that would once again seal off the community, at least the people who already lived there, from the waterfront. However, the plan and the resulting zoning text is deeply imbued with the urban thinking that emerged in the 1970s: encouraging access, view, and physical corridors, and discouraging megastructures or towers, certainly towers on the piers. The new zoning set minimum coverage and height limits for building on piers, limits that would have precluded the high-rise residential proposals for Brooklyn's Piers 1 through 5 in the 1980s and which will be put to the test if Gehry's proposal for the Guggenheim on Piers 11 through 14 on the East River goes forward.

The Comprehensive Plan is by its nature more framework than implementation agenda. Its scale of recommendations has not been matched by specific programs such as the city's relatively modest 1997 Waterfront Revitalization Program or its environmental double, the New York / New Jersey Harbor Estuary Program adopted the same year by a range of federal, state, and city agencies. Does there need to be an overall plan for revitalization at the scale of change in, say, London? Perhaps, but the first task is to understand the city's current condition. As for its natural systems and human networks, water quality and ferries have had the most powerful impact. The first massive project of the past thirty years was to clean the water, and without the change in that system's water quality, the best it has been in fifty years, any

20. ESPLANADE, BATTERY PARK CITY, MANHATTAN, COOPER, ECKSTUT ASSOCIATES: FIRST SEGMENT, 1983; NORTHERN SECTION (SHOWN), 1992

21. PROMENADE, BROOKLYN HEIGHTS, BROOKLYN, OPENED 1957

change on the waterfront would be moot or at best desultory. As long as raw sewage was pumped into the Hudson, the grand or modest plans for the waterfront would have no takers.[16] A waterfront where kayakers would paddle around the docks of the West Side was almost unimaginable thirty years ago, but the kayakers are there now thanks to the increasingly clear water that brought this about (fig. 19). Yet in calculating the future of the water and the waterfront, it is frustrating to note that there is still raw sewage, because when it rains hard, the water level in the storm sewers rises to the level of the waste water sewers, and the lot flows into the harbor. The great ecological project of bringing the harbor back to a status where shellfish—not to mention swimming humans—thrive has far to go. A permanent solution runs into the billions of dollars and would require a colossal act of civil engineering, but a necessary one for the next wave of waterfront designs. McClellan's plan for the seawall took forty-five years to accomplish; treating the city's water, which began in 1972, may take as long.

The use of ferries and the ferry system, or the lack thereof, was a fittingly melancholy subject in the 1960s and 1970s, when the only ferry running was the Staten Island route, with its grim terminals at both the Manhattan and Staten Island depots. The near demise of the ferry system was a glum counterpoint to memories

of when more than a hundred steamer and ferry routes plied the harbor at the turn of the nineteenth century. Thanks to increasing traffic at the city's tunnels and bridges, office complexes at the waterfront like Battery Park City's World Financial Center, and a growing New Jersey population living at the Hudson riverfront, the ferry has experienced a great revival. In 1986, the New York Waterway fleet started its service with one line from Weehawken to Midtown Manhattan, and by the end of the century had expanded the operation to seven New Jersey terminals and three in New York, including Battery Park City and Pier 11 at Wall Street.

The systems of waterborne transit and water treatment are paramount for the waterfront's future, as is the Comprehensive Plan, yet so are the designs of specific projects for places and buildings and the cultural, financial, and regulatory environment that defines the city's approach to and appreciation of design. The Battery Park City esplanade has had and will continue to have an enormous influence on the imagination and implementation of the city's waterfronts (fig. 20). It was the dominating design principle of New York's waterfront plan of 1992, with its insistence on waterfront access, and it was the guiding principle of the Manhattan Comprehensive Waterfront Plan of 1995, commissioned by Borough President Ruth W. Messinger. It is the organizing idea of Hudson River Park, the successor to Westway, whose

22. QUEENS WEST, PLAN, LONG ISLAND CITY, QUEENS, 1984, GRUZEN,
SAMTON, STEINGLASS WITH BEYER BLINDER BELLE

first section opened at the end of the 1990s. It led to the design and execution of the East River Esplanade in the late 1990s under the sponsorship of the New York City Economic Development Corporation. It is part of a larger vision for New York's waterfront, not just for Manhattan or the Queens and Brooklyn waterfronts directly across from it, but also for Staten Island, where it led to the long-desultory, yet now being realized, esplanade north from the ferry terminal at St. George.

The esplanade as a formal and functional construct should not be underestimated. In its design, the esplanade at Battery Park City drew on a New York approach of radical infrastructural conditions rendered with the forms of a less than radical urbanity. The clear source for the Battery Park City walkway is the Brooklyn Heights Promenade, originally called the Esplanade.[17] The Brooklyn promenade is a resolutely modern phenomenon, with a long landscaped platform built above two levels of the Brooklyn Queens Expressway and a pier access road in 1951 (fig. 21). This is an ingenious cap to a major piece of infrastructure; before the Battery Park City esplanade, it provided a model diagram, if not a model design expression, for future projects that could work at the mixed scales that are inevitable and part of the energy and interest of the waterfront.

A major development project in New York that drew on Battery Park City is Queens West, a mixed-use community shaped by the long list of players incorporated in the Queens West Development Corporation: the Port Authority of New York and New Jersey, the Empire State Development Corporation, and the New York City Economic Development Corporation, with guidelines and input from the New York City Department of City Planning and the Queens Borough President's Office (fig. 22). The 1984 proposal for seventy-four acres on the Queens shore of the East River, designed by architects Gruzen, Samton, Steinglass with Beyer Blinder Belle, relies on a strong waterfront esplanade. As had occurred at Battery Park City, the project's backers, with only one lone building in place—a residential tower designed by Cesar Pelli—put their faith in a new public space, Gantry Plaza State Park, which opened in 1998.

In a review of Gantry Park at the end of 1998, *New York Times* architecture critic Herbert Muschamp declared that the era of the Battery Park City esplanade was over: "The evil spell is broken.... The curse that reduced New York's landscape architects to creating Disney versions of Central Park has been at least temporarily lifted."[18] The designers of the park, Thomas Balsley Associates, Sowinski Sullivan Architects, and Weintraub & di Domenico, who created the first two acres of what is scheduled to become twenty acres of public space in Queens West, had an advantage over their counterparts at Battery Park City, where landfill stretched from the bulkhead to the pier-head line: the river site allowed Balsley and his partners to build piers, install riprap, and create

23. GANTRY PLAZA STATE PARK, QUEENS WEST, LONG ISLAND CITY, QUEENS, 1998, THOMAS BALSLEY ASSOCIATES, SOWINSKI SULLIVAN ARCHITECTS, WEINTRAUB & DI DOMENICO

a more informal edge than the seawall in Manhattan would allow. While the Battery Park City esplanade has the ambience of a genteel late-nineteenth-century park, suited to late-nineteenth-century strolling, Gantry Park is more rugged, keeping its twentieth-century industrial float bridges (gantries) as a key element of the design (much to the frustration of the developer of the housing tower behind it when it opened) and encouraging fishing—even supplying a fish-gutting table—in its design (fig. 23).

Other critics were not as sure that Balsley and his colleagues had evaded theme-park disingenuousness: Michael Wise, a critic who writes on design and politics, complained that the leftover float bridges turned the site's industrial heritage into "an incongruous fig leaf," subsuming history and the possibility of a more complex, less white-collar, mixed-use development.[19] At first, the community was less impressed than even Wise. Community activists had a strong sense that a waterfront should have less pavement.

Gantry Park was a new idea and one extraordinarily suited to its site, allowing for people to get down to the water on a rough tidal strait and serving as a memorable urban place with the twin lift bridges as icons. It incorporated history, even as it defined itself as a contemporary park in the selection of its materials, its crisp geometries, and its focus on providing its visitors with as direct an experience of the water and the waterfront as possible. Part of why it stood out was that so few alternatives to Battery Park City and its planning and design strategies—and expression—have been completed in New York. There have been few alternative models, good or bad, for architecture and landscape on the waterfront in the last three decades of the twentieth century in New York, and little evidence, in Gantry Park or elsewhere, that the waterfront's future might be something other than leisure's green edge for the city.

Both the planning gurus and development enthusiasts of highest and best use, and the community activists calling for unlimited access and the renaturalization of the waterfront, ignore the waterfront's persistent industrial character at their peril. It has taken decades, and much of the industry now at work there is very clean indeed, but the waterfront has undergone an industrial evolution, not elimination. Service industries have always been at this waterfront, and will continue to be so, and the tourist and recreation industries, which are today's shipping industries, are critical to an active economy of exchange. For New York's waterfront to thrive, it is essential for the public sector to value planning and design and to dedicate the intellectual and fiscal capital necessary to carry out what is, effectively, a continuous campaign for urban culture and civic identity. Private investment, community support, and a sense of cultural engagement are key. In the end, design matters, and it is not at odds with the urgent necessities of modern life but is one of them. The esplanade is a driving planning and design force in New York, but there are also vivid alternatives for the form, scale, and program of the waterfront throughout the world, from zoos in Barcelona to courthouses in Boston, organized into districts drawn from mental maps dating back to the nineteenth century and forward to the rest of this one. New York can give its exceptionalist rationales for inaction a rest and learn from waterfront cities around the world.

NOTES

1. Kevin Bone, ed., *The New York Waterfront: Evolution and Building Culture of the Port and Harbor* (New York: The Monacelli Press, 1997), 267.

2. "The Monumental Treatment of the End of Manhattan Island," program by John Wynkoop, suggestion for four-mile extension by T. Kennard Thomson, Esq., Paris Prize Committee Chairman James Otis Post, for Final Competition for the 10th Paris Prize, Society of Beaux-Arts Architects, 1913, Van Alen Institute Archives, New York, attached to 174–75.

3. For a recent summary of Moses' waterfront impact, see Gina Pollara, "Transforming the Edge," in Bone, ed., *The New York Waterfront*, 177–89.

4. Kenneth Silber, "The Wasted Waterfront," *City Journal* 6/2 (Spring 1996): 58–69.

5. Angus Kress Gillespie, *Twin Towers: The Life of New York City's World Trade Center* (New Brunswick: Rutgers University Press, 1999), 182–201.

6. Mary Miss, quoted in Christian Zapatka, "The Art of Engagement in the Work of Mary Miss," in *Mary Miss*, comp. Christian Zapatka (New York: Whitney Library of Design, 1997), 26.

7. *Art on the Beach* was inaugurated by Creative Time in the summer of 1978. In 1983–84 each project involved a visual artist, an architect, and a performer. By 1987 Creative Time moved the project to the Hunters Point District of Queens on the East River. *Art on the Beach* (New York: Creative Time, 1984); *Art on the Beach 1983–85* (New York: Creative Time, 1986); *Creative Time 1987–1988* (New York: Creative Time, 1989).

8. Kay Larson, "Sculpture in the Sand," *New York*, 30 July 1984, 42. The piece incorporated the performances on August 19 and 22 by performance artist John Malpede.

9. The broadest definition of the ecosystem includes not only the estuary but the New York–New Jersey Bight, from Cape May, New Jersey, to Montauk Point, New York, a 16,266-square-mile area. See "Coast" (a bistate committee established in 1993), www.nynjcoast.org.

10. Ann L. Buttenwieser, *Manhattan Water-Bound: Manhattan's Waterfront from the Seventeenth Century to the Present* (1987; Syracuse: Syracuse University Press, 1999). See Map 15, Waterfront Projects, Manhattan, 1980–1998, 232.

11. The 1985 competition proposed adding an office tower and reusing the landmark Battery Maritime Building, designed by Walker & Morris in 1909 as the Municipal Ferry Building, once servicing the Brooklyn ferries but after World War II used chiefly for the Governors Island run.

12. David L. A. Gordon, *Battery Park City: Politics and Planning on the New York Waterfront* (Amsterdam: Gordan and Breach Publishers, 1997), 55–56.

13. This reflects the author's experience of sitting on design and planning review juries for architecture and planning graduate-degree programs at Columbia University and other New York–area schools of architecture.

14. Craig Whitaker, *Architecture and the American Dream* (New York: Clarkson N. Potter, 1996), 77. Whitaker reserves his greatest condemnation for the waterfront esplanade in New Jersey, which has battled with privatization efforts, and concedes that the density of Battery Park City somewhat redeems its waterfront esplanade's backyard status.

15. "Harbor Park: A New York State Heritage Area," information sheet (Conservancy for Historic Battery Park, 2001).

16. See Ginger Webster, primary author, "Summary of the Comprehensive Conservation and Management Plan," *The New York–New Jersey Harbor Estuary Program*, March 1996, 8–10. The Clean Water Act of 1972, which mandated new sewer construction, initiated water improvements in the 1980s and 1990s. Anecdotally, in 1988 Seagate Beach on Coney Island opened for the first time in forty years.

17. Andrews, Clark & Buckley, engineers; Clarke & Rapuano, landscape architects.

18. Herbert Muschamp, "Where Iron Gives Way to Beauty and Games," *New York Times*, 13 December 1998, Arts 35.

19. Michael Z. Wise, "Modest Endeavors: Reclaiming the Shoreline," in Bone, ed., *The New York Waterfront*, 249.

THE WORLD'S NEW CULTURE OF

WATERFRONT DESIGN

2

New York sees itself as a place where in design, as in all else, there is nothing to learn from anywhere or anybody. There is no place like it, so no other experience can apply. The city prides itself on being the place where culture is produced, not consumed. Yet even the most adamant believer in the city's unique conditions has to admit that part of the genius of the place is its ability to interpret and synthesize the experiences of other cultures and other places. Rather than take the events of September 11, 2001, as more justification for chauvinistic exceptionalism, New York has more reason than ever to analyze, interpret, and apply experiences from elsewhere.

Han Meyer, a planner and urban designer instrumental in the transformation of Rotterdam in the 1980s and 1990s, saw the great shift in the form and use of waterfronts as beginning in the 1970s, intertwined with the beginnings of urban design as a practice. Meyer placed changes in waterfront planning and design within a larger movement that recognized the primacy of "human sensibilities" and suggested that the morphology of the waterfront had to be interpreted more as a cultural than technological or functional condition.[1] In center cities, in Rotterdam and around the world, the dock and harbor areas, which had been designed to meet the specific demands of shipping, when deprived of their original function had to be looked at again, had to be appreciated as a part of the culture of the city that went beyond their technological use.

In Meyer's analysis, mid-twentieth-century planning drew sharp distinctions: "The design of the socialized part of the public domain [housing, for example] is seen as a task for urban planning, and the design of the functional part [the highway or port]—or 'technocratized public space'—is left to civil engineers."[2] This can be changed in the center city, which has lost its most intense industrial uses, yet it is an open question whether twenty-first-century shipping—with its requirements for containers, petrochemicals, and grain, necessitating enormous ships and huge acreages for off-loading and storage—can legitimately be integrated into the life of a city or will remain, perhaps inevitably, in the hands of civil engineers. The seaside Starbucks will never find a home next to the petroleum tanks.

Yet there is the potential, in the center city and beyond, to overcome these sharp distinctions and create waterfronts where different scales of social, economic, cultural, and ecological activity take place. The scale of a harbor is in itself more than local, and it demands metropolitan-scale activities—highways, ferries, or recreation centers—serving far more than the immediate local population. Successful waterfront initiatives are able to work at neighborhood and metropolitan scales at the same time, and they must encompass even the most intimate scale of detail of the architecture and landscape architecture of public spaces and buildings. Many cities around the world have been able to retool and redesign their waterfronts to operate successfully at different scales as icons, infrastructure, and exceptional urban places.

AMSTERDAM: ARCHITECTURE AT THE HARBOR'S SCALE

Amsterdam began to grapple with the redevelopment of its outmoded industrial waterfront in the late 1970s. Like many port cities, it had a host of islands, piers, and wharves dedicated to shipping that had undergone a vast build-up at the end of the nineteenth century but were now irrelevant to trade. It had dedicated the waterfront to work, cutting it off from the general public, not only with warehouses but also with the railroad running between the city center and the IJ River; in fact, the 1889 Central Station, a neo-Renaissance-style edifice designed by P. J. H. Cuypers and A. L. van Gendt, rose smack in the center of the city's waterfront. Together with the tracks running through it, the station cuts central Amsterdam off from views and access to the broad expanse of the IJ. Yet there are ample waterfront sites near the core, to the east and west and across the IJ to the north, and Amsterdam has moved forward in redeveloping these. Some of the first sites to be cleared and opened for new design were on the north bank, including the 1981–1988 IJ-plein scheme by Rem Koolhaas and his partners at the Office for Metropolitan Architecture (OMA). For the 6.5-acre, 1,375-dwelling neighborhood on a former shipyard, Koolhaas showed an ardently geometric pattern of bars arranged perpendicular to the waterfront, with extruded forms sheared off as the program demanded (fig. 1). His communiqué was lean and glib: the future of social space would not be the perimeter courts of prewar Dutch social housing, and it would certainly not be the ringed pattern of canals of traditional Amsterdam just to the south. Realized by several architects, the scheme included public space, recreational facilities, shops, a community center, and a school.

One of the more architecturally complex buildings in OMA's master plan was one that at first appeared to be yet another extruded bar, but on closer inspection the Oost III mixed-use complex had a layered program housed in discrete volumes. Running directly along an inlet, designed by Koolhaas and a team of collaborators, its residential slab rises on pilotis above retail buildings in bold geometric shapes—circle, triangle, and square. In its siting and form, Oost III hinted at a complex urbanism that might offer more than a formal polemic on the future of waterfront life.

In the 1980s, Amsterdam began planning its waterfront in earnest, both reusing derelict warehouses and creating enormous new urban districts. It was not a smooth process: squatters, artists, and others fought to maintain the uses they had established for abandoned industrial buildings, and a weak economy worked against the city's grand strategy of public planning coupled with private development. In the end, many warehouses were preserved and reused, thanks first to public protest and then to a recession. By 1995, with the economy returning in strength and the Dutch government under pressure to produce hundreds of thousands of new units of housing for its citizens, the City of Amsterdam did not hesitate to reenergize the redevelopment process, relying less on one grand master plan for the harbor than on a series of major projects. These have gone ahead and produced remarkable new waterfront environments, even with the intense public review and discussion typical of projects in the Netherlands. The Dutch stress that they have sophisticated urban design processes because they have no choice: to develop infrastructure in a country built on lowlands and marsh next to the North Sea inevitably involves public, private, and community cooperation.[3] The cooperation it takes to build and sustain a polder—land that was formerly underwater kept dry through a system of pumps and dikes—has become a metaphor for the culture of consensus. The "polder model" approach to urban planning and design, which involves extensive community and public agency review, has critics who worry that it inhibits original design.[4] Whatever the process, the Dutch seem remarkably able to

2. NEWMETROPOLIS SCIENCE AND TECHNOLOGY CENTER, AMSTERDAM, NETHERLANDS, 1997, RENZO PIANO BUILDING WORKSHOP

sustain the resilient generating diagram of their major projects, and Amsterdam has been able to produce both individual projects and districts of great distinction. These design initiatives operate at the scale of the harbor in their architecture and urban form, and at the same time, they pay keen attention to the particular experiences of living, working, or visiting the waterfront. Atop the tunnel to the north bank of the IJ stands the deliberately iconic newMetropolis Science and Technology Center, completed by the Renzo Piano Building Workshop in 1997. It staked a claim for a waterfront architecture that demanded attention at the scale of the harbor. It also identified itself as operating as part of the city's working infrastructure more than part of its traditional urban fabric. The tunnel siting played up the center's relationship to this major piece of infrastructure in its form and expression. As the ramp for the tunnel roadway goes down, the angle of the copper-clad structure's roof goes up (fig. 2). Alessandra Rocca wrote when it opened: "It is a gigantic object, a conspicuous excrescence of the system of infrastructure."[5] The interior has a resolutely 1990s program of exhibits on communications and technology, presented as games. But the exterior is not locked in time, with its overt presence and inventive public space. To capture views of the harbor and the city, Piano experimented with a public plaza on a raked roof riding the wave of the building's blue-green swell of oxidized copper cladding below. But as the *Netherlands Yearbook* noted dryly, Piano's elevated plaza has had "the problem that this type of public space tends to hold a special attraction for such city dwellers whom nobody wants here."[6] It works at the scale of the harbor, yet if it produces public spaces that are so cut off from the rest of the city that they are, ironically, antisocial, some aspects of its program have to be rethought.

Just east of the city center, the Eastern Harbor District has been one of the first parts of the city to rebuild. The urban design by Adriaan Geuze and his West 8 colleagues for the Borneo and Spoerenburg peninsulas in Amsterdam's harbor, slightly more than a mile east of the newMetropolis Science and Technology Center, allows housing blocks to have an iconic role as powerful as Piano's, intent on operating at the scale of the harbor, yet also garnering a distinct character for a new residential district. From its first translucent model glowing with design life in 1996 to its fully built-out reality in 2000, the redevelopment of Borneo and Spoerenburg has realized much of its promise: Geuze acknowledged the density requirements of forty units per acre for the two razed, former port sites, which normally would have made row houses impossible. He reviewed the expectations for the types of housing (low- to mid-rise multifamily dwellings) that would normally be used to meet that density goal. He did not throw out the rules, or diminish the value of public space, but he used those requirements and

3. BORNEO-SPOERENBURG HOUSING, AMSTERDAM, NETHERLANDS, 2000, ADRIAAN GEUZE/WEST 8

expectations creatively. First, he proposed three-story row houses as the main element, and second, to meet the overall density requirements, he insisted on a handful of very large, taller housing blocks, rising in the path of the almost pre-twentieth-century urban fabric created by the row houses (fig. 3). On the southern peninsula, Borneo, the housing block designed by Frits van Dongen and completed in 2000, more than fulfills Geuze's goal of defying the urban pattern of the lower building in its form as well as its cranked siting. Dongen's Whale housing development, with 214 units, is highly sculptural, an inescapably iconic silver-gray box whose sloping underside gives it the sense of straining to rise up from its pilotis for an even better view of the harbor.

West 8's design is taut with exercised intelligence, operating in the theater of the urban waterfront, yet providing intimate relationships between the row houses and the street and waterfronts. It is a bracing diagram made rich in execution, juxtaposing ideas about urbanism and the public realm, commonality and the individual, shared experience and the unique. As such, Geuze's is a cultural idea, full of promise for any city or site, but especially appropriate in a city as densely populated as Amsterdam and on a waterfront in a flat country where the only landmarks are constructed. It is an idea that is more than a zoning diagram, yet it allows far more flexibility than many master plans and urban design schemes.

Amsterdam continues to push the experimental in its development of waterfront housing, a type that is often a victim of the conser-

vatism of market research. Less than a mile to the northwest of Amsterdam's Central Station, MVRDV, a Dutch firm best known for the stacked landscapes of the Dutch Pavilion at the Hannover 2000 exposition, has built what it calls a "housing silo" on a twelve-hundred-foot-long jetty jutting into the IJ. The Western Islands District is an area where artists and others moved to warehouses past their industrial use, some of which have been preserved. Silodam Housing is, in part, a commentary on how to create an industrial-scale waterfront building that serves postindustrial purposes. It manages, like the waterside warehouses it evokes, to produce an urban form while supporting a less uniform program than the industrial and housing projects of the twentieth century. First designed in 1995 but not constructed until 2002, it mixes housing and commerce, as well as building and town, by composing "mini-neighborhoods" striving to get a "house with a garden" feeling, all within what is essentially a midrise apartment block.[7] MVRDV has taken one of the ineluctable housing types of the twentieth century—the Unité blocks designed by the Swiss-born painter and architect Le Corbusier, which had streets in the sky and a terrace for everyone—and remade it in its own contemporary Dutch image.

The structure fills the narrow site, rising sheer from the waterside (at a different scale but much like the combined

4. SILODAM HOUSING, AMSTERDAM, NETHERLANDS, 2002, MVRDV

commercial/industrial pre-twentieth-century houses along canals in Dutch cities). It takes on the dimensions of a colossal industrial building (like the grain silos once on the site), assuming an enormous presence on the harbor, even as it breaks down the interior into a complicated puzzle of 157 different residential units, from lofts to studios to two-story maisonettes, with public spaces at different elevations throughout the system as well as commercial spaces at the ground level. At close inspection, the exterior reveals as much diversity as the interior sections and plans, shifting through colors, materials, and open public and private decks (fig. 4).

The bar-shaped Silodam Housing is energized by its site, using water views to dramatize its narrative of negotiation among the different types of families and other users that will occupy the building, avoiding monoculture at all cost—a polder model of consensus turned into an uncompromising design.[8] For MVRDV, repetition, stacking, and compression are not strategic means to a rationalist end but an opportunity to barter diagrams of use and occupation into social and formal complexity—a visualization of social exchange that is the antithesis of the gated housing of many contemporary waterfront developments. Whether the architects' passionate social analysis—and social engineering—will result in the experiences they anticipate can only be judged over time, but it can be understood as an astutely rendered work of architecture, as able as Geuze's proposal to revitalize the waterfront as a place to live in an entirely unexpected form.

The most impressive aspect of the Amsterdam waterfront is the willingness of the public sector to appreciate design's role in remaking the city. This effloresces in seemingly superficial ways, as when the planning office in charge of these projects produces luxuriously printed figure-ground plans of the projects, printed on magnetized tiles so that as the designs evolve and are executed, the maps throughout the office can be updated. The illegible and worn physical environment of New York's Department of City Planning and its visual representations of its work, usually constrained in quality by budgets and priorities, reveal a starkly different cultural and political value system. The difference in presentation carries through in the results. Amsterdam is transforming its waterfront in a compelling way, with both an overall plan and visually, conceptually, and pragmatically impressive projects that resonate at the scale of the city and the neighborhood and that value new building over razing and reuse. New buildings—and not only the patronage projects of museums—seem diagrams of ideas made real.

5. VIEW OF WILHELMINA PIER AND KOP VAN ZUID FROM EUROMAST, ROTTERDAM, NETHERLANDS, MASTER PLAN 1987, RIEK BAKKER, TEUN KOOLHAAS, HUBERT DE BOER

ROTTERDAM: FROM EDGE TO CENTER THROUGH ICON AND INFILL

Rotterdam, unlike many other world ports, has actually survived as a major industrial center because of its commitment to accommodating the scale of contemporary shipping, rail transport, and trucking—outside of the center city. Rotterdam expressed its modernity in 1960 with its soaring Euromast tower, the highest elevation in the Netherlands, an expression of the city's ambition sited in a park overlooking what was then an active industrial port.[9] It also overlooked many areas still undeveloped, a testament to the scale of the bombing at the beginning of World War II, which leveled the center city and its waterfront. Fifty-seven years after the war, the view from the Euromast includes vast urban redevelopments, with the latest, Kop van Zuid, still incomplete (fig. 5). The first major plan for the destroyed inner city came in 1946, when it was assumed

that the waterfront would be largely dedicated to shipping. Like New York's Battery, the Boompjes, which had functioned as the city's front yard, was seen as largely for vehicular traffic, much the way Robert Moses saw most of the waterfronts of Manhattan and Brooklyn.

Two very different visions for the future of the Rotterdam waterfront developed in the late 1970s and early 1980s. At the project scale, there was the redevelopment of Oude Haven (the old harbor) as a largely pedestrian waterfront—including old ships and a marine museum—with a mix of historically inspired and unusual architecture (including architect Piet Blom's Cube Houses, bright-yellow diagonal boxes on stilts proposed in 1978 and completed in 1984) that presented the waterfront as a new pleasure ground for the city. For the Office of Metropolitan Architecture, from the start, Oude Haven was moving in an uninspired, retroactive direction. The 1979–82 proposal for the Boompjes TowerSlab by Rem Koolhaas/OMA for the City of Rotterdam offered an alternative to the ethic of architectural entertainment apparent in the novelty buildings, historical or new, on the old harbor. The TowerSlab, which was never built, offered a very different vision for the front yard of Rotterdam on the north bank of the River Maas. Koolhaas described the proposal in "Soft Substance, Harsh Town" in his collaborative

6. ERASMUS BRIDGE, KOP VAN ZUID, ROTTERDAM, NETHERLANDS, 1996, UN STUDIO; FOREGROUND, KPN TELECOM TOWER, 2000, RENZO PIANO BUILDING WORKSHOP

1995 book *S, M, L, XL* with an acerbic commentary on the process of the Boompjes scheme that skewered the postmodern urban vision for the city.[10] In a famous, much published series of drawings of acute-angle towers leaning over the still dangerous, heavily trafficked, and polluted Maas, Koolhaas put OMA's more dangerous vision of the harbor into the mental map of world architecture. The port was losing its props of industry, yet OMA, rightly, believed that the harbor should recognize the dynamic complexity of its present—charm, modern or historical, had to be tempered with reality. Rotterdam's 1985 plan for its inner city was the first major planning effort since the 1946 reconstruction plan. The Waterstad Plan, completed in 1986, called for a mix of activities to strengthen the connection between the center city and the waterfront, which would once again function as Rotterdam's front yard. The largest development area, Kop van Zuid in South Rotterdam, arrived at its core plan in 1987 with a design by Riek Bakker with Teun Koolhaas and Hubert de Boer. The plan called for the reorganization of the district and the construction of a new bridge linking Kop van Zuid to the center city on the north bank.

The Kop van Zuid plan consisted of two major areas. For the Wil-

helmina Pier, six hundred feet across and a half mile long, directly south of the Boompjes, there were rows of tall buildings. The pier, three narrow blocks wide, was dedicated largely to tall buildings, including Norman Foster's World Port Center, completed in 2000, which had a programming philosophy not unlike that of New York's World Trade Center built twenty-three years earlier: the physical port was gone, but its intellectual activity could continue at the city's core. Some of the past was preserved, including the headquarters of Holland America Line, in service from the beginning of the twentieth century to the 1980s. It is an imposing twin-towered structure at the tip of the pier that now houses the Hotel New York, a restaurant opened in 1993. (While it abandoned its historic headquarters, Holland America secured its ongoing identity in Rotterdam with the revival of the cruise ship industry in the 1980s. Passenger ships continue to dock at the pier, at the restored arrival and departure terminal that reopened in 1997.) Many local Rotterdammers have little love for the restaurant: they cannot face another ride on the launch across the Maas with their out-of-town guests, yet they have to concede that it is an instructive example of how historic preservation and adaptive reuse can be the introduction to a new idea of the waterfront, not its demise. Wilhelmina Pier kept its signature building yet undertook a massive new building program as well.

The second part of Kop van Zuid, a mile-long wedge from the waterfront inland, with two inlets, is largely dedicated to

7. KOP VAN ZUID AND CENTER CITY, MODEL, ROTTERDAM, NETHERLANDS, IN PUBLIC PLANNING OFFICE, DEPARTMENT OF URBAN PLANNING AND HOUSING

housing, organized into mostly perimeter blocks (with continuous and broken courtyards). The most engaging architecture happens at the joint between the two parts of the Kop van Zuid reclamation plan, where a new bridge reaches the south bank. Here, Renzo Piano's KPN Telecom tower, completed in 2000, with its leaning facade bearing down on a twelve-story strut, is a distant echo of OMA's never realized Boompjes TowerSlab designed two decades earlier (fig. 6).

Rotterdam has an active civic tradition of engaged debate in developing its architecture. This means that it looked to the successes of Baltimore in turning its harbor into an entertainment center—declaring itself a sister city in 1986[11]—even while it invited the most ambitious urban design thinkers and designers of the time, who were far less American in their outlook, to address its future. Among other efforts, Architecture International Rotterdam, an assembly of architects and urban planners held in phases from 1979 into the 1980s, included Francesco dal Co, Giorgio Grassi, and others who were then at the cutting edge of urban thought. Josef Paul Kleihues, who would go on to set the urban design pattern for Berlin, as well as Aldo Rossi, Oswald Matthias Ungers, and other stellar urbanist architects entered their ideas for the master plan of Kop van Zuid. Yet there was a point when, as F. Scott Fitzgerald's last tycoon tells the pilot in flight over the Sierra Nevadas, "It does not matter which of several options you take, just that you take one."[12] Neither Rossi's plan for Kop van Zuid nor Koolhaas's Boompjes TowerSlab were the option chosen, but the city benefited from their engagement, visualizing how design could be a generator, not a decorator, of urban life.

Rotterdam's planning department, like its counterpart in Amsterdam, is committed to presenting its work and its progress to local citizens and the world. With the effusive stamina of a second city, which happens to have the largest port in the world, Rotterdam documents its progress in models, maps, and publications (fig. 7). There is a commitment to communication that bears out the seriousness of the built artifact, as in the Department of Urban Planning and Housing's map of the city, region, and port, which contains a virtual seminar in urban information.[13] On its cover is the 1996 Erasmus Bridge that links central Rotterdam and Kop van Zuid, designed by the team now organized as UN Studio.

8. ERASMUS BRIDGE CENTRAL TOWER BEING BARGED INTO PLACE, ROTTERDAM, NETHERLANDS, 1996, UN STUDIO

UN STUDIO: FLOWS AND FORM ON THE MAAS AND BEYOND

The most important work of architecture in the Kop van Zuid project is not technically architecture at all but the bridge designed by the firm then known as van Berkel & Bos Architectuur Bureau, now operating an interdisciplinary practice as the UN (standing for United Network) Studio. The Erasmus Bridge, named for perhaps the greatest freethinker of the Northern Renaissance (1466–1536), is a single-tower, cable-stayed structure. The form, designed through technical equations yet imbued with reference to the port's industrial past, rises in the middle of the harbor, serving pedestrians, bicyclists, and cars. It functions as both an icon of the city and a physical link for redevelopments to the south (fig. **8**).

UN Studio principal Ben van Berkel is, however, leery of calling the bridge an icon, seeing the term as too reductive given the com-plexity of programmatic and structural analysis that went into the bridge and its form. He speaks of the "2,000 facades" of a bridge that was designed to be visible from two thousand sides using contemporary engineering and design software to go far beyond right angles and delineated elevation, plan, and even three-dimensional perspectives.[14] Such software, in van Berkel's view, is part of a postperspectival vision of design and experience in which projects can never be simplified to a two- or even three-dimensional figure. To him, the bridge is of a piece with the Möbius House, completed in 1998 with partner Caroline Bos, in which the never-ending Möbius strip, "a one-sided surface that is constructed from a rectangle by holding one end fixed, rotating the opposite end through 180 degrees, and applying it to the first end," became three-dimensional.[15] In the house, program, circulation, and structure are interwoven. Nonetheless, the two-dimensional image of the Erasmus Bridge—the beautiful, upright wishbone of pale blue steel strung with cables—seems ready-made for today's version of Rotterdam's seal, reproduced on every map and guide to the city.

UN STUDIO IN THE AMERICAN CONTEXT: NEW YORK AND PITTSBURGH

The conceptual approach and experiential benefits of UN Studio's method are playing out on several waterfronts, each with valuable lessons for New York, a city that has yet to commission the firm. UN Studio did, however, participate in 1999 as a finalist in the ideas competition sponsored by the International Foundation of the Canadian Centre for Architecture (IFCCA) to redesign a major portion of Manhattan's West Side, including a stretch of waterfront from 30th to 34th Street. Looking at the edges of New York, van Berkel comments: "This question is related to goods coming in, production—even high finance is related to the mechanical system of the grid and the piers. This is an equipotential that belongs to the industrial era."[16] His firm concentrated on sustaining a "twenty-four-hour cycle of liveliness, accessible to the public." UN Studio did not win the competition, yet New York's City Planning Commission chairman at the time, Joseph Rose, who had served on the competition jury, was intrigued enough to invite van Berkel's team to his office, where they further illuminated their vision of information. It was the first time the planners had seen a contemporary animation of the statistics the department itself had compiled (fig. 9).[17]

How a sophisticated understanding of contemporary cultural and economic activity, of data and flow, can translate into waterfront architecture since the breakthrough Erasmus Bridge is an ongoing challenge for UN Studio. In Pittsburgh, Pennsylvania, for example, it was again a finalist in an international competition, this time for a science center, and it won the competition for the reinvention of the main wharf in Genoa, Italy. For a site at the mouth of the Allegheny as it flows into the Ohio, UN Studio lost the competition to French architect Jean Nouvel, whereas in Genoa, it won the two-round contest to complete a design for one of the most prominent waterfront sites on the Mediterranean.

While it will not be realized, the Carnegie Science Center design by UN Studio illustrates many crucial concerns for waterfront projects. The center plans to renovate and expand its existing quarters by 160,000 square feet, on a site with thirteen acres

10. CARNEGIE SCIENCE CENTER COMPETITION, RENDERING, PITTS-
BURGH, PENNSYLVANIA, 2001, UN STUDIO

11. HEINZ FIELD, PITTSBURGH, PENNSYLVANIA, 2001, HOK
SPORT+VENUE+EVENT

overlooking the river. The center is adjacent to major new developments on the city's North Shore, including waterfront baseball and
football stadiums, a major park, and the private development generated by these high-profile facilities. The center was explicit about its
goal to have the project be as memorable as the Sydney Opera
House in Australia, which opened in 1973, or the Guggenheim Bilbao
in Spain, which opened in 1997. As if to emphasize the desire for a
waterfront icon equal to the opera house and the museum, the center's chairman declared that "we want this building to be related in
large measure to the river, perhaps cantilevered out over the water."[18]
For van Berkel, this urge for an iconic monument cannot be the driving principle, although he concedes that Pittsburgh had a need for,
"as some politicians say, something that could start to attract you.
There are these black holes in the city that need an attractor. People
make choices. It is like the eyes in the face—the eyes attract you."[19]
Starting with the 200,000-square-foot existing building and a program that needed to incorporate and express science and technology with space for exhibitions and educational programs, UN Studio
developed a "circle of experiences" for the visitor (fig. 10). The firm
produced a scheme for the project that effectively avoided touching
the center's existing building. It conceived of the new 160,000-
square-foot project as a tube that turns back on itself, forming a

Y with one leg down to the ground and two cantilevering above the
site and the river. For van Berkel, this does not "refer to moving
along the ramp in a cinematographic and perspectival series";
instead circulation creates an "implosion of visual experiences."[20]
The waterfront is an important place to see, and it should be a primary place for architecture that, as van Berkel puts it, is always "giving information back to you from another point," about its program,
about its structure, about its site, and, at its most ambitious, about
the real complexity of contemporary life.[21]
UN Studio could not have proposed a more aggressive contrast to
the relatively staid program, structure, and siting of the nearby stadiums. The contrast between what the center and the sports facilities will "give back" is informative. Much was demolished to make
way for the stadiums, from warehouses to senior housing and a river
rescue center to town houses and a union headquarters, as well as
the existing Three Rivers Stadium.[22] The new 64,500-seat stadium
for the Steelers football team, Heinz Field, just east of the science
center, was completed by HOK Sport+Venue+Event (HOK S+V+E) in
2001 (fig. 11). A football stadium, to the chagrin of urban planners
everywhere, tends to operate as dead space for most of the year,
coming alive for less than a score of Sundays in season no
matter who plans or designs it, and often its seating strategy

12. PONTE PARODI COMPETITION—WINNING ENTRY, AERIAL COLLAGE, RENDERING, GENOA, ITALY, 2001, UN STUDIO

UN STUDIO IN GENOA

precludes leaving an end open to its site. At Heinz Field, however, there is a direct effort to orient the project to its waterfront site, with a horseshoe seating arrangement that leaves the river side open (with the scoreboard at its center) and looks south across the river to Point Street Park. Sited to the west of the science center, PNC Park, the new 38,000-seat stadium for the Pirates baseball team, also designed by HOK S+V+E, also opened in 2001, has an even stronger relationship to the city and the waterfront. From the walkway leading from downtown across the bridge, to the design of the seating, the stadium offers spectators an open view of the water and the city.

In looking at the flows of contemporary life, which UN Studio so decisively analyzes, and the special character of urban waterfront sites, it is important to reevaluate whether a stadium is as important an opportunity for architecture as a science center or museum. Van Berkel, like his Pittsburgh cofinalists Jean Nouvel and Daniel Libeskind, designed his proposal in the context of patronage, while the stadiums, civic-minded as they may be, are designed fundamentally within the value system of business. There is no reason to jettison HOK S+V+E's formidable expertise and urban sensibility for the sake of UN Studio, but there is every reason to insist that cities look to stadiums for cultural expression as bold as they expect from art museums.

UN Studio's waterfront projects, built and unbuilt, are in the business of finding meaning and yielding form to the future of public life. The methods of collection and analysis so fruitfully developed in UN Studio's IFCCA scheme and the waterfront-engaging, interactive environment of its proposal for Pittsburgh are applied to a work commissioned by the City of Genoa, where the firm won an extraordinary opportunity to design a piazza on the harbor (fig. 12). "We looked at the students, tourists, overnight visitors, residents," explains van Berkel, "and asked, How could attractors for all these different groups be linked?" He explored "the programming of a three-dimensional square on the water, a [town] square made more spatial." UN Studio looked at it in terms of "a volume program." The goal was not to bring "the harbor

13. PONTE PARODI COMPETITION, PERSPECTIVE RENDERING, GENOA, ITALY, 2001, UN STUDIO

to the city" but rather to bring the "liveliness of the city" to the harbor.[23]

In Genoa, UN Studio found itself in a city, like Rotterdam, determined to engage contemporary design as part of its identity. Like the Kop van Zuid, Genoa's disused industrial docks and piers were targets of redevelopment in the 1980s. The Italian city decided to regenerate its former port area, including, among other projects, an international exposition that opened in 1992. The Renzo Piano Building Workshop undertook the expo-driven redesign of the port, managing both the reuse of existing buildings and the construction of new buildings. The reestablishment of a connection between the port and the city at the Piazza Caricamento was a major part of Piano's plan. *Bigo*, Piano's huge sculpture of a derrick with cables and booms, is seemingly intent on still doing the work of unloading ships.

A decade later, the City of Genoa, together with the city's Port Authority and Porto Antico, a public company, continued efforts to renew the harbor through culturally ambitious planning and design. The competition for the reuse of the Ponte Parodi, a breakwater at the midpoint of the port, anticipated the removal of two huge cargo warehouses and the possible retention of the iconic 266-foot-high disused grain silo built in the 1960s. The reuse of the 1886 breakwater, which was named after its engineer, Adolfo Parodi, and holds

the status of the most important monument of the early industrialization of Genoa's port, is a potent symbol for a new urban life in the twenty-first century.

The UN Studio design uses all the tools of transparency and circulation to be read in three dimensions, if not also the fourth dimension, time (fig. 13). Not surprisingly, given the studio's commitment to multiple perspectives, the "square" is broken off and opened up into an imperfect, layered cube. The breached cube reaches up into an amphitheater open to the harbor, sloping over the glazed section of activities underneath its top. It is a strategy of three grounds: water, deck, and the undulating exterior upper deck echoing the building and topography of the city.

As finalists, UN Studio explained that the 3-D square "is not seeking the cosmetic effect of an isolated object" but is an "event in a chain of multiple connections."[24] It named the square Piazza del Mediterraneo, a "generator of contemporary urban experience." To achieve this, van Berkel hopes to produce the "piazza effect," which makes a place not just space to go through but to come to and use. Acutely conscious of trying to bring the dimension of time to the project, UN Studio's mission is to make it busy throughout the day and evening, because now the port is busy only intermittently when passengers board and debark cruise ships. The new design will still accommodate cruise ships at one of the upper levels of the square, where the project will also house auditoriums and exhibition space for technology-oriented programs. At the wharf level, there will be cinemas, discotheques, restaurants, as well as the tug service of the working waterfront. On the roof, there will be an amphitheater and a city park with sports, games, and a swimming pool. In brief, Piazza del Mediterraneo is a reexamination, or cross-examination, of public life on the waterfront, and the design outlines the results.

F. O. ARCHITECTS: ON YOKOHAMA BAY

UN Studio is not alone in its emphasis on analyzing the flows of contemporary programs and inscribing them in the form of their designs. This approach to architecture, an effort to bypass the discussion of building types and urban form that dominated the 1970s and 1980s, had a dazzling premier in the results of the 1995 competition for an International Port Terminal twenty miles southwest of Tokyo in Yokohama, where Japan first opened to foreign trade in 1853. The winning scheme by F. O. Architects, the London-based partnership of Farshid Moussavi and Alejandro Zaera-Polo formerly known as Foreign Office Architects, was rigorously situated in the world of ideas. Set atop the level plane of the existing eight-acre Osanbashi Pier in the city's inner harbor, the project is to house cruise ship facilities and public spaces in which the

14. AND 15. INTERNATIONAL PORT TERMINAL, YOKOHAMA, JAPAN, OPENING 2003,
F. O. ARCHITECTS

flow of program and passengers will become the defining measure of the structural system, the circulation pattern, and, ultimately, the form of the terminal (fig. 14).

Yokohama has already built waterfront icons in its gargantuan redevelopment program, the Minato Mirai 21, including the convention center complex dominated by a sail-shaped high-rise. The city's master plan was conceived in 1981 to build a new city center that would connect Yokohama's two waterfront business districts by way of a seventy-five-acre inner harbor infill site. It set the stage for the kind of inventiveness so richly played out in F. O. Architects' scheme.

Among the harbor's other new landmarks, the terminal scheme is unique in its profoundly interactive physical and programmatic engagement with the city. Entered at ground level, the terminal is designed as an extension of the city, shifting the flow of movement from Yamashita Park into the harbor. Just as the standard expectation of boundaries between the city and the pier would be overcome by the terminal's modulating topologies, so would the folded plates of its structure overcome boundaries between ceiling and floor, interior and exterior. In fact, in preparing construction documents and building the pier, some of these boundaries did return (the floors, for example, became wood, distinct from the ceiling,

which exposed its steel structure). Yet it was not a matter of throwing out the design ideas and building a conventional structure. As Zaera-Polo puts it, "Japan allows architects to evoke design throughout the construction process," and he adds that the Japanese engineer referred to the design of F. O. Architects's pier as "a fish that kept moving until it was finally stopped."[25]

In the visual rhetoric of drawings and text, F. O. Architects asserted that it was not the expressive characteristics of the architecture but its performance that drove the design. As Zaera-Polo puts it, architecture is based on "the capacity to coherently integrate materials—materials in the broad sense."[26] When architects say that they do not care about the way things look, only how they perform, and at the same time produce ravishing drawings that win competitions, it is a recklessly dissociative statement, yet, as with F. O. Architects as much as with UN Studio, the proof is in the result. By breaking from deliberations of precedent, such as questions of heritage—what is the heritage of terminals? of piers? of Japanese building?—F. O. Architects arrived at an extraordinary scheme. The exploration of how to redefine what is the ground for architecture in one of the core design projects of the last century is a compelling study, especially on a waterfront site where "the ground" is inevitably open to change. This $100 million project began with the hallmarks of a brilliant paper architecture that would never go forward, and now it will open in 2003 (fig. 15).

LONDON BY THE
MILLENNIUM

16. "LONDON AS IT COULD BE," MODEL, *NEW ARCHITEC-TURE: FOSTER, ROGERS, STIRLING* EXHIBITION, LONDON, ENGLAND, 1986, RICHARD ROGERS PARTNERSHIP

The major London waterfront project in which F. O. Architects was involved, a 2001 proposal to add new outdoor spaces and media-related programs to the existing south bank cultural center, has been put on hold, one in a long line of schemes sought and shelved for the South Bank Centre since the 1960s. London, however, has not stood still; like Yokohama, it has undertaken a relentless program to remake its waterfront. London was the world's largest port from the early 1800s into the twentieth century, and it developed miles of docklands and related industrial uses along its waterfront. With containerization, as in Rotterdam and New York among other cities, London could only maintain its shipping by moving it far out of the city, leaving behind thousands of acres of suddenly redundant port and port-related buildings and spaces. The first forays into

reconstruction in the late 1980s and early 1990s included the thick towers of Canary Wharf, converted warehouses, and the rare elegant modern move of Norman Foster's 1991 glazed office and residential block rising eight stories on the south bank, near Battersea Bridge, which included the architect's own office. Yet these efforts pale compared to the work that was first imagined in the 1980s but not executed until the latter half of the next decade.

London has long benefited from the presence of architects of stature, not only Foster, but also Richard Rogers, who in the 1986 *New Architecture: Foster, Rogers, Stirling* exhibition at the Royal Academy envisioned the Thames as a steel-and-glass-bordered ribbon of modernity running through the city. Rogers's scheme, "London as It Could Be," exhibited a new waterfront, complete with a North Embankment Linear Park connected to the south bank by the technologically expressive replacement for the Hungerford Railway Bridge—a pedestrian bridge with a tram slung underneath connected to futuristic islands and walkways (fig. 16). With the 1993 legislation assigning a quarter of the national lottery income to cultural projects, with the establishment of the 1994 Millennium Commission, and with the 1997 election of Labor's Tony Blair, a charismatic leader determined to put his mark on the UK's

17. MILLENNIUM BRIDGE, LONDON, ENGLAND, 2000 (REOPENED 2002), FOSTER AND PARTNERS/ANTHONY CARO/ARUP ASSOCIATES

18. THE LONDON EYE, SOUTH BANK, LONDON, ENGLAND, 2000, MARKS BARFIELD ARCHITECTS

capital, London was poised to build its new identity. People who believed in the power of design to improve urban life had access to the prime minister. Even before his election, Blair, as leader of the opposition, had secured a life peerage for Richard Rogers, who in 1996 became the Lord of Riverside. Contemporary design was back as a popular symbol for the United Kingdom. (Prince Charles had to put his own house, rather than the architecture of the kingdom, in order.)

However shallow or short-lived the "Cool Britannia" moment that began with Blair's election in 1997 and petered out before the millennium, with the problem that anything "cool" must never aver that it is so, there were architectural and cultural consequences alongside the moment when government and the ineffable buzz of a city in change were in tandem. Foster and especially Rogers took on the Thames as a cultural and ecological point of reference for the type of architecture—and city—that they advocated. Following up the 1986 exhibition, as well as the 1992 publication *A New London*, Rogers stated that he saw "the millennium as the carrot to bring the city back to the river and from there nourish the entire metropolis itself."[27] Rogers's enormous contribution to the new vision of the Thames has been undermined by the failure of his greatest commission, the Millennium Dome in Greenwich, which was to be the city's ready

embrace of the twenty-first century. The ill-fated dome by the Richard Rogers Partnership was not an architectural failure but rather the victim of a strange blindness to contemporary culture in its programming. For all its disappointments, the project laid the ground for redeveloping the former brownfields of the Greenwich peninsula. Foster, too, suffered the temporary debacle of a high-profile project when the thirteen-foot-wide pedestrian Millennium Bridge, closed seventy-two hours after its opening in June 2000, became a shaky icon for the new century (fig. 17). Designed with sculptor Anthony Caro and Arup Associates, the bridge that crosses the Thames at the foot of the Tate Modern reopened in February 2002. London had only eleven bridges in its central six miles along the Thames; it was time for a new one, even if after a hundred years it took a while to get it right.

Most millennium projects did not threaten to collapse, at least not physically. There are mixed critical responses to the British Airways London Eye, the 450-foot-high wheel on which visitors are taken, with all the cornpone world's fair-ist imagination that current marketing can provide, on a "flight" above London. Yet unlike the Millennium Dome, this temporary project, sited on the south bank, just above Westminster Bridge, has been a great popular success. While it does not engage the waterfront directly, it is a formi-

19. GREATER LONDON AUTHORITY HEADQUARTERS FROM RIVERSIDE WALK, PHOTOMONTAGE, SOUTH BANK, LONDON, ENGLAND, 2002, FOSTER AND PARTNERS

dable waterfront building. Lifted almost 500 feet above London, "passengers" cannot help but see the "River City" that Rogers has long wanted them to see (fig. 18). In a media-saturated era, the tools for "seeing" the city, for understanding its ecology, its potential, its public life, its architecture, sometimes have to be as blunt as a ride, hundreds of feet into the sky, in order to get a new perspective, or perhaps a new kaleidoscopic vision. The Eye was an entry in a competition sponsored by London's *Sunday Times* and the Architecture Foundation that asked for a millennium project and left it to the competitors to decide what that might be. The winning team, the partnership of Marks Barfield Architects, created an idea, a program, and a design for a contemporary Ferris wheel. This is design engaged, not as an afterthought but as integral to reimagining a city. (Whether or not the Eye survives, Marks Barfield's approach will be permanently visible by the end of 2002 in the new Millbank Pier, on the north bank, a thirty-meter welded steel structure that will provide a dock for boats shuttling back and forth from the Tate Britain in Westminster to the Tate Modern in Southwark.)

Just to the south of the Eye is the London Aquarium, the adaptive reuse of what had been the Greater London Council, the government body eliminated by the Thatcher administration in 1986. For the resurgent London government, elected in 2000, there is a new structure designed by Foster and Partners, six bridges downstream and opposite the Tower of London. The Greater London Authority (GLA) building, completed in 2002 and sited toward the east, where

London is redeveloping, serves as a working icon for the first London government of this generation (fig. 19). Just like the Houses of Parliament, the symbolic importance of being on the Thames is vital. The new glazed city hall has the rhetoric and reality of ecologically thoughtful design, from the slope and angle of its south elevation to its use of Thames water for cooling. As Foster puts it, the ten-story building "will be ideally positioned to allow the development of a fully integrated environmental agenda, exploiting the natural resources of wind, sun, and water."[28]

From a New York perspective, it is an arresting move in its aggressive relationship to existing landmarks. The GLA building is part of the privately developed "More London" urban design scheme, with master plan by Foster and Partners, for thirteen acres with riverside walks, public squares, offices, hotels, and stores. It is also adamantly expressive, determined in its memorable form to become as much an icon as the adjacent 1894 Tower Bridge. As with the Eye, in Foster's Greater London Authority there is a clear ideology of the importance of views. The design includes London's Living Room at the top of the structure and a rooftop garden. In this, it echoes the Tower Bridge itself, with its high pedestrian walkways, 140 feet above the Thames. Yet the GLA stands out and in so doing makes clear that if the waterfront is to be the city's front yard,

20. TATE MODERN, SOUTHWARK, LONDON, ENGLAND, 2000, HERZOG &
DE MEURON

it cannot be driven by discreet or banal urban design projects. The waterfront has to be energized by extraordinary, memorable projects, whether buildings, landscapes, or entire districts, but with focused ambition that operates at the scale of the waterfront.

The new vision for a Thames-oriented London received a spectacularly successful rush of realization when the Tate Modern opened in 2000, with a design by Herzog & de Meuron (fig. 20). The firm, based in Basel, Switzerland, won an international competition for the commission, demonstrating an adaptive reuse that does not diminish the visual and structural force of its past incarnation as the Bankside Power Station. Inside or out, the Tate Modern sustains the pragmatically sublime scale of Giles Gilbert Scott's original design, which was conceived shortly after World War II, fully complete by 1963, and out of commission as a power plant by 1981. In the annals of adaptive reuse of industrial structures, two decades is a very brief fallow period. As with seemingly every new project along the Thames, the former industrial behemoth has become not only a monument to look at but a building to look from, with a café above the turbine hall looking across the new bridge to St. Paul's Cathedral. The same spirit is in evidence with the adaptive reuse of the Oxo Tower, a former power-generating station for the post office on the south bank just west of Blackfriars Bridge, designed by Lifschutz Davidson and completed in 1997. There, above three commercial floors and five floors of apartments, the ninth floor has two restaurants looking out at the Thames. As with the Eye, as with the Greater London Authority, this is a city that cannot stop looking at itself.

21. FERRY TERMINAL, HAMBURG, GERMANY, 1993, ALSOP ARCHITECTS

ALSOP ARCHITECTS: ON THE RIVER THAMES AND OTHER WATERFRONTS

Closer to street level, London will be better able to look at itself from the proposed remaking of Blackfriars Bridge, an inhabited structure intended to span the Thames just west of the city of London. Representing the next generation after Rogers and Foster, the elder statesmen of London's architectural community, there is a waterfront thinker and practitioner with a keen view of his city, its river, and its future. Will Alsop's perspective on the changes in London, and on architectural design for waterfronts and urban life, is a remarkable one in that he is a fearless form-maker with a taste for structural bravado and is highly versed in urban planning, urban design, and community involvement. He brings this sensibility, and the ability to evolve projects from intense planning processes to highly articulate architecture, whether to the north bank of the

Thames or to the master plan for the redevelopment of Rotterdam Centraal now on the boards, a long-term, mass-transit-based mixed-use project under way since 2000.

One of Alsop's first major projects was the ferry terminal in Hamburg, with a design first proposed in a competition in the late 1980s and completed in 1993 (fig. 21). Like most of the projects in this discussion, the terminal was sited in the part of the city that had once been an active port that was made redundant by container shipping in the early 1960s. The six-story, six-hundred-foot-long building situated along the length of the quay has an anthropological profile, with a high waist at the fourth floor and a swelled chest of glass above its concrete frame, where offices and public spaces with views of the Elbe are found. Alsop's ability to integrate a highly tectonic language with what can only be described as the experiential pleasures of architecture—decks stayed by thin cables, boarding through glazed tubes, an aggressive, memorable profile that has a technical and cultural relationship to its site—is unparalleled.

The opposite condition prevails at the existing Blackfriars train station, which, in Alsop's terms, is "buried under development" in the existing Puddle Dock area.[29] Alsop Architects is looking at ways to improve the entire area around the station, noting that in a post–World War II mixed-use redevelopment it was cut off

22. BLACKFRIARS BRIDGE, RENDERING, LONDON, ENGLAND, 2001, ALSOP ARCHITECTS

from the water and "lost its appeal…it didn't have any sex, no ambiance."[30] Looking at the whole north bank of central London, he notes: "It is ironic that the wealthiest real estate in Europe has the worst waterfront facilities. In the late 1960s and in the early 1980s, they built lots of housing, but there was no public concern about being on the river's edge."[31]

His most original contribution to the waterfront will be the redesign of the 1869 Blackfriars Bridge itself, which will serve as a rail platform and observation deck (fig. 22). For Alsop, who has never felt that an engineering program should interfere with formal and experiential invention, the redesign of Blackfriars to serve the new configuration of train lines in and out of London offers the chance to invent an occupied span across the Thames. It will be a bridge that also serves as the station platform as well as the most dramatic observation deck since the elevated pedestrian crossings on the Tower Bridge of more than a century before.

The main ticketing area will still be on the north bank, as it is today, but the design, built on an existing rail bridge, recognizes that travelers, for the first time since rail served the capital, are as likely to want to go to the south bank as the north, so a ticketing hall will be added to the south end. Just to the east there is the Tate Modern and beyond that the Globe Theatre. To meet the programmatic needs of the station over the river, Alsop had to add an independent structure off the existing bridge to the west, a light steel element resting on the disused bridge piers in the river below. Transparent

in its structural logic and lightness, Alsop's design is simultaneously aggressive and sensitive in its reuse and expansion of a piece of London's infrastructural past.

The platforms, not thoroughly enclosed but with a glazed and metal roof high above and glass windshields on the sides, will offer the people waiting, changing, or just traveling through an open view of the Thames. Alsop's design imagination is driven by the experience rather than the abstraction of buildings and spaces he has designed. He wants travelers to feel the wind or at least a gentle breeze. He wants people to feel only a minimal enclosure, which was part of the rationale for his first proposal of a much higher roof than English Heritage would allow. (He argued, without success, that there was a view of St. Paul's under the roof.)[32] Alsop likes to point out that every train running on the bridge violates the view rules, as does his proposed structure, but while he cannot build as high as he wanted to, as infrastructure Alsop and his team "got a dispensation."[33]

Alsop's project has been delayed, but integral as it is to the remaking of rail service in London and the United Kingdom, it is expected to go ahead. It will be finished in a London far different from that of the early 1990s, where a conspicuous embrace of contemporary design, focused on the River Thames, has symbolized London's successful transition into a global city. Without the bombast of the Parisian *grands projets*, and with sensitivity to its far different role as a port, London is demonstrating that it will not be frozen as a museum, even as it increases its public life. The ability to combine this kind of formal and tectonic imagination with a powerful vision of public life is Alsop's great strength. He states, "What interests me is working with the people who are actually going to use [a project], and the people around it....We use very painful methods...to discover where the architect might be able to avoid debris" and to literally "get everyone painting." The technique has led him to realize that "people are much more inventive" than planning authorities. Sometimes he wonders "who the planners think they are protecting on esthetic grounds." He reports that the method leads to "finding something that you genuinely would not have found when you started," yielding a "collective creativity."[34]

LONDON BEYOND THE MILLENNIUM

To Alsop, the making of good architecture can be summed up by his philosophy for the design of the North Greenwich Underground station on the Jubilee Line Extension, where "the main job was to brighten up somebody's mundane job, jamming on the subway at 8:00 a.m. It is all about lifting the spirits." Not the easiest task at North Greenwich, where the station that opened in 1998 was no longer open to the air above, but under future development.[35] Nonetheless, the station has an airiness and glamour in its steel and blue mosaic surfaces, and it shows not only Alsop's commitment but that of a client with an attitude and a budget reflecting a similar value system, articulated throughout the Jubilee Line Extension project by Chief Architect Roland Paoletti. A formidable political, financing, and engineering achievement, the extension, first

23. GREENWICH PENINSULA URBAN DESIGN PROPOSAL, RENDERING, LONDON, ENG-
LAND, MARKS BARFIELD ARCHITECTS

fully presented in 1992, became by accident of delays the most important millennium project of all, serving as the infrastructural and urban backbone for major projects along the Thames.

The North Greenwich station serves the Greenwich peninsula east of central London, site of the derided dome scheduled to be dismantled. As with the dome itself, there is an opportunity here for far larger, more ecologically and urbanistically transformative projects than in the heart of London. After the success of their controversial but ultimately successful London Eye, Marks Barfield Architects has turned its sights to the area where, with its recently decontaminated soil, new development is possible. Their proposal, largely for housing, is a potent speculation that poses an alternative to the less-than-promising first colonization of the site—the Millennium Village was meant to embody progress—as well as a contrast to Canary Wharf's dockland "city" across the river.

With an attention to landscape and habitat, and a reminder that sometimes towers in a park are all right, the scheme pulls together ideas about the river, the viability of tall buildings, and the relationship between indoors and out, producing a novel ecology of public life (fig. 23). Whether it is ever built or not, the Marks Barfield proposal is emblematic of an urban culture that is committed to seeing itself, an idea at the very core of what a waterfront city can be about—a communication between the larger scale of urban living and the intimate scale of daily life, between the global and the local, between the urban and the natural.

Not every speculation is a good idea. Not every large, intensely designed project is brilliant. Not every urban design that encourages a list of signature buildings is worthwhile, but London's recent history of design should serve as an influential model for major waterfront cities, especially New York. London's reinvention has required enormous investment: a mid-1990s estimate put the investment of public and private funds at $8 billion along thirty-five miles of the Thames. The city's revival was aided not only by funds, but also, like Rotterdam, by a simple big idea: that the city's north and south banks needed to be tied together by their one common amenity, the animated, open space of the Thames. Parts of the city long left to a depressing postindustrial decline were reined in by this new vision, not only on the south bank but also to the east. Even in London, a city more obsessed with its heritage than New York will ever be, and with local communities and environmental regulations as intense, there is room for the new.

24. OLYMPIC VILLAGE, BARCELONA, SPAIN, 1992

BARCELONA: THE EVENT AND THE PROJECT

When government values design and planning, as it so evidently does in London, Amsterdam, and Rotterdam among other cities, the special opportunity of the waterfront—freed from freight cargo, ready to be the working icon of urban life—rises exponentially. In Barcelona, architecture and urban design have been an elemental part of the city's modern identity since the mid-nineteenth century. First was the urban design plan for L'Eixample (the expansion) in 1869, which laid out a street pattern with distinctive 440-foot-square blocks with chamfered corners at every intersection. *Modernisme* architecture filled in that grid from the 1880s into the first decades of the twentieth century. *Modernisme*'s greatest architect, Antonio Gaudí (1852–1926), exemplified the role of architecture in demonstrating a nationalist, Catalan identity, which was also dis-

tinctly modern and European. With the political release that came with the fall of Francisco Franco in 1975, Barcelona slowly reconnected to its history and legacy of design sophistication. Recently, the director of foreign economic promotion for Barcelona City Hall, Mario Rubert, declared: "In Barcelona, we cherish design. Our buildings, public spaces, street lighting, and signage are not only functional but reflect aesthetics and our architectural history."[36]

In the 1980s, Barcelona began the transformation of its waterfront, beginning with the Port Vell (old port) at the base of the Rambla, the broad street that cuts from L'Eixample to the Plaça Portal de la Pau at the water. Here, what was an undistinguished blockade of roadways next to a dismal loading dock has become an urban showpiece. In a design by Manuel de Sola-Morales, a seminal figure in Spain's reemergence as an internationally significant center for design and urbanism, the infrastructural functions were preserved by reorganizing the roadways and trolley tracks into a layered assemblage that gives primacy to the seaside view while allowing industrial and commercial traffic to coexist—without an elevated highway obstructing the view—with pedestrian walkways at both the upper city level and sloping down to the water. A one-third-mile-long waterfront plaza, the Moll de la Fusta, gridded with palms, and raised footpaths connect the city and the water. The result took advantage of the necessary infrastructure to

25. UNIVERSAL FORUM OF CULTURES, RENDERING, BARCELONA, SPAIN, OPENING 2004

create the type of vantage points that define successful waterfront projects. It also set up a model, and an approach, for allowing Barcelona to reclaim its waterfront for recreation even as it maintained its beltway, either through partially burying the highway or decking over it with parks running straight to the shore.

Barcelona, even before the Olympics, had a government and an architectural culture committed to improving the city and harnessing its greatest experiential resource—the Mediterranean coast—at the heart of the city. Planning and design for the 1992 Olympic Games spurred projects throughout Barcelona, yet it provided a special impetus to further reunite the city to the sea, and in the process, brought new housing, hotels, office buildings, and nightlife to the waterfront. The Olympic Village, by Martorell, Bohigas, Mackay, and Puigdomenech, was deployed as an extension of the city, cutting through the old industrial edge. In particular, the Olympic Port, less than a mile east of the Moll de la Fusta, became the joint between two urban scales: one, the dense historic core; the other, the broader scale of what had been the industrial sector of the city, the Poblenou (fig. 24).

Barcelona typically combines a sophisticated sense of urban design with a passion for the individual building, inviting scores of talented architects, local and international, to contribute designs. It craves the distinctive—as with the waterside shopping center,

topped by a 177-foot-long fish sculpture by Frank Gehry—as well as the sober and the urbane.[37] Yet not all critics were impressed; some felt that in the 1992 Olympics rebuilding effort, urban design's gain was building design's loss. Critic Joseph Giovannini wrote: "The underlying achievement of the Barcelona Olympics is that Barcelonans reclaimed their neglected city by impressive works for infrastructure, but the regret is that the architecture might have been allowed to make a more significant contribution."[38] The greatest legacy of the games may be the reanimation of the waterfront beyond the Olympic Village. West of the village, a very urban waterfront along the Barceloneta was built: the marina in the center, and to the east a long, undulating parkway running along a series of sandy coves that serve as a city beach at the scale of the region. Barcelona's commitment to urban design and designers works, though not always perfectly, at the multiple scales that an urban waterfront demands.

By 1995, plans for a second phase of waterfront redevelopment—as ambitious as the first—were under way. Once again, the city was using the vehicle of a major international event to push forward a vast rebuilding agenda, determined to combine the highest standards for both its architecture and its urban design. Endorsed by UNESCO in 1999, the Barcelona 2004 Universal Forum of Cultures, sponsored by the Barcelona City Council with the support of the Catalan and Spanish governments, is "conceived as an international gathering to discuss issues of peace, cultural diversity,

26. BIODIVERSITY PAVILION, RENDERING, BARCELONA, SPAIN, OPENING 2004, MVRDV

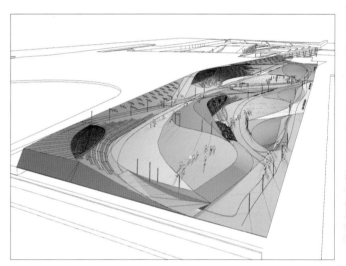

27. SEASIDE PARK/AMPHITHEATER, RENDERING, BARCELONA, SPAIN, OPENING 2004, F. O. ARCHITECTS/TERESA GALI

and environmental sustainability," and less universally, "as a way of boosting town planning in blighted areas."[39]

The first major move for this second round of waterfront renewal involves the Poblenou, an area once known as a manufacturing center, dubbed the "Manchester of the Mediterranean," where the grid of L'Eixample is maintained yet never completed as planned. The Avenue Diagonal, intended to reach from the heart of the late-nineteenth-century city, the Plaça de les Glories Catalanes, to the sea, finally reached its destination in 1998, laying the groundwork for the area's reinvention.

The site for the Universal Forum is at the east edge of the Poblenou—at the end of the Diagonal where it meets the Mediterranean shoreline—and extends east to the shore of the Besos River (fig. 25). Together with redevelopment plans for the Besos riverfront, the Universal Forum occupies a 1.5-mile Mediterranean shoreline and 247 acres, and while it will run for 155 days, its built impact will last for decades (fig. 25). A series of competitions in 2000, with a jury including Josep Acebillo, chief architect of the Barcelona City Council, as well as Barcelona-based architects and historians such as Ignasi Sola-Morales, led to commissions for twenty-four architecture and engineering firms chosen out of the 157 who competed. Several innovative designers with a special talent for waterfront

sites were selected, including Herzog & de Meuron, designers of the Tate Modern on the Thames, here landlocked yet with the main building and plaza for forum events as their commission. MVRDV, architects of the Silodam housing on Amsterdam's waterfront, were chosen together with Barcelona-based Enric Massip to design the biodiversity pavilion at the waterfront zoo. Their design draws on MVRDV's Dutch Pavilion at the Hannover 2000 exposition; in Barcelona, the playful multilevel landscapes of the pavilion now include water as an artificial ground plane (fig. 26). A similarly acute sense of the artificial construction of nature is borne through in the proposed "dunes" of the 1,650-foot-long, 330-foot-wide coastal park and open-air auditorium design by F. O. Architects with Barcelona-based landscape architect Teresa Gali (fig. 27), designed with the same convictions regarding created topographies as the firm had used in Yokohama.

The forum's master plan does not eliminate infrastructure but modifies it, expanding public transport along the newly opened stretch of the Diagonal, adding a photovoltaic solar-energy generating plant, and upgrading the wastewater treatment plant enough to build an esplanade beside it. The Catalans have shown that one way to make great architecture, or great urban design, is through the program of a major, if temporary, international event. It is impressive how a world's fair approach actually leads to permanent improvements in Barcelona, and the brilliant range of talents that are brought to bear on a site is also impressive. This time, as well, in an era when the strictures of responsible urbanism have been loosened, the architects may be able to express a fuller range of contemporary design than with the 1992 Games. Yet perhaps the most critical lesson of Barcelona's waterfront is the commitment to "the project," to understanding that a master plan doesn't change cities, projects do, and that projects require a campaign approach, from the cultural event to which they are attached to the selection of architects to construction. The method advanced in Barcelona beginning in the 1980s established the importance of the project, meaning a comprehensible, large-scale urban design initiative in which transportation needs are met yet at the same time subsumed in larger urban goals. Acebillo is adamant on the importance of staying focused on creating specific, concrete additions to the city: "Personally, I don't believe in the master plan, but only in the project."[40] The focus on the project gives the public a clear sense that the product—the building, the place—actually matters, that it is not merely a calculation of attendance, or increased leasing rates per square foot, that has to be measured. It is this conviction about the product, both at the scale of urban design and the building, that does not always yield perfect waterfront architecture, but sets up the expectation of quality without which extraordinary design cannot happen.

BILBAO: THE CULTURAL ICON AS DRIVER

Bilbao, on the Nervión River that flows into the Atlantic, remains a significant industrial port, yet, like far larger ports, it has found that industry no longer functions at the heart of the city. At the beginning of the 1990s, following a long economic decline, Bilbao was focused on rejuvenating itself and determined that new design could not only reconnect its own citizens to their civic identity but also generate foreign and national investments and tourist dollars. Three hundred miles to the southeast, the Catalans had Barcelona; perhaps the people of the Basque region could, even in a down-at-the-heels industrial city without a Mediterranean shore, have the same.

In 1997, the city completed Frank Gehry's ineffably affecting Guggenheim Museum Bilbao on the Nervión, a project that

28. GUGGENHEIM MUSEUM BILBAO, BILBAO, SPAIN, 1997, FRANK GEHRY.

began design in 1991. In Bilbao, the free forms of the building-size sculpture of a fish that Gehry did in Barcelona were abstracted, expanded, and integrated into a complex urban structure that cannot be identified as sculpture or architecture but only as both. The best-known view is from across the Nervión and shows the subtly glistening curves bunched together in an iconic knot of art and architecture on the river, packed into a dense city. Yet there are other, critical views down the river, showing how the Guggenheim is part of a much larger urban renewal program to transform its 1950s industrial center into a mixed-use district characterized by high-caliber architecture and landscaped open spaces. In fact, the folly of the marble-clad tower on the other side of the bridge was kept in the design to make sure that the museum had a presence from vantage points up and down the river. In Bilbao, as in Barcelona, a unified program is at work, supported and energized by public sector involvement, to identify the city as a cultural capital.

Beyond the glittering titanium of Gehry's museum, Bilbao's cultural revival is in evidence at every beautiful Foster and Partners–designed subway entrance, completed in 1995, the most memorable urban infrastructure since Hector Guimard's Metro entrances appeared on the streets of Paris a century ago. The city's reinvention also includes work by Spanish architects: an airport renovation completed in 2000 by Santiago Calatrava, who is also the author of

a 1996 footbridge across the river, and a new conference and performing arts center by Federico Soriano and Dolores Palacios, which opened in 1999.

The conference center and the Guggenheim Museum are at opposite ends of the Abandoibarra district, which is at the center of the city and not far from its old downtown. The district, a landfill site along the Nervión, is to provide a pedestrian-oriented link between the downtown and the river, with public spaces and new offices, housing, and shopping. Initiated in 1993, the publicly funded urban plan involves a reopening of the city to the waterfront. The plan was led by Cesar Pelli & Associates and Balmori Associates, both based in the United States, and Aguinaga & Associates of Spain.

The Guggenheim is tightly tied into its site, both in the waterfront bending out over the river and in the galleries and ramps slipping underneath the Puente de la Salve bridge (fig. 28). The building is an urban connector, linking city streets with the riverbank fifty feet below grade. Yet it is folly to overemphasize the context of the Guggenheim Museum Bilbao. Gehry is acutely conscious of the front yard–backyard site and gave the front yard a startlingly successful finish, allowing his clattering mix of orthogonal, windowed architecture for the elevations off the river, back behind the titanium swirls. Bilbao's image in the world has been irrefutably transformed not by the overall master plan, or even the high caliber of the infrastructure and other designs that went with it, but by one overwhelming waterfront design. When the novelty of

Gehry's design wears off, Bilbao's new identity will still resonate, with a citizenry and an international audience expecting great buildings, great public spaces, and the reuse of what seemed to be devastated, irrecoverable districts. "In Bilbao," says Gehry, "they had the problem that no one knew where it was. They asked for a Sydney Opera House, they asked to establish Bilbao with an art museum."[41] And establish Bilbao they did, attracting 1.3 million visitors to the museum, and the city, in its first year.

LOOKING AGAIN AT AMERICAN WATERFRONTS

From a planning perspective, the United States has been a leader in urban waterfront renewal, regeneration, and reclamation, whether in turning the inner harbor from desolate docks to an urban playground in Baltimore, Maryland, starting as early as the 1960s, or in the relentlessly urbane endeavors on the peninsula of Charleston, South Carolina, led by its mayor of almost three decades, Joseph Riley. For lessons in getting new activities and new people to the waterfront, several cities along the country's coasts, lakes, and rivers are unparalleled.

Some waterfront projects are exceptional, some are not. Many fall into the second category, from the drably unimaginative reuses of old warehouses at the Charlestown Navy Yard on Boston Harbor to the 1980s projects on the Hudson waterfront in

Jersey City, New Jersey, that read as crude diagrams of leasable space, jammed up against the Hudson. There are always explanations: tight money, a bad decade in architectural culture, a developer's or community's unenthusiastic response to a city's or state's public access requirements, as with a public walkway that is punishingly grim (or pleasant enough but locked).[42] And then there are the mass-market blended cocktails of mixeduse, poured out in city after city. The programs of shops, restaurants, and entertainment that typify these are fine; the dilemma comes in their numbing sameness among cities, even countries. The waterfronts they create are dull to the bone.

On the flip side, there are waterfronts that are unquestionably exceptional by virtue of their urban performance, in which the overall range of activity, adjacency, and use build an irresistibly vibrant place. More rare is the virtue of the design of the built artifact itself. Pittsburgh undeniably excels in the category of performance. Not only did it build a new baseball stadium on the water, drawing on a once-lost American tradition of baseball as a game integrated into the life of its cities, it even built a new stadium for football—a sport whose schedule, audience, and history are far more suburban—as part of a campaign to reanimate the riverfront as much or more than the proposed expansion of the Carnegie Science Center. The precise architectural resolution does not always meet a contemporary eye's expectations, but projects like these show that the waterfront can be both foreground and background, a place to travel through, across, and along, as well as a place to go. Museums are often extraordinary works of architecture, driven by their patrons' need to erect a monument as nuanced and startling as the art or science it contains, but American cities and programs can also show that there is more to life in the public realm than eating pastries in the museum café. Three urban-scale projects, in San Francisco, Boston, and Philadelphia, illuminate the strengths and weaknesses of American design approaches to the waterfront.

29. HARRY BRIDGES PLAZA, SAN FRANCISCO, CALIFORNIA, 2000, ROMA DESIGN GROUP

SAN FRANCISCO: WATERFRONT CROSSROADS

Of all American cities on the water, San Francisco has an incomparable natural advantage in the beauty of its harbor and the most terrible disadvantage in its vulnerability to earthquakes and the fires that can follow them. After the 1906 earthquake and fire, San Francisco did rebuild, but it chose to largely ignore the grand plans that the leader of America's City Beautiful movement, Daniel Burnham, and his collaborators Edward H. Bennett and Willis Polk had been working on for two years. San Francisco passed on the opportunity afforded by the tragedy to unify the city through diagonal avenues and grand squares.[43] The city did little to modify its basic double grids—one up and down, the other at a diagonal—with the two patterns meeting at Market Street. Market Street ran through the heart of the city down to the docks of the Embarcadero, in a

direct line to the 240-foot clock tower of Arthur Page Brown's 1898 Beaux-Arts monument to urban transportation, the Ferry Terminal Building. The city already had an appetite for grandeur, and Burnham, known for the 1902 McMillan Plan for Washington, D.C., wanted to give them more by keeping the grids but rationalizing—and beautifying—them through a system of diagonal avenues.

San Francisco held on to its basic layout of streets until 1956, which brought an overlay far less elegant in form and function than the City Beautiful boulevards envisioned a half century before: the highway, including the double-decker Embarcadero Freeway from the Bay Bridge past Market Street to Broadway, separating downtown from its piers, and blocking the view of the Ferry Terminal Building. In a city where, since the building of the Golden Gate and Bay bridges in the late 1930s, ferries were no longer important and were even abandoned by the 1950s, it was not surprising that the view was devalued. What had been one of the busiest transportation hubs in the world had gone quiet. In 1989, the Loma Prieta earthquake, while less devastating than the 1906 disaster, battered the elevated roadway blocking the view of the terminal, and it also, in damaging the Bay Bridge, forced the city to reassess not only the symbolic role of a civic building as important as the Ferry Terminal Building but also the value of the function it once housed: using the water as a serious transportation alternative to

30. PACIFIC BELL STADIUM, SAN FRANCISCO, CALIFORNIA, 2000, HOK SPORT+VENUE+ EVENT

roads and rail. Ferries had come back slowly since the 1950s, but with the Bay Bridge closed, ferry use quadrupled, and while the number came down as the highways were repaired, it remained higher than before. The ferries were running, and if they would tear down the damaged Embarcadero Freeway, San Franciscans would see their icon of harbor travel, the Ferry Terminal Building, down the length of Market Street again. In 1991, they razed the freeway. San Francisco had been preparing for a radical change for its waterfront since 1979, when the city completed the Northeast Waterfront Plan that called for the creation of South Beach, in the South of Market area. In a district that had been the city's industrial backyard, fronted by decaying docks, ROMA Design group and its agency and citizen advisors proposed more than two thousand units of new housing, hundreds of units more in renovated warehouse buildings, a million square feet of commercial development, and a seven-hundred-slip marina.[44] By the 1980s it was well under way, and while the dot.com revolution came and went in the 1990s, it ensured the reality of South Beach as a new waterfront neighborhood in the city.

After the earthquake, ROMA Design took the helm again, with a design for what had suddenly become the most important public space in San Francisco, Harry Bridges Plaza directly in front of the Ferry Terminal Building, which opened in 2000. Boris Dramov, the firm's president, notes that he had to consider "how to scale spaces so they work for people on a daily basis and also for major events—so they are not only successful if you have a hundred thousand people in them."[45] The plaza by its program and design works at those levels: the F-Line runs through it, connecting it to the entire waterfront; there are "light cannons" that can rise up and shoot beams of light six hundred feet into the sky, operating at the scale of the whole city; and there is the renewed ferry terminal in front of it and mass transit stations nearby. ROMA resisted proposals for separating the different transportation infrastructures, insisting that an urban place could successfully handle all that activity on one level. Their design renders a crossroads where the multiple transportation systems of the city work together, whether for tourists, commuters, or residents, untethered from the isolated levels of mid-twentieth-century planning and design, and the grand half circle imagined by Burnham has been rendered at last (fig. 29). The plaza also connects to a wider system. To the northwest, the Embarcadero roadways now run along a broad, palm-lined median, with trolleys and pedestrian paths running its mile length in the direction of Fisherman's Wharf, two miles away. To the southwest, the 2.5-mile-long waterfront promenade leads along the length of the South Beach area, reaching its end at China Basin and the Pacific Bell Stadium (fig. 30). The walk from the major transit stops at Harry Bridges Plaza to the stadium has already become a game-day tradition (and by 2003 a waterfront trolley, the E-Line, is planned for the same route) as has coming by boat to the marina at the 41,000-seat ballpark, designed by HOK S+V+E and opened in 2000. The experience inside the stadium, too, takes advantage of the bayside location. Fans in the stands can look out beyond the field to the bay, and batters can hope to hit a home run out of the park—into the water. In the future, the old-timey details of the stadium entrance may grate, but the success of the siting, which defies the notion that mass entertainment is at odds with a vital urbanity, overcomes that concern for many.

The most important work of architecture at the Embarcadero is the turn-of-the-last-century Ferry Terminal Building, yet there is nothing irrevocably nostalgic or touristic, twentieth-century trolleys or not, about the revived Embarcadero's capacity to operate simultaneously at different scales of use and infrastructure. In the plaza, which stretches into a mile-long palm-lined median between the Embarcadero's traffic lanes, in the promenade on the water, in the use of a trolley line, and in the boulevard and walkway that emanate from it, San Francisco has laid down the armature for future architecture and urban experience that is unquestionably pleasurable and could be culturally exhilarating. But is it yielding new architecture as compelling and as connected to the spirit of the time as that created at the turn of the last century?

The armature is more than the physical artifact of the promenade, the plaza, and the grand median. San Francisco has heavy public

involvement in waterfront planning and design decision making, usually more confrontational than the polder model of the Dutch. In 1990, the year after the earthquake, citizens voted in Proposition H, which forbid the building of hotels on the piers. The Port of San Francisco, a special agency run by the City and County of San Francisco, controls the piers, which are for the most part no longer relevant to industry, and continues to promote real estate development on the piers. After struggling with public opinion and agencies, including the other chief ruling body for the waterfront, the Bay Conservation and Development Commission, which represents the counties of the Bay Area, the Port joined an agreement on future development that among other issues calls for creating a waterfront historic district to "encourage preservation and appropriate redevelopment of the piers."[46] Yet even in the year that the parties reached consensus, the Port defied citizen expectations, proposing a waterfront amusement park on Pier 45, where the commercial fishing industry still docks and works. Citizens of San Francisco voted three to one for Proposition R against the plans the Port had made, preferring instead a center for education about the Bay. They were also responding to the fear that Fisherman's Wharf just was not big enough to handle any more "fun." Despite all the tourist gimcrackery already there, the wharf is still the center of commercial fishing in Northern California, complete with a modern fish processing center.[47]

Proposition R had no legal binding impact, but the popular

opinion it rallied derailed the amusement park plans, and in the end San Francisco is contemplating a proposal by shopping mall developers that, like the worst compromises, appears to make no one happy.[48] It seems that the foray into a polder model consensus has already broken down. It may take a reconsideration of the armature of the 2000 plan. Historic districts have been invaluable in American cities, yet San Francisco may be trying to operate within the strictures of "appropriate" architecture, as well as appropriate uses, that are more confining than liberating for the waterfront. At the start of this century, it would be very difficult to build a design as powerful as the 1898 Ferry Terminal Building and even harder to create a functioning monument with the vigor of Will Alsop's ferry terminal in Hamburg.

BOSTON: TRYING TO LOOK LIKE BOSTON

Boston, like San Francisco, found most of its downtown waterfront industry—like much of the rest of it along the 180-mile edge of its harbor—redundant by the 1960s. Between the leftover docks and the roaring corridor of the John F. Fitzgerald Expressway, Boston had a hard time sustaining or enhancing its immediate character as a waterfront city. By the end of the twentieth century, the situation was much different. There had been early moves, past the highway and at the water, such as the mixed-use complex of Rowes Wharf, designed by Skidmore, Owings & Merrill and opened in 1987, with its great portal cut through the building wall. Designed in the contextualist style of the time, it will probably realize its full potential as an urban gesture—that bright gleam of water visible from the city through the portal, that dense knot of city visible

31. JOHN JOSEPH MOAKLEY UNITED STATES COURTHOUSE AND HARBORPARK, BOSTON, MASSACHUSETTS, 1998, PEI COBB FREED & PARTNERS

from the water—now that the elevated roadway has been razed to make way for the Big Dig project, which by 2004 will offer the grade-level Rose Kennedy Greenway instead.

A decade after Rowes Wharf, Boston Harbor had far more to offer, because, like the water in New York, it was exponentially cleaner than it had been, thanks to a $4 billion campaign in the 1990s. The city saw its greatest opportunity to exploit this new appeal just a thousand feet across the Fort Point Channel from Rowes Wharf, at Fan Pier. The pier, where coal had once been loaded, formed the edge of the declining industrial waterfront of South Boston. It had originally generated interest at the same time as the Rowes Wharf project: in the mid-1980s prominent architects including Robert A. M. Stern drew up schemes for towers along it, but the recession brought plans to a stop. By the late 1990s, projects, not just plans, had begun on the pier, starting with the brick-and-glass John Joseph Moakley United States Courthouse and Harborpark completed in 1998 by Pei Cobb Freed & Partners (fig. 31). The program of a courthouse on the waterfront was a welcome innovation. Looking across to Boston's financial district, it anchors its own area with a reminder that "public" does not always equal "recreation" but rather can have a more complex profile.

In late 1997, while the courthouse was under construction, the Boston Redevelopment Authority (BRA) released its version of how development should continue beyond the confines of Fan Pier in an interim report of The South Boston Seaport: A Master Plan for the Fort Point and South Boston Waterfront. Its chief illustration, a view toward Fan Pier, barely showed the new courthouse, and instead displayed a gawky build-out of massive new buildings, unhappily rendered. The local press was merciless in response. Robert Campbell, architecture critic of The Boston Globe, wrote: "The buildings—our planners' vision of Boston's future—look like a random heap of misshapen shoe boxes. They belly up to the water like overfed hogs at a trough. None of them looks the least like Boston."[49]

The sense of what "looks like Boston" is intense in New England's largest city, which has as strong a sense of self and history as San Francisco, and nowhere is the feeling more acute than on its waterfront. In response to the colorless BRA report, architects and civic leaders began to push for a more visionary, less crowded, district. The Boston Harbor Conference, begun in spring 1998, argued that the thousand-acre seaport area could be "the centerpiece of the harbor revival—or just another skirmish in the city's tribal wars."[50] The Boston Society of Architects addressed the issue in plans and forums, and their Web site on the topic opened with a cry against towers on the water, saying, "The Mayor [Thomas M. Menino] has frequently said, 'It would be a huge mistake to Manhattanize the waterfront.'"[51] Architecture critic Jane Holtz Kay declared that it was time to follow her seaside maxim: "Nothing higher

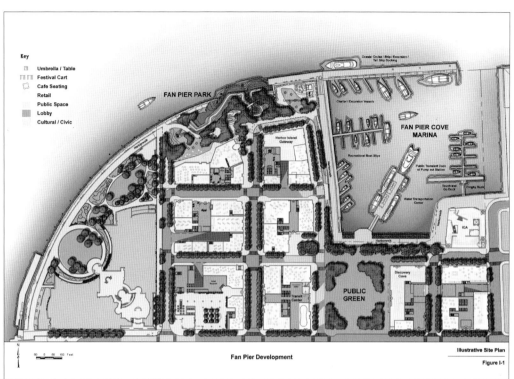

32. FAN PIER PLAN, BOSTON, MASSACHUSETTS, 2002, KEN GREENBERG, MICHAEL VAN VALKENBURGH ASSOCIATES, URBAN STRATEGIES, CBT/CHILDS BERTMAN TSECKARES

than a whale by the water," a height limit she sets at fifty feet.[52] Boston prides itself on being the rare walkable city, without the tolerance for shadows and density of New York. The BRA, despite the poor reception of its interim report, soldiered on, preparing the Public Realm Plan (PRP) of 1999 that made the more respected case that the whole character of the district would hang on public space improvements. The Municipal Harbor Plan, released in 2000 by the BRA, incorporated state waterfront law that made the PRP enforceable.

So what will constitute a place that "looks like Boston" in its public spaces and buildings on the waterfront? At the Fan Pier site, the Hyatt Development Corporation, led by the Pritzker family (patrons of the Pritzker Architecture Prize), is proceeding with its plan for the twenty-one-acre site between the courthouse and Pier 4 to the south, with an urban design proposal led by Ken Greenberg and Michel Trocme of the Toronto-based Urban Strategies group, in collaboration with CBT/Childs Bertman Tseckares, a Boston firm (fig. 32). The Hyatt master plan does look more like Boston than Manhattan, in part because of long negotiations with public agencies, including the BRA, community groups, and the public realm of the media. The power of these stakeholders in the future of Boston has influenced the height, character, and programs of the project. The buildings meet the tree-lined streets with shops and restaurants, striving to create an amenity-drenched critical mass of activity on the way to the fully public pleasures of the waterfront, which will

include a hundred-foot-wide arc-shaped park overlooking the Boston skyline, designed by Michael Van Valkenburgh Associates, landscape designers based in Cambridge, Massachusetts. At the north side of the inlet, there is a marina and a fishing pier, and at a corner of the inlet, the Pritzkers donated a .75-acre site for civic or cultural use. In 1999, the City of Boston selected the Institute of Contemporary Art (ICA) to build a new home on the donated site, and two years later the institute announced that it had chosen the MacArthur Prize–winning partnership of Diller+Scofidio to design the sixty-thousand-square-foot museum. Elizabeth Diller and Ricardo Scofidio were selected for their conceptual verve, not a design proposal. A review of their most significant waterfront project—the floating cloud of Blur, an exposition pavilion whose only walls are the mist of a synthetic cloud hovering above Lake Neuchâtel for Swiss Expo 2002—indicates that their museum will probably not look anything like Boston, if that is defined by the red brick with white trim that holds so much of the city's imagination in its grasp.

In 2004, the year the ICA opens, Boston's Big Dig project to bury the highway running through its downtown and along the waterfront of the financial district will be done. By then, the South Boston Convention and Exhibition Center by HNTB/Rafael Viñoly Architects—at 1.7 million square feet the landlocked behemoth of South Boston—will be open, and the new Seaport District, complete with some distinguished works of architecture and some flashes of original programming, will be under way. Yet this accomplishment will pale if Boston's public agencies, private developers, and designers are unable to pull off the greatest promise of the overall plan—to sustain the industrial port just to the south and keep maritime activities in the heart of the new mixed-use district. Visitors to the museum, conventions booked at the center, full restaurants, and leased floors all matter, but by the standard of the waterfront—a uniquely dynamic and varied zone—it is by the ability to bring in this new population while keeping the maritime one that South Boston's seaport will be judged.

Proposals like the Commonwealth Flats Strategic Plan of 2000, released by the Massachusetts Port Authority (Massport) and prepared by Chan Krieger & Associates of Boston, cover seventy waterfront acres of Massport property for commercial development on the South Boston waterfront. The port's urban planning consultants say that their client can have it all: be a mixed-use developer and sustain and enhance cruise ship landings, seafood processing, and cargo handling. At the entry to the Massport-owned Fish Pier, where the fleet will still dock, according to the strategic plan, there will be a park designed by the architects of New York's Robert Wagner Jr. Park, Machado and Silvetti. Less than a half mile away, the Conley Container Terminal will still handle freight. To have a highly designed park for a largely white-collar population, and the activities of a contemporary port and fishing industry in almost direct adjacency is a hard row to hoe, but it is one that will distinguish Boston as a city genuinely able to develop a waterfront that is both the civic front yard and the vitally necessary backyard that together render a compelling waterfront. As MVRDV warned in their descriptions of the Silodam housing project in Amsterdam, "monoculture" can kill any project, or any district. Fan Pier promises to break out of its monoculture in design terms with the ICA by Diller+Scofidio, and the South Boston waterfront overall may stave off uniformity by a genuine commitment to keeping its still productive maritime industries alive.

PHILADELPHIA: INSTEAD OF A MASTER PLAN

Like many cities that have watched their central port districts decline, Philadelphia has seen many initiatives for its waterfront. Since the 1960s the city has been trying to create a waterfront destination at Penn's Landing, on the Delaware just below Society Hill and a quarter mile south of the Benjamin Franklin Bridge. But Philadelphia has never come close to the success of other revived northeastern waterfronts like Baltimore's. Along the Delaware River, the city formed a public-private partnership in the late 1990s to replace the outdoor amphitheater for public events with a more heavily programmed family entertainment center scheduled for completion in 2004. Ehrenkrantz Eckstut & Kuhn are leading the urban design process for the site, which will also be programmatically and physically tied into the river by an aerial tram to

Camden, a city that, so far, no amount of money and effort has been able to help shake off its postindustrial malaise. By the end of the century, Penn's Landing had ferry service—traveling back and forth to attractions like the New Jersey State Aquarium in Camden on the opposite bank—and cruise ship terminals, a hotel, a sculpture garden, a seaport museum, and an active schedule of events. Farther south, where the Delaware meets the Schuylkill River, the 1994 plan for reusing the Philadelphia Naval Base and Shipyard is slowly being realized.[53] The plan calls for keeping some of the yard for such specialized manufacturing as propellers, while the rest will be developed into an "industrial park of the twenty-first century," in a vision prepared by the city and a team of consultants, including Kohn Pedersen Fox Associates for architecture and planning.

Penn's Landing and the Naval Base both operate at the scale of the river; they are connected to it by waterborne transportation, by interstate programs, and by maritime activities. Yet they have no impact on the stretch of the Delaware north of the Benjamin Franklin Bridge, a ten-mile natural border for North Philadelphia, a district hard hit by declining industrial activity. If there is a model for urban waterfront design at multiple scales, it has to be one that allows extraordinary landscape and architecture to happen with a clear sense of the relationship between the two. In a recent Philadelphia project, there is a meeting of minds and purposes that engages the ecology of public life and sets the boundaries and character of a field where a meaningful urban architecture could take place.

In a bold decision, the City of Philadelphia and the executive director of its planning department, Maxine Griffith, hired Field Operations, the Philadelphia–New York partnership of landscape architect James Corner and architect Stan Allen, to lead a team to prepare a concept plan for the Delaware riverfront, from Benjamin Franklin Bridge in Center City to Philadelphia's northern boundary. Commissioned in late 2000, the North Delaware riverfront planning project team had to deal with ten miles, 3,500 acres, three bridges, two creeks, industrial detritus, "natural" shorelines, a neighborhood and a gated community, the interstate highway, and the cultural slough of despondence from years of waiting for something to replace the maritime-related industries. Among the principal reasons it was ready for redevelopment was that, as in New York, the Delaware was increasingly clean, benefiting from the decline in industrial uses and the rise in sewage treatment along its edge.

The selection of Corner and Allen, who both have significant professional experience but have never led a project at this scale, was insightful. Corner has been thinking through landscape's increasingly close relationship to architecture in his designs and writing, illuminating how it is as much a constructed environment as buildings. Allen has been a leader in architecture's increasing understanding of how buildings need to be considered integral to the infrastructure of transportation and services that cities depend on, which leads to a recognition that buildings have to be thought of as larger urban landscapes, a concept relevant to the North Delaware Riverfront project. Both are concerned about how their respective design disciplines can be part of a strategy for change beyond the unique building or exterior space. For Corner, it is important for landscape designers not to fall prey to the illusion that their work is an elitist diversion when it focuses on anything short of saving the Earth. He argues: "Unfortunately, environmental advocates continue to attend to an objectifiable nature that they believe remains external to culture. In so doing, they fail to consider the profound consequences of the world's *constructedness*—its schematization as a cultural idea and, therefore, its subjugation."[54] In his view of landscape, the practice of landscape architecture "may still embrace naturalistic and phenomenological experience but its full efficacy is extended to that of a synthetic and strategic art form, one that aligns diverse and competing forces (social constituencies, political desires, ecological processes, program demands) into newly liberating and interactive alliances."[55] For a city with what has so far proved to be limited resilience from industrial decline, faced with ten miles of beat-up riverfront and a diversity of existing uses and community aspirations, such an approach is more necessity than novelty.

For Allen, architecture, too, especially when it focuses on infrastructure, thrives as a strategic art. His seminal essays in *Points+Lines: Diagrams and Projects for the City* (1999) advance a theory of "infrastructural urbanism" for his work,

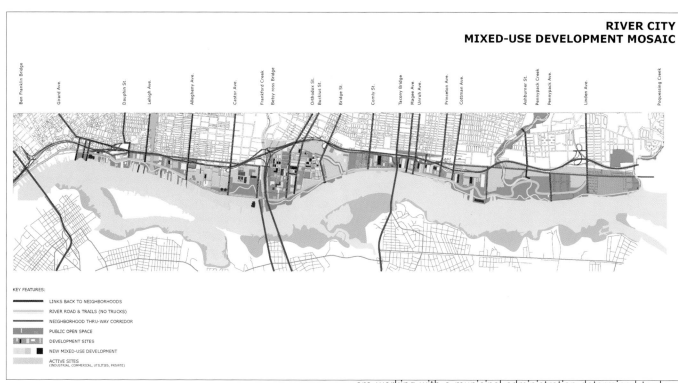

Ben Franklin Bridge · Girard Ave. · Dauphin St. · Lehigh Ave. · Allegheny Ave. · Castor Ave. · Frankford Creek · Betsy ross Bridge · Orthodox St. · Bucklius St. · Bridge St. · Comly St. · Tacony Bridge · Magee Ave. Unruh Ave. · Princeton Ave. · Cottman Ave. · Ashburner St. · Pennypack Creek · Pennypack Ave. · Linden Ave. · Poquessing Creek

KEY FEATURES:

LINKS BACK TO NEIGHBORHOODS
RIVER ROAD & TRAILS (NO TRUCKS)
NEIGHBORHOOD THRU-WAY CORRIDOR
PUBLIC OPEN SPACE
DEVELOPMENT SITES
NEW MIXED-USE DEVELOPMENT
ACTIVE SITES
(INDUSTRIAL, COMMERICAL, UTILITIES, PRIVATE)

33. RIVER CITY MIXED-USE DEVELOPMENT MOSAIC, DELAWARE RIVER PLAN, PHILADELPHIA,

PENNSYLVANIA, 2001, FIELD OPERATIONS

advocating a move beyond the failed postmodern architecture of "images and signs" that tried unsuccessfully to compete with media and move "away from instrumentality." As a designer, he proclaims his dedication to producing "directed fields," wherein designs are "flexible and anticipatory," incorporate "artificial ecologies," and, while "static," are able to "manage complex systems of flow."[56]

While some of this language has the special character of the design studio, the two partners, Corner, who teaches at Columbia University, and Allen, who became dean of the School of Architecture at Princeton University in 2002, presented their ideas for the Delaware project to Philadelphia's planning department and the broader community with sophisticated yet comprehensible and visually arresting documents. By the end of 2001, the project had been heralded in the Philadelphia press for its "brilliance," with reporters writing that the proposal made "a gargantuan undertaking seem manageable—and even affordable." Field Operations had laid out "a six-step process that would add middle-class housing for ten thousand persons and create a new public park."[57]

The team's plan incorporates an adamant argument for an urban life that is, in Allen's terms, diverse, mixes public and private, incorporates mobility, is driven by and drives technology, and has sites based on density and proximity.[58] In Philadelphia, Allen and Corner are working with a municipal administration determined to draw people back within in its borders for the fiscal and cultural health of the city. To meet the city's expectations, Field Operations' analysis and proposal did not rely on the kinds of animations and terms that, for example, UN Studio used in the IFCCA competition, but rather harnessed many of planning's more direct tools, with their findings arranged into telling juxtapositions. They collected information on the site infrastructure of vacant lands, existing parks and recreation, the major streets, the highway network, the rail network, and even a figure-ground diagram of the site (fig. 33). They broke down the analysis into portions of the site, looking at what was there, what bordered the water, and on the inland side, how it connected to the city. They also demonstrated that the properties available for redevelopment, about 1,160 acres out of the 3,500-acre parcel equaled about 70 percent of Center City Philadelphia's acreage. Their mandate was not to build another Center City, but to think through the type of housing, recreation, and commercial activity the area could sustain.

This is not planning with a commitment of billions of dollars waiting in the city's bank account. It is, instead, a strategy that has to envision the long term. In the end, Corner and Allen proposed a design strategy that could "develop a new river city, allow for long timelines, and establish new mixtures and programs" gathered into a thoughtfully named series of sequenced interventions: "Seed+Link, Clear+Plant, Construct New River Parkway,

RIVER SWATH DIAGRAM - ALT1

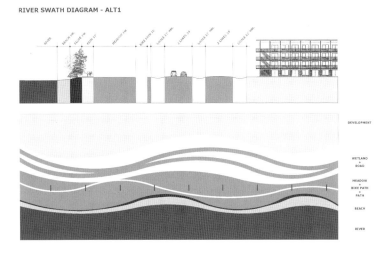

RIVER SWATH DIAGRAM - ALT2

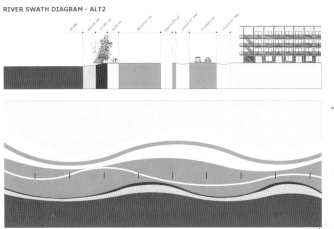

34. RIVER SWATH DIAGRAM, DELAWARE RIVER PLAN, PHILADELPHIA, PENNSYLVANIA, 2001, FIELD OPERATIONS

Establish Two Separate Fronts, and Adaptively Manage."[59] While there is an almost punning pleasure in terms like "seed+link" and "clear+plant," the first two phases' names are deliberate in their integration of seeding, clearing, and planting, with the cultural and economic sequence of first drawing on the strengths of the property already in use. In the second, the program proposes actively expanding that resource to include phyto-remediation, which occurs when plants remove toxins from the soil. Visually, this remediation stage will create a variety of open meadows and landscapes, some of which will ultimately be redeveloped for building. The third phase, constructing the proposed river parkway, a 150- to 250-foot-wide-swath to be located in an abandoned railroad right-of-way, would be the organizing principle for the following phases of development (fig. 34). On the one hand, this undulating band for circulation establishes a precinct for both road and open space, bordering the river, while on the other, it defines the access routes for new residential developments and areas for public recreation. But it is not meant to erase the industrial and commercial programs serviced from North Philadelphia's arterial roadways. The industrial routes and the parkway are envisioned as interlocking along the length of the site, which becomes a "mixed-use development mosaic" in the overall plan.[60] In Corner's terms, "The parkway gives the develop-ment parcels a new front door, without which they are unlikely to be funded given the derelict state of the current 'back door.'"[61] Corner adds, "The parkway front door also ensures that the river remains a continuous public domain."[62]

Reflecting on the term "Field Operations" and its application to this project, Corner views "the entire choreography from site seeds to clean-up and remediation to early stage development and later stage densification," as "one huge series of field operations" (fig. 35). Like many current proposals, the Delaware project is conceived as a post-zoning, post-monotonous urban vision. Corner believes that multiple uses can be sustained, that pier sheds and new housing can sit cheek-by-jowl: "The idea of establishing new mixtures is simply to provoke the possibility of juxtaposition...the industrial sector wants to keep the whole thing industrial. Others want it all to be some kind of new residential community. We want to suggest that there is enough space to accommodate a mixture of both, and that indeed such a mix would help bring a distinctive and unique character to the place."[63]

35. NEW LAND COLLAGE, DELAWARE RIVER PLAN, PHILADELPHIA, 2001, FIELD OPERATIONS

CONCLUSION

Waterfronts in the United States and around the world can be measured by roughly the same standards of performance: the civic, or how many people go there; the commercial, or how much money people spend there to live or work or shop; and the environmental, either how lightly a project impacts the water around it or how much the project remediates the once industrial land it occupies. American waterfronts often score well on the first two and are doing better on the third. Yet there are other, overarching standards: how well the spaces and buildings serve as icons of the urban life they frame, and how well they serve the working needs of a city's infrastructure best met at the water.

By those standards, most waterfronts fall short, but there is still a rich panoply of examples that are inspiring in their ability to harness an urban design vision that accommodates the complex range of programs and the raw verve of architectural and landscape design that the best planning can help happen. It is a two-sided effort: without a liberal perspective on possible juxtapositions of use for the waterfront combined with an openness to applying a culturally ambitious standard of design to civic programs from stadiums to terminals that cities either never applied or have forgotten they did, it is difficult to move the waterfront forward.

New York, in recent years, has shown a new attitude, not only to learning from elsewhere but in applying that knowledge by design initiatives, including international competition. In December 2001, for example, the competition jury charged with assessing proposals for the transformation of New York's vast landfill, Fresh Kills on Staten Island, unanimously found the scheme by Field Operations, leaders of the Delaware Riverfront planning project in Philadelphia, the best among six finalists. The jury saw the scheme as ecologically sound and daring in its vision for a natural lifestyle that firmly connects human experience to the systems, manmade and natural, that it cycles through. With Fresh Kills, as well as other initiatives, New York City is on the verge of making a waterfront for its time.

NOTES

1. Han Meyer, *City and Port: Urban Planning as a Cultural Venture in London, Barcelona, New York, and Rotterdam: Changing Relations between Public Urban Space and Large-Scale Infrastructure* (Utrecht: International Books, 1999), 13.

2. Meyer, *City and Port*, 37.

3. "Transforming Amsterdam: The Dutch Way of Urban Redevelopment," round-table discussion, New York, 1 June 2001.

4. Hans Ibelings, *The Artificial Landscape: Contemporary Architecture, Urbanism, and Landscape Architecture in the Netherlands* (Rotterdam: NAi Publishers, 2000), 65.

5. Alessandra Rocca, "Urban Surrealism: A Green Box in the Bay of Amsterdam," *Lotus* 95 (December 1997): 12.

6. "Metropolis and Naturalis: Urban Beacons," *1997–1998 Architecture in the Netherlands Yearbook*, ed. Hans Ibelings (Rotterdam: NAi Publishers, 1998), 25.

7. Winy Maas and Jacob van Rijs, with Richard Koek, eds., *MVRDV FAR MAX: Excursions on Density* (Rotterdam: O10 Publishers, 1998), 534.

8. Maas and van Rijs, eds., *MVRDV FAR MAX,* 535.

9. The original design for the Euromast completed in 1960 rose 350 feet, but in 1970, to ensure the tower's identity as the highest vantage point in all of the Netherlands, a space needle was added, giving the tower its current height of 607 feet.

10. OMA, Rem Koolhaas, and Bruce Mau, *S, M, L, XL* (New York: The Monacelli Press, 1996), 518–43. Meyer presents this comparison visually in *City and Port*, 333.

11. Meyer, *City and Port*, 337.

12. F. Scott Fitzgerald, *The Love of the Last Tycoon* (1941; reprint, New York: Scribner, 1993), 20.

13. Department of Urban Planning and Housing, Martin van Vliet, concept and design, Rotterdam: The City, the Region, and the Port (map, City of Rotterdam, 1997).

14. Ben van Berkel, interview by author, 30 May 2001.

15. *Webster's New Collegiate Dictionary* (Springfield, Mass.: G. & C. Merriam Company, 1979).

16. Van Berkel, interview.

17. Van Berkel, interview.

18. Frank Lucchino, quoted in Tom Barnes, "Science Center Announces $90 Million Expansion," *Pittsburgh Post-Gazette*, Web site, www.post-gazette.com, 25 October 2000.

19. Van Berkel, interview.

20. Van Berkel, interview.

21. Van Berkel, interview.

22. "Timeline to 2001," *Pittsburgh Post-Gazette,* Web site, www.post-gazette.com, 2 December 1998.

23. All quotations in this paragraph are from van Berkel, interview.

24. All quotations in this paragraph are from UN Studio Project Presentation, Port Antico/Ponte Parodi, Web site, www.portantico.it, 16 May 2001.

25. Alejandro Zaera-Polo, lecture cosponsored by Van Alen Institute and the Architectural League of New York, New York, 19 October 2001, author's notes.

26. Zaera-Polo lecture, author's notes.

27. Richard Rogers, quoted in Gordon Sander, "London's Millennium Fever," *Preservation* (May/June 1997): 71.

28. Greater London Authority Headquarters project description, Foster and Partners, Web site, www.fosterandpartners.com, December 2001. Foster's assesment of the design's sustainability may not hold; according to the *Guardian*, a governmental report anticipates mediocre air quality and energy efficiency in the design. David Hencke, "Capital's Glass Globe Fails Green Test," *Guardian*, Web site, www.guardian.co.uk, 30 July 2001.

29. Will Alsop, interview by author, 4 June 2001.

30. Alsop, interview.

31. Alsop, interview.

32. Alsop, interview.

33. Alsop, interview.

34. All quotations in this paragraph from Alsop, interview.

35. Design credit for the station goes to Alsop Lyall & Störmer through 1993 and the Jubilee Line Extension team through completion in 2001.

36. Barbara Wagner, "The Buzz on Barcelona," *Grid* (July/August 2001): 39.

37. This project was done in conjunction with Skidmore, Owings & Merrill.

38. Joseph Giovannini, "Olympic Overhaul," *Progressive Architecture* (July 1992):66.

39. *Barcelona: New Projects* (Barcelona: Agencia Metropolitana de Desenvolupament Urbanistic i d'infrastructures, 1999), 16–17.

40. Josep Acebillo, Future+Cities Conference: Design+Urbanism+Philadelphia, panelist comments, Graduate School of Fine Arts, University of Pennsylvania, 23–24 March 2001, author's notes.

41. Frank Gehry, interview by author, 20 July 2001.

42. The Hudson River esplanade in New Jersey suffered this sort of project: see Anthony DePalma, "The River Beckons, But It's Not Easy to Get There," *Reclaiming the Waterfront: A Planning Guide for Waterfront Municipalities* (Hoboken: The Fund for a Better Waterfront, Inc., 1996), 4–9.

43. The drawings of Burnham and his collaborators, begun in 1904, were damaged in the 1906 fire, but the team was able to produce a full, finished plan a month later. This was a project undertaken for a civic group—the Association for the Improvement and Adornment of San Francisco. Mario Manieri-Elia, "Toward an 'Imperial City': Daniel H. Burnham and the City Beautiful Movement," *The American City from the Civil War to the New Deal* (London: Granada, 1980), 81–82, 85–89.

44. Bonnie Fisher, "From the Water's Edge," *Urban Land* (January 1999): 73–77.

45. Boris Dramov, quoted in "Millennial Face-Lift: ROMA Design Re-creates the Embarcadero," *Landscape Architecture* (May 1998): 32.

46. Charles Lockwood, "On the Waterfront," *Grid* (April 2001): 84–88.

47. Chris Martin, cochair of the Bay Center Alternative for Pier 45, quoted in Jessica Materna, *San Francisco Business Times*, Web site, www.bizjournals.com/sanfrancisco/, 6 November 2000.

48. Aaron Peskin, "Working Waterfront," *San Francisco Bay Crossings*, Web site, www.baycrossings.com, Port of San Francisco, October 2001.

49. Robert Campbell, "Waterfront Sprawl: The City's 'Master Plan' Should Go Back to the Drawing Board," *Boston Globe*, 11 January 1998, N1, N4.

50. "Water's Edge," special magazine supplement, *Boston Globe*, 25 October 1998, 6; see also "National Panel Recommendations," The Boston Harbor Conference, The Boston Harbor Town Meeting, 21 May 1998.

51. "What Can We Learn from Manhattan?" Boston Society of Architects, Web site, www.architects.org.seaport/chapter8.htm, 2001.

52. Jane Holtz Kay, "Vision for a Livable Waterfront," *Boston Globe*, 16 March 1998, A17.

53. City of Philadelphia, Mayor's Commission on Defense Conversion, Community Reuse Plan for the Philadelphia Naval Base and Shipyard (September 1994), 3.

54. James Corner, "Introduction: Recovering Landscape as a Critical Cultural Practice," *Recovering Landscape* (New York: Princeton Architectural Press, 1999), 3.

55. James Corner, interview by author, 5 July 2001.

56. All quotations in this paragraph are from Stan Allen, "Infrastructural Urbanism," *Points+Lines: Diagrams and Projects for the City* (New York: Princeton Architectural Press, 1999), 46–57.

57. Inga Saffron, "Riverfront: Land of Opportunity," *The Philadelphia Inquirer*, Web site, www.inq.philly.com, 2 November 2001.

58. Stan Allen, Future+Cities Conference panelist comments, author's notes.

59. Field Operations, PowerPoint presentation to the City of Philadelphia, May 2001.

60. Field Operations, presentation.

61. Corner, interview.

62. Corner, interview.

63. All quotations in this paragraph are from James Corner, interview.

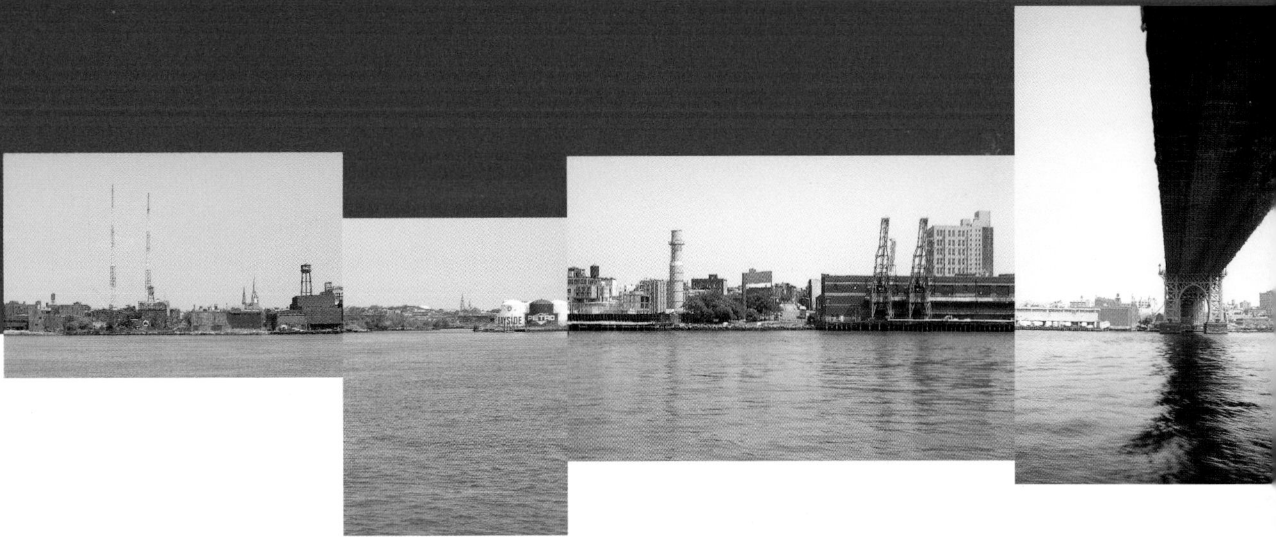
PETRO

NEW YORK CITY ON THE VERGE

I. KEYSPAN PARK, CONEY ISLAND, NEW YORK, 2001, JACK L. GORDON ARCHITECTS

3

New York has the opportunity to generate extraordinary design for its waterfront, but to achieve this it needs both to absorb lessons from port cities around the world and to learn from its own recent failures and successes. What distinguishes the nascent approach of Field Operations in Philadelphia, and the decade-long theory and practice of Barcelona, is the ability to set up a framework for translating regional-scale issues at the most macro level of infrastructure, culture, and environment into projects on the ground. As the Barcelona Regional agency (BR) declares: "Ad hoc solutions to territorial issues (such as those in which we are now implicating practically every large city in the world) are just not enough." Moreover, generalities about the territory are not enough either: BR presents a triangle of approaches including studies and proposals, strate-

gies, and projects: "This working process of reformulating solutions to regional issues culminates in the design of projects that will turn strategies into reality."[1]

New York's waterfront is hardly a tabula rasa, and it has plans, policies, and initiatives that together form more than just a series of ad hoc moves. The plans for the harbor by the bistate Port Authority and for New York City's waterfront by its City Planning Commission, as well as a slew of master plans for multiacre districts of shoreline in New York and New Jersey, reflect "territorial" concerns, and they have had consequences of great impact for the entire metropolitan region. However, the translation of regional issues into projects has not always gone smoothly, and the final version of New York's waterfront is still only a murky vision. In part, this is because the future is beyond even the most determined technocrat's reckoning. The pace and range of change is beyond the control of planners and strategists, however gifted. Change happens in the disastrous negative, with unimaginable events like those of September 11, 2001. Change happens as the unanticipated downsides of otherwise beneficial initiatives, like the return of the marine borer worms to the harbor's cleaner water, where they now destroy historic docks and barges. On the positive side, there has been the impact of communities and individuals who have served, through projects as small as a museum on a barge, a converted warehouse, or an art installation on an abandoned industrial site, as catalysts for change in delimited but powerful ways.

New York may need to reinvent its regional imperatives and its methods of responding to them, but it cannot do so without understanding the energy and vision of these local enterprises on the waterfront. At best, the visions that civic and community groups sponsor, which often do propose an overarching response to metropolitan issues that the public and private realm have yet to address fully, are tempered by a knowledge that moves both up and down the piling. To grasp its potential, New York needs to look at itself right now, in flux, with projects listed as part of long-term plans, on the drawing boards, or under construction, and to understand how these connect to the evolving systems of infrastructure—transportation and services—and systems, or at least trends, of culture, such as sports, arts, and recreation. This exercise in self-reflection, modulated by an analysis of waterfront designs worldwide, requires moving back and forth among questions of systems, plans, and projects and a continual dialogue between sites and issues, experience and themes, the big picture and the small.

CONEY ISLAND: RENEWAL BY ICON AND INFRASTRUCTURE

Coney Island, the legendary New York playground by the sea, is not as sad and sick a place as it is portrayed in the 2001 film *Requiem for a Dream*, but it is a ghost of its glory days in the early twentieth century when it had Steeplechase Park, Luna Park, and Dreamland along Surf Avenue, with a million visitors a day during the summer. The last of the amusement parks, Steeplechase Park, closed in 1964 and was reborn in 2001 as KeySpan Park, the 6,500-seat beachfront home field of the Brooklyn Cyclones baseball team (fig. 1). The value and optimism of the stadium is thrown into relief by the still decayed district and by the history of Steeplechase Park, whose remains have been cleared except for the iconic Parachute Jump just to the west of right field. (Not actually a relic from early Coney Island, the 360-foot-high steel Parachute Jump was first erected at the 1939–1940 New York World's Fair held in Flushing Meadows in Queens.) The team chose another amusement park icon for its name: the Cyclone roller coaster, a few blocks east of right field, in operation since 1927.

In its setting on the boardwalk, the ballpark capitalizes on nostalgia for long-lost amusement parks as well as the borough's unending love affair with baseball despite the Dodgers' exit to Los Angeles in 1957. Built with the support of the New York City Economic Development Corporation (EDC) for the Mets' single-A minor league farm team, the stadium's seats with ocean views did not come easily. There was a long and bitter dispute between the Brooklyn borough president and the mayor over the stadium, with the borough president advocating a larger sports center and voicing other objections from local constituencies, some of whom argued that the $39 million would be better spent on high school facilities. In the end, the stadium was built, and the seats are sold out.

Jack L. Gordon Architects, designer of the ball park, sensibly focused on getting the fans up to a level where the view of the ocean was open and then located the retail portion of the project on the concourse level, which connected the stadium to Coney Island's still famous, and perhaps resurgent, two-mile-long boardwalk. The spirit of the amusement park comes through in the "lollipop" light poles, with rings of neon around the main floodlights for the field. However much nostalgia is key to its success, KeySpan provides an inimitably urban experience of a natural site

and exposure to the game far more direct than in a major league stadium.

The stadium was developed as part of a much larger transportation and infrastructure project for the redevelopment of long-depressed Coney Island, where hundreds of millions of dollars are being spent on subway station renovations where multiple lines come together—a once important transportation hub that had been dark, decayed, and dripping with rot for decades, a negative symbol of how disconnected Coney Island had become from the life of the larger city. For architecture and urbanism critic Alex Marshall, it is important to note that the infrastructure investment is more valuable to the future of this waterfront district than the baseball stadium. He sees KeySpan as having a relationship to its surrounding area parallel to the Guggenheim Museum Bilbao, which in his words is "a bauble on top of a mound of infrastructure," while the Coney Island stadium is a "bauble on top of some serious infrastructure."[2] This is a significant point, given that the media and public often discount the importance of infrastructure and focus on iconic buildings and programs, declaring them generators of change. However, mocking the stadium and the museum as baubles runs the risk of a twentieth-century truism that can damage our understanding of cities and places by implying that individual projects or buildings do not matter; that infrastructure is central to cities and architecture marginal—a cliché that has to be unlearned.

Guggenheim Bilbao is the "bauble" that transformed the

identity of the city in the world's consciousness, not the new subways and bridges. The museum—in all its shimmering titanium glory—brings the tourists; it changes international investor attitudes; it encourages the talented and the productive to stay rather than leave. That is what one can do in a city's front yard, its waterfront. Similarly, KeySpan Park is the bauble that brought 247,000 people to Coney Island for the Cyclones' first season and has already changed the perception of Coney Island as a whole, which still has the potential to reclaim its role not only as a waterfront playground but also as a place to live.

In the question of what is merely decorative and what is substantive in a city's life lies the calculus of the successful waterfront project: not to be fooled into building special projects without thinking through their relationship to the systems of the city, while never forgetting that the whole enterprise is in vain without the production of special experiences, which are defined by program and design. At KeySpan there is an infrastructure move, of less consequence in numbers of passenger trips but of great power in terms of experience. On game days there is a ferry from Coney Island to the second new minor league waterfront stadium built in New York by the end of the last century, in St. George, Staten Island. When their respective teams are playing each other, fans can enjoy the minor league version of the major league subway series: the ferry series. The play is not as good, but the trip between the rival home fields is a lot more fun.[3]

ST. GEORGE, STATEN ISLAND:
SPORTS, CULTURE, AND REVIVING THE EVERYDAY

The ferries, like the stadiums, are more than mere window dressing; they are part of redefining the identity of waterfront locations year-round, even when they only operate on summer weekends. For Staten Island, the commuter ferry to Manhattan has been a serious part of the transportation infrastructure since 1816, and it now has more than fifty thousand passengers trips a day. Yet, for decades, the terminal and the depressed district behind it have been places that workers and tourists wanted to get through as quickly as possible. The new Richmond County Bank Stadium, completed in time for the Yankees' farm team's 2001 season, designed by HOK Sport+Venue+Event, has given a new identity to the area where the ferry lands, St. George. The stadium, whose main entrance is off Richmond Terrace, Staten

2. RICHMOND COUNTY BANK STADIUM, STATEN ISLAND, NEW YORK, 2001, HOK SPORT+
VENUE+EVENT

Island's waterfront avenue, is also only a short walk west from the ferry terminal. Its siting allows it to be part of St. George and Staten Island yet also easily accessible from other boroughs, and from the stands it reinforces that transportation connection with a spectacular view of the New York harbor (fig. 2). The still industrial waterfront of Bayonne, New Jersey, is over left field, while the skyline of Lower Manhattan stands behind the scoreboard in center field. Game day is an urban design diagram of a public experience made real, from the ferry, along the waterfront, to the game, and back. It is the whole urban experience, not just enthusiasm for minor league ball, which sells out the stands.

Experience is difficult to measure in dollars, but the price of a stadium is not, and there were many concerns about both the Coney Island and especially the Staten Island project. Mayor Giuliani was roundly criticized for the cost overruns of the Yankees' stadium in St. George, as when City Comptroller Alan Hevesi commented, during his mayoral campaign in 2001, that "all New Yorkers learned a lesson from the mayor's [Giuliani's] deal over the minor league stadium in Staten Island....It was a $29 million deal that actually cost nearly $80 million."[4] As a matter of management, such an overrun is hard to justify, yet if it were an art museum, with the same or even a smaller level of attendance, would the complaints be as loud? In the equation of reclaiming St. George as a place to live, work, and visit, the stadium's cost may make sense in the long term, and if it does, it will because it showed that the city valued the urban experience of its citizens, and in doing that, so transformed the identity of the place that a whole new generation of waterfront programs flourished in its wake.

PETER EISENMAN ON THE ST. GEORGE WATERFRONT

As with KeySpan Park on Coney Island, the stadium is only one part of a major infrastructural upgrade. The long-awaited improvement of the Staten Island Ferry terminal now under way, with HOK as the lead architecture firm, will give the building an open, glazed waiting room to replace the grim vault it has known since its construction in the 1950s. Plans for improving St. George also go well beyond the stadium and the renovated terminal, to museums and renovated historic structures. In the mid-1990s, Peter Eisenman Architects joined with HOK to develop a preliminary master plan for the whole gateway area, and while Eisenman did not take part in the final stadium and terminal renovation designs, he did keep his focus on a new branch for the Staten Island Institute of Arts and Sciences (SIIAS). Eisenman's design, first released in the late 1990s, is sited

at the joint between the streets of St. George, the terminal, and the waterfront path to the stadium (fig. 3). It is a startling vision for Staten Island. A project for a small cultural entity, it has global ambitions in its scope and is as architecturally ambitious as, for example, Renzo Piano Building Workshop's newMetropolis in Amsterdam. In the original scheme, Eisenman's museum was conceived as the Center for Electronic Culture, in which the ferry terminal waiting room did double duty as the lobby of the center, integrating infrastructure and cultural programs. The folded planes of roof and section spoke a mantra of movement, with literal and metaphorical flow to turn on the visitor's experience.

In its current design development stage, the project is no longer formally for "electronic culture" and has become more discrete—it does not share its lobby with the terminal.[5] Its front plaza, however, on the route from the terminal to the stadium, maintains its role as a crossroads, offers an arresting view of New York Harbor, and will also occupy a very prominent site on Staten Island's low skyline. The city's fiscal crisis, well under way before September 11, may deal a harsh blow to the center designed by Eisenman, yet even as a proposal, it was a breakthrough image of waterfront identity for New York, especially refreshing in a borough that has not traditionally had the same cultural ambition, not to say pretension, as Manhattan.

Eisenman offered the most determined expression of contemporary culture he could, although the glamour of digital

3. STATEN ISLAND INSTITUTE OF ARTS AND SCIENCES, RENDERING, STATEN ISLAND, NEW YORK, 2000, PETER EISENMAN ARCHITECTS

anything has worn very thin with changes in the economy. A significant cultural expression on the waterfront, with the support of the most important local politician, Guy V. Molinari, the Staten Island borough president from 1989 to 2001, marked a new attitude in New York. Molinari takes pride in having blocked the VSBA and Anderson/Schwartz Architects' "clock" and "sign" proposals for the Staten Island Ferry's Manhattan terminal. Eisenman fared far better with Molinari, perhaps having learned from the clock designers that "architects, icon-building architects, cannot stay out of the political process."[6]

For an architect of Eisenman's intellectual drive, a waterfront project in New York is an astonishing opportunity. He has been designing for and thinking about New York's waterfront for decades, first with the project he did in 1967 with Michael Graves for the Museum of Modern Art's *The New City: Architecture and Urban Renewal* exhibition. The architects proposed a thirty-block megastructure along the Hudson River from Columbia University to 155th Street with "shops, housing, and light industry, which would have the effect of creating a lagoon between the new structure and the existing neighborhood."[7] Since that time, Eisenman has completed relatively modest projects in New York, including a fire station in Brooklyn and an office building in Queens. At the end of the 1990s, he turned his attention to New York's waterfront again, first with the Staten Island museum project (for which images were first released in 1997) and then, at a much larger scale, with a stadium on Manhattan's West Side for the IFCCA competition, whose multiblock scope struck many as too huge for a city and beyond the neighborhood's capacity. Yet for Eisenman, it was only a lemonade stand compared to what he and Graves had dreamt of in Harlem three decades before.

Eisenman brings intensity worthy of thirty blocks to the 120,000-square-foot branch of the SIIAS, seeing it in the context of the harbor. Discussing waterfront projects, Eisenman comments that "because of the scale of New York City's waterfront, we have not known what to do. This is not like the Thames, or the Seine, or the Tiber, where the scale of the river keeps the context in place. The scale of the harbor, the scale of the Hudson, even the East River imposes its own scale problem."[8] Eisenman's Staten Island project is a response to these various dilemmas of scale and shows an acute awareness of its site. Its forms are part of an international architectural language about movement and flow that he has helped to generate, in evidence around the world from the River Thames to Yokohama Bay. Marco Galaforo, an architect who worked on the design, writes: "The flow of itineraries molds the space, the form envelops and twists on a central void."[9]

The design is also, in spite of its international language, very contextual in its form's response to the terminal's existing cat-o'-nine-tails of bus ramps and bays. In its siting, the museum takes up an unfinished but open dialogue with the town's stately early twentieth-century Staten Island courthouse and borough hall, by the gifted Beaux-Arts partnership of Carrère & Hastings, over-looking the terminal and its workings from the rise of Richmond Terrace. With competitive candor, Eisenman focuses on the harbor scale, asserting that first and foremost his design will be iconic. He asks: "Do they go to Bilbao for the exhibitions? People come for the building. I've been to the Sydney Opera House five times, but I haven't heard an opera there. It's an icon. The world depends upon icons. It also needs workspace, and living space, but everything isn't architecture."[10]

If Eisenman's design goes forward, it will be part of a very different St. George than when it was first conceived. To the southeast, the tower/bridge base of Bay Street, with artist Siah Armajani and landscape architects Johansson & Walcavage, will finally lead to more than an abandoned site and little-used waterfront esplanade, thanks to the opening of the National Lighthouse Museum in 2002 in what had been an abandoned and decayed former Coast Guard headquarters now being renovated under the design direction of Jan Pokorny Architects. In its mix of programs, spaces, and expression, St. George is a microcosm of evolving systems of the city. On the one hand, there is Eisenman fighting for contemporary culture and iconic architecture; and on the other, there is a stadium where the city has rediscovered the pleasures of attending "local" games at a new baseball stadium. To the south, there is an example of the late-twentieth-century public art movement in Armajani's stair tower and a celebration of the harbor's heritage in the adaptive reuse of the museum dedicated to the historic role of lighthouses along America's shores. In the midst of this largely pedestrian zone, there is the major transportation infrastructure of the reno-vated ferry, where the dignity of the daily commute has been rec-ognized, as it was so successfully by the Jubilee Line Extension in London. Finally, as if to contain almost the entire front yard of a city, the borough has announced a design competition for a Sep-tember 11 memorial—and Eisenman has proposed a design—on the walkway between the terminal and the stadium.

NEW JERSEY:
THE MASTER PLAN AND
ITS EXECUTION

No part of New York Harbor has been the focus of a more expansive vision of and strategy for reinvention than New Jersey along the harbor and the Hudson River. The most obvious evidence is the range of offices and condominiums crowding the waterfront, most of very limited architectural merit, that have erased the low-rise port facilities of an earlier era. Yet whatever the mixed message of individual buildings and places, New Jersey planned, designed, and is soon to complete the most ambitious armature for waterfront transformation in the region. Despite the involvement of multiple municipalities, despite community disputes as vociferous as New York's, despite an even weightier industrial heritage than most of New York, the towns along New Jersey's waterfront are where you can find the boldest sustained idea for

urban design: a continuous pedestrian ribbon 18.8 miles long. The Regional Plan Association foresaw River City in 1966 in its Plan for the Lower Hudson.[11] Fourteen years later, legislation was passed to build the waterfront walkway connecting municipalities from the Bayonne Bridge north to the George Washington Bridge, with the Philadelphia-based design and planning firm of Wallace Roberts & Todd as master planners, with the New Jersey Department of Environmental Protection (NJDEP) Division of Coastal Resources. In 1988, NJDEP adopted regulations requiring construction of a thirty-foot-wide public walkway at all new waterfront developments (five years after the first stretch of Battery Park City's esplanade opened and four years before New York completed the same type of regulations as part of its Comprehensive Waterfront Plan). The Hudson River Walkway Conservancy, a coalition of public and private groups, was founded to ensure that developers and the public sector met the mandate of public access to the water.

The walkways started strong on public lands, as at Liberty State Park, but things did not go as well on private property. As architect and author Craig Whitaker has written, developers, even after the passage of the 1988 law, "disguised public walkways by installing gates, adding barbed wire, or letting the weeds grow. In one large project a developer even constructed the required public walkway inside his building."[12] Nonetheless, the almost twenty-mile-line on the map was drawn, and it is nearing completion, paralleled by the other new line on the New Jersey map, the Hudson-Bergen Light

4. HUDSON-BERGEN LINE LIGHT RAIL, EX-CHANGE PLACE, JERSEY CITY, NEW JERSEY, 2000

5. HARBORSIDE PLAZA X UNDER CONSTRUCTION, JERSEY CITY, NEW JERSEY, 2002, HLW INTERNATIONAL

Rail, which started its first service in 2000; ultimately, it will run from Bayonne north, traveling only a few blocks from the waterfront through Weehawken, then turning inland the final stretch of its 20.5-mile run to Ridgefield. The light rail, expecting up to one hundred thousand passengers a day when complete, travels on both dedicated rights-of-way and city streets, connecting its New York–bound users to PATH stations and a number of new ferry landings. Planning for the thirty-two stations the system will require, the architecture and urban design partnership of Jambhekar Strauss (in association with the engineers and planners for the overall project, Parsons Brinckerhoff Quade Douglas, Inc.) first designed a series of handsome stations. The same partnership, merged with Fox & Fowle Architects in 2000, is completing designs for the Hoboken and Union City stations, using an architectural language in tune with their understanding of light rail as a contemporary, rather than quaint, transit system.

Together with the Hudson River Walkway, the rail line demarcates a new public realm, a double edge that marks out a new, twenty-first-century ground for these waterfront cities. The architecture that occupies the ground between the rail line and the waterfront walkway has had its ups and downs. Despite the marinas, the con-dominiums, the low-, mid-, and high-rise buildings, the ferry service and rail, plans by municipalities and private developers seem to have been slow to generate the urban vibe of complexity and opportunity. This is partially due to the slow rise to critical mass, which may come with the final build-out of both smaller projects and huge districts like six-hundred-acre Newport (almost as large as the "square-mile city" of Hoboken next door), which has a thoughtful master plan by Ehrenkrantz Eckstut & Kuhn Architects completed in the mid-1980s. Newport has, however, generated enough critical mass to have its own newsletter and community activists who, like the site's developer, the Lefrak Organization, want to rename their home "Newport City," not just "Newport," and at the same time are attending Jersey City town hall meetings to raise their voice against, ironically, overdeveloping the waterfront. Having already spawned its own opponents from within its own boundaries, perhaps Newport is not so far from that urban vibe.[13] Yet the name issue is a contentious one because it is driven, in part, by a desire to disassociate the development from Jersey City's lower-income identity, now literally on the other side of the tracks. The mayor of Jersey City, Glenn D. Cunningham, elected in 2001 after the 1980s and 1990s building boom pushed by the mayoralty of his predecessor, one-time conservative Republican *wunderkind* Brent Schundler, believes that his city risks settling into the Atlantic City phenomenon of a gold coast completely detached from the intractably poor areas behind it. He has spoken of the need

6. PIER A, HOBOKEN, NEW JERSEY, 1999, ARNOLD/WILDAY LANDSCAPE
ARCHITECTS

to review the tax abatements that have helped fuel waterfront development, to make sure that there are benefits inland, too.[14] There are, however, incidents of urban design and architectural integrity that promise to be engaging environments. Exchange Place south of Newport, in Jersey City's traditional downtown, now offers the satisfying urban spectacle and infrastructure of the light rail line stop from which there is a harbor view framed by buildings, harnessing the visual and experiential power of the site and the infrastructure that gets one there (fig. 4). The Harborside Development in Jersey City, between Exchange Place and Newport, which sealed off stretches of its waterfront in some urbanistically unhappy early phases and generally offers little architectural satisfaction, has turned over a new leaf with the Plaza X project, opening in 2002, by HLW International. Its nineteen-story curtain wall shows more verve than has been seen in commercial building on the New Jersey shoreline for years (fig. 5).

A noncommercial waterfront project of great merit in Jersey City south of Exchange Place is not yet moving toward construction. The New York partnership of Weiss/Manfredi Architects, well known for their 1997 Women's Memorial and Education Center in Arlington National Cemetery in Washington, D.C., designed Veterans Park in 1999. Sited where the Morris Canal flows into the Hudson, it covers 2.5 acres once occupied by a coal depot and, later, by military barracks. Rather than leave it a level plane, firm principals Marion Weiss and Michael Manfredi, who often work at the boundary

between landscape and architecture, built up the site to a twenty-foot rise, a landform recalling a "relic of military fortifications."[15] In the design, the hillock is created by a series of terraces that together serve as a shallow amphitheater with an unfettered view of the Manhattan skyline, castle batteries, Ellis Island, and the Statue of Liberty.

New Jersey has been faster to recover from the Port Authority's overly ambitious development plans of the 1980s than, say, Brooklyn Heights. In 1989, Hoboken's citizens voted down the Port's proposal for waterfront towers. After years of community meetings and civic group actions, the city has allowed new construction in exchange for a public park, open to the waterfront. Just north of the renovated Erie Lackawanna Railroad and Ferry Terminal (a copper-clad 1907 edifice partly restored in the 1990s), South Waterfront Park has seven acres, including Pier A and a stretch of Hudson River walkway (fig. 6). Arnold/Wilday Landscape Architects, based in Hoboken, kept it visually simple: a clear division between a grove of plane trees and a lawn, running along a diagonal on axis with the view of the Empire State Building. For a passive park, it is very active, with sunbathers, fishers, and the children under the copper-topped pavilion designed by Dmitri Sarantitis Architects.

The park may also become the dock for a long-delayed floating swimming pool designed by Jonathan Kirschenfeld Architects for the Parks Council, a New York–based civic group led by waterfront scholar and planner Ann L. Buttenwieser. The plan was for the pool to be moored anywhere in New York Harbor and was inspired by the city's own history of floating pools, which flourished from 1817 until 1935, when the construction of public pools on land and the decline in the harbor's water quality brought their era to an end. Yet it is in New Jersey, not New York, and most likely at Pier A for the short term and adjacent Pier C for the long term, that the first floating pool in almost seventy years is likely to find its twenty-first-century dock. Buttenwieser is a passionate advocate of the floating-pool idea, which she sees as both a symbol of and a program for an active waterfront. The study of affordable, feasible construction solutions led Kirschenfeld and Buttenwieser to envision using a retired, refurbished garbage barge, an act of urban recycling in itself, as the base for an artful, almost minimally construed 50-by-115-foot pool.

FERRIES: REGIONAL FUNCTION AND LOCAL IDENTITY

The interdependence of New York's and New Jersey's waterfronts is underscored by incidents like the New York floating pool finding its home port in Hoboken. There is a full armature to support this interaction with the activities of the port, administered by the bistate Port Authority. The environmental definition is also clearly beyond municipal or state boundaries—this is the Hudson-Raritan Estuary. Yet the common interests of the two states, separated by a river and a harbor, are not always preeminent in the minds of citizens and their leaders. New Jersey's new developments need New York; many of their residents are there because of the easy commute to Manhattan. And New York needs New Jersey; its leading role as a financial center is now intertwined with the score of major companies that have relocated not to the deep suburbs of

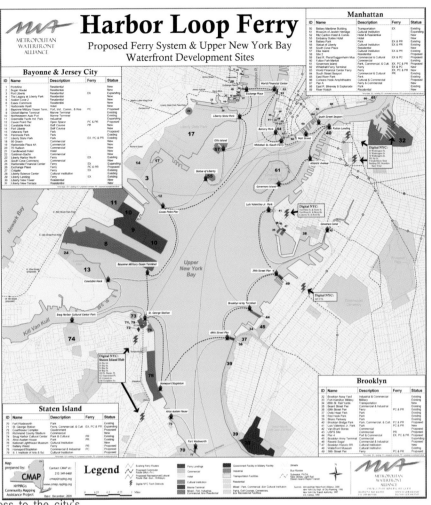

7. HARBOR LOOP FERRY PROPOSAL, NEW YORK CITY, 2001, METROPOLITAN WATERFRONT ALLIANCE

New Jersey but to the shorelines with easy access to the city's downtown and midtown central business districts.

Sometimes it takes the private sector to overcome the inhibitions of opposing political entities, and sometimes it takes a direct, physical connection to make the point that two places are inextricably bound. The ferry system, or the lack thereof, was a fittingly melancholy subject during the twenty-five years when the only ferry running was the Staten Island route, with its grim terminals in Manhattan and Staten Island, a sad counterpoint to memories of the era before World War II when scores of steamer and ferry routes traversed the harbor. Yet since the introduction of the privately operated New York Waterway fleet in 1986, transporting passengers between its property in Weehawken, New Jersey, and the company-owned pier at 38th Street on the West Side of Manhattan, ferry use has grown to thirty-three thousand passengers a day in addition to the more than fifty thousand traveling the Staten Island-Manhattan route before September 11, 2001.[16] The company did not initiate the service to win civic kudos—it looked at its property in Weehawken and realized that it could never develop it successfully without a ferry connection to Manhattan. For Arthur Imperatore, Jr., New York Waterway's president, the success of reintroducing New Jersey-New York ferry service is a testament to the enlightened self-interest of a private company. He has remarked that when it started, his company not only owned the land in Weehawken but held control of Pier 78 in Manhattan, where it had the flexibility to move far faster than the public sector could have in installing a ferry landing—the first new one since 1959—and would never have succeeded if it had required public investment to get started.[17]

After September 11, private ferry operators' daily ridership—largely New York Waterway but also including other services such as the route between Manhattan and Monmouth County, New Jersey—rose to fifty-nine thousand, with the number of routes up from thirteen to twenty-two, landings up from seven to nine, and boats from thirty-seven to fifty-one.[18] Some of this is temporary: when the PATH train station that was knocked out by the World Trade Center attack returns to service, the ferry will be less essential for New Jersey commuters, although many expect the ferry to play a larger permanent role, including Mayor Michael Bloomberg, who in his 2002 "State of the City" address argued that "improved ferry service is critical...new, faster ferries are needed."[19]

Many in New York were already planning an expanded role for ferries before September 2001. Earlier that year, the Metropolitan Waterfront Alliance, headed by Carter Craft and founded by Municipal Art Society president Kent Barwick, announced a formal plan for an integrated ferry service, which they called "Harbor Loop Ferry" (fig. 7). The proposal includes twenty-five landings on Upper New York Bay (from the Verrazano Narrows to the openings of Arthur Kills, the Hudson, and the East River). The business loop for the weekday would have sixteen stops, including new ones along the New Jersey shore, Staten Island, Brooklyn, Governors Island, and the East River; a supplemental "cultural and recreational" loop adds nine more stops on weekends, reaching into Staten Island's Snug Harbor Cultural Center, down to the same borough's Alice Austen House on the Narrows, and up to South Street Seaport and Battery Park in Manhattan. Like the bid for the 2012 Olympics, this is not a city-endorsed or -funded plan but rather a "noble logical diagram," in planning visionary Daniel Burnham's famed but undocumented phrase.

Both the loop idea and a more general commitment to increasing the harbor's ferry service have gained strength since fall 2001.[20] The first impact on the cities and boroughs that border the harbor has been in the designs for new ferry terminals by a variety of architects, but the larger question is the ferry system's impact on the waterfront districts beyond the immediate needs for waiting rooms and terminals.

PIER 40: COMPETITION, CHARRETTE, AND PLAN

New York is confident enough in the future of ferry service in the harbor to sponsor the construction of the West Midtown Intermodal Ferry Terminal on the publicly owned Pier 79, now functioning as a ventilation tower for the Lincoln Tunnel and a bus garage for New York Waterway, which still controls Pier 78. The design, by William Nicholas Bodouva & Associates, is a solid essay in contemporary transportation infrastructure, with multiple berths and glazed waiting rooms anticipating an increase in service and demand. The new terminal lies at the middle of the long, narrow line of Hudson River Park, the vast, controversial reclamation project on Manhattan's West Side waterfront from the Battery to 59th Street that has been opening incrementally since 1999.

Hudson River Park, 550 acres along almost five miles of

8. HUDSON RIVER PARK CONCEPT PLAN, MODEL,
MANHATTAN, 1999, QUENNELL ROTHSCHILD & PARTNERS
AND MATHEWS NIELSEN

Manhattan's West Side waterfront, reflects the astonishing patience and commitment of the public officials and designers who endured thousands of agency reviews, community meetings, design reviews, and funding increases and decreases, from the demise of the Westway highway and development proposal in 1985 through the 1992-1999 Hudson River Park Conservancy, for which Quennell Rothschild & Partners/Mathews Nielsen completed the master plan. The plan set the outline of continuous public access, restoring more than a dozen piers (and removing others) and allowing for a range of active and passive recreation, public education centers, and, what always generated the most controversy, "park-compatible commercial development." It also offered a number of strategies for design that kept the spaces at the waterfront open yet fit in enough activity to keep it animated (fig. 8). By 1999, the Conservancy, as its mission changed from planning to building, was restructured as the Hudson River Park Trust (HRPT), which opened the first stretch of the park, across from Greenwich Village, in 1999.

By 2001, HRPT had moved its headquarters to Pier 40 at the end of Houston Street, the vast, unplanned, fifteen-acre question mark for the park's future. In general, most of the Hudson River Park is a thin if interesting ribbon, which is often too exiguous to make public spaces for anything more than walking, running, skating, or bicycling through. Pier 40 is the exception. Completed in the early 1960s, Pier 40 is one of the largest relics of the shipping industry in Manhattan, which left almost as soon as the huge reinforced concrete structure was completed. Today, the pier largely serves as a parking lot graced by water views from its thirty-seven-foot-high top deck, with the relatively recent addition of soccer fields on its roof and interior as well as special recreation rooms and fishing sites along its southern edge.

The focus of an ideas design competition led by Manhattan's Community Board 2 and Van Alen Institute (VAI) in 1998-1999, the pier is both the embodiment of and a vantage point on the future of adaptive reuse of existing structures on the waterfront. The roof deck is rimmed by a thirty-foot-high fence of gantries towering above the parked cars, all dashing steel and catwalks angling out over the water to unload the phantom ships that once docked there, briefly. For many observers, and probably the majority of architects and designers, there is something irresistibly functionalist about the gantries, which are light and expressive of purpose and strength, and the concrete structure supporting them. But for years, the gantries, and the building as a whole, inspired little sympathy from a community that demanded its replacement with a park. The park was also a point of contention, with some locals campaigning for an open green space and others advocating facilities for organized sports as well as some commercial activity.

9. PIER 40 WATERFRONT CHARRETTE, HUDSON RIVER, MAN-HATTAN, 1999

10. PIER 40, PLAN OF POST-CHARRETTE PROPOSAL, HUDSON RIVER, MANHATTAN, 1999, SEBASTIAN KNORR, MICHAEL TRIEBESWETTER, MAJID JELVEH, CHRISTIAN JOIRIS

The competition opened up the community and public agencies to different ideas for the pier. Choosing a jury of largely design professionals who lived or worked within its boundaries, Community Board 2 sent out a powerful message that local concerns would be addressed. The local not-for-profit, the Pier Park and Playground Association (P3), which had forced the city to provide sports fields on the pier in the mid-1990s (even as it continued to function as a parking garage), supported the process. The competition received a strong response, with hundreds of submissions entered from the immediate neighborhood and around the world, by a full spectrum of the profession, from students to well-known practitioners. The Cooper Union sponsored an exhibition of the entries before the jury, as did the Hudson River Park Trust, the public authority in charge of the whole park's development, which offered space at Pier 40 for an exhibition and the jury itself, which took place on the artificial turf of the second floor indoor soccer field.

The work on display provoked great interest and mixed reviews from the community. Cumulatively, it galvanized a demand for something more than the everyday. Most entries proposed some greening of the pier. Not the passive green park that some demanded but a complex greening, one that reused the powerful industrial frame of the building. Brooklyn-based architect Richard James, for example, provided the purest collage of concrete frame intersecting lawns and gardens. Deamer/Phillips, an architectural partnership with offices within blocks of the pier, and one of the three winning entrants, harnessed much of the frame, but instead of "greening" it, "blued" it into an aquatic center. Another winning entry, this one by New York architects Majid Jelveh and Christian Joiris, offered a series of grid and garden scenarios—a sand beach under the columns, basketball in between. The team of Sebastian Knorr Architects, with Liu Liang Landscape Architects, Nicole Kroehling, and Michael Triebswetter, drew a "rain forest," taking away the structure to build in a relentlessly interactive relationship with the site, cutting the pier away from the bulkhead and inserting a Hudson River swimming area within a boomerang-shaped buoy.

The summer after the competition, two of the teams agreed to work together with P3 to take the scheme further, volunteering their time and energy for the extraordinary opportunity to work on site, in the glazed finger pier at the southwest corner of Pier 40 (fig. 9). Through the heat of a New York summer in a six-week charrette, Knorr and his partners, including the German firms Brandi & Partner Architects and GTL Landscape Architects, the cofinalists Jelveh and Joiris, and P3 president Tobi Bergman, kept their commitment to retaining much of the structure of the pier and

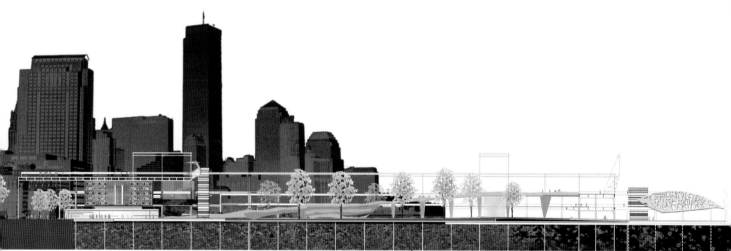

11.PIER 40, SECTION OF POST-CHARRETTE PROPOSAL, HUDSON RIVER, MANHATTAN, 1999,
SEBASTIAN KNORR, MICHAEL TRIEBESWETTER, MAJID JELVEH, CHRISTIAN JOIRIS

providing sports fields, yet beyond that began with an open mind toward a design for the pier. During the charrette, the public came in and out, both informally and through a series of structured meetings. The designers let go of their preconceived ideas for the pier. They undertook a close analysis of the site's ongoing uses for fishing, baseball, soccer, and other recreation as well as for parking. The team reviewed plans for the esplanade running between it and Route 9A (also known as West Street and the West Side Highway) as well as for Hudson River Park to the north and south, and it also uncovered the original engineering drawings for the pier's reinforced concrete structure designed by David P. Billington, who went on to become a distinguished civil engineer and scholar of reinforced concrete structures.[21]

The designers invited hundreds of people to the site for interviews, and then they drew, built models, and as they learned more from the community, revised and redesigned. Every day, they worked on site, getting to know how people use the pier, and how the weather, water, and river traffic impact the structure, all the while envisioning how people might use the pier in the future. The team concluded that this was an opportunity to design a new kind of urban waterfront park. The park could reuse rather than raze the pier's superstructure, transforming it from a closed box into an open system (fig. 10). The

team's research showed that they would be restoring the open, flexible system that the structure had been designed to be historically. They realized that they could successfully organize the park into layers, both horizontally, out eight hundred feet into the Hudson from the city's edge, and vertically, from a fully open ground level to a mix of sports and cultural programmatic elements on an intermediate level and open decks and sky above (fig. 11). They could take the solid reinforced concrete "bones" of the structure and humanize them with materials ranging from boardwalk to green lawns, a baseball diamond at grade, and soccer fields on the roof. The scheme also proposed a radical idea for parking—replacing the self-service garage with an automated parking system that got almost two thousand spaces into the front of the pier. By focusing on the park's three-dimensional potential, they could accommodate a range of voiced community needs, from a soccer game to a waterfront stroll, and with less fanfare, equal in program and experience to projects like the Ponte Parodi in Genoa.

The designers and P3 found a way to design a waterfront park that, instead of "suburbanizing" the city, creates a park that is thoroughly urban, meets a complex overlay of community demands, and provides green open space. In fall 1999 the community board endorsed the plan, and in spring 2000 the Hudson River Park Trust Design Advisory Committee did the same. The following year, the trust agreed to have a plan to replace the existing parking garage by 2003. The ideas competition led to a vision for a programmatic synthesis that expanded the notion of reuse. The competition led to a workshop, the workshop led to a community and public authority endorsement. The design initiative as a whole suggests that reuse of recent structures, not just of those built before World War II, is fertile ground for waterfront-related programs and architectural expression, and that an open design process engaging the community, while at odds with much of current practice and sometimes leading to nothing more than a bitter dead end, can be invaluable to a design's development and acceptance. For Pier 40 it may ultimately have only the power of influence rather than policy, yet the plan that P3 and the designers completed through the on-site charrette has raised the bar for the program and design of whatever project the Hudson River Park Trust finally endorses.

RIVERSIDE SOUTH: HIGHWAY IN THE PARK

Just north of Hudson River Park begins Riverside South's stretch of waterfront park, from 59th to 72nd Streets. The linear park sits between Riverside South, a development spearheaded by the Trump Organization through a long and tumultuous review process, and the Hudson. A consortium of civic groups who entered the cooperative planning process in the early 1990s felt that it was time to demonstrate that New York was a place where major projects were possible, but where they had to be good. The civic groups agreed that first, in return for a more sensitive (and smaller) development, and second and most importantly, in return for a spectacular waterfront park for the West Side, they would lend their support to Trump's project. Yet even in its scaled-down version, the development encompasses sixteen residential

12. PIER 70, RIVERSIDE SOUTH, HUDSON RIVER, MANHATTAN, 2001, THOMAS BALSLEY ASSOCIATES

buildings and one commercial project, with an estimated total cost of $3 billion.

In spring 2001, Riverside South met some of its commitment to build waterfront open space. It completed seven acres of park, including the 750-foot-long, diagonal Pier 70, in the first phase of what will in the end be more than twenty acres of public space (fig. 12). Thomas Balsley Associates designed the park, calling on some of the same design language and program the firm used at Gantry Park in Queens West, including fish-cleaning tables and planning to keep, rather than demolish, an industrial artifact—a float bridge. With a smaller budget than the one available for the Long Island City park, the float bridge has yet to be touched.

Like the bridge, the heavily trafficked viaduct of the Miller Highway, which cuts above and across the park, had been left in place, despite an agreement between the civic groups and the developer, and an understanding between the state and city, that the highway would be razed and its lanes rebuilt in a tunnel and a cut burrowed into the park. The Miller Highway, a piece of the same structure eliminated from New York's waterfront south of 59th Street after its decay and demolition in the 1970s, was in fact recently repaired for $85 million in the 1990s, and there was no political consensus that it should be removed, with Congressman Jerrold Nadler, among others, determined to prevent it, whatever consensus the civic groups had reached. Michael W. Bradley, who was a key member of the staff of the Hudson River Park Trust (and its predecessor,

the Hudson River Park Conservancy), before becoming executive director of the Riverside South Planning Corporation, faces a dilemma with his board. The decision to build sections of the park with the highway still in situ has made it a popular place, admired for its setting and design, but the better one makes the park without tearing down the highway, the less imperative its demolition becomes. The attention of the developers and the Riverside South Planning Corporation has shifted to another focus since September 11: how to turn their rotting float bridge at 69th Street into a landing for a fast ferry down to Wall Street, which would take pressure off the overcrowded Broadway subway line. A downtown ferry would also give a boost to the revival of Lower Manhattan by providing a more enjoyable way to get there. New York Waterway, the major private ferry operator in the harbor, for one, believes it is a plausible option, and Riverside South's Bradley believes that a terminal could be in operation by fall 2003. Members of the local community have voiced their wariness of transportation infrastructure entering a park, but need may prevail. In the right design and planning hands, an inspired adaptive reuse of the ninety-year-old structure would serve as a vivid model of waterfront iconography, connecting past and present, serving a maritime function, and enhancing the experience of daily life.[22]

HARLEM ON THE HUDSON RIVER: COMMUNITY, COMMUNICATION, AND DESIGN

At the beginning of the twentieth century, the Harlem waterfront from St. Clair Place, just north of Riverside Park and south of 125th Street, and on up to 133rd Street included recreation and industry, with piers used for freight and excursion boats. Streetcars ran up the diagonal of 125th Street, formed by a valley, to the ferry landing for Fort Lee, in the midst of a mill town of breweries, meat-packing plants, and other industries. By the 1940s, those functions were gone, and by the late 1950s, the piers themselves had been demolished.[23]

More than three decades after Eisenman and Graves anchored their MoMA exhibition megastructure on this same stretch of the Harlem waterfront, and after years of proposals and counterproposals, a strong conceptual design is emerging for the site. In the late 1990s,

after a false start, there was a move toward consensus. New York City's EDC, a public agency involved in virtually all of the city's waterfront projects, developed a request for proposals (RFP) for the site. The responses, including among other ideas a waterfront motel, alarmed community activists, including Peggy Shepard, a forceful voice on issues of environmental justice who led the battle over the odorous waste treatment plant that sits beneath Riverbank State Park on the waterfront just north of the EDC's Harlem site. The organization she heads, West Harlem Environmental Action (WE ACT), partnered with Manhattan's Community Board 9 in opposing the motel plan, and most importantly, in working with dozens of community groups to put forward an alternative. The Harlem on the River Steering Committee offered its ideas in workshops, forums, and a public exhibition in 1999, having worked closely with Abeles Phillips Preiss & Shapiro as their planning consultant and Thomas Balsley Associates as their landscape architect. The alternative plan the team developed looked beyond the EDC site to two blocks north (131st to 133rd streets), a site occupied by waterfront parking, as well as two blocks inland, to envision how the soaring 1901 Riverside Drive viaduct over Manhattan Valley (125th Street) could be used to help define the district. The plan included three recreational piers, docks, learning centers, and a range of ideas for the scale and character of the district. It was an impressive, inclusive exercise in community process, especially because participants insisted on a high caliber of planning and design.

13. WEST HARLEM WATERFRONT MASTER PLAN, RENDERING, HARLEM, 2001, W ARCHI-
TECTURE

The Harlem on the River group's position was clear, as when it prepared a protest postcard for potential advocates of the response to the EDC's RFP. The card, addressed to Manhattan's borough president, read in part: "I am very concerned that you are considering approving a plan that would privatize the Harlem Piers area by placing a large motel—which is not water dependent—along the Harlem waterfront," and added, "Doing so would eliminate significant public access, unlike communities downtown that are benefiting from the development of waterfront parks that provide open space and recreational activities."[24] In other words, the community was telling its elected officials and other powerful players: We took the sewage plant; we're not going to take this. And their voices were heard.

The EDC announced a new master plan process for a West Harlem Waterfront Plan in 2001, demonstrating that they were an agency flexible and open to input from concerned citizens and willing to work together for an appropriate and mutually appealing solution, tempering their community concerns with their responsibility to foster economic development. The master plan area includes the city-owned waterfront property between St. Clair Place and West 133rd Street and continues up to 135th Street. The EDC selected Ten W, a partnership of architect Enrique Norten and architect and landscape architect Barbara Wilks, together with economists from the firm Ernst & Young, to develop the plan. Wilks and her collaborators began in March 2001 and acknowledged and utilized the Harlem on the River planning work that had already taken place, but they also brought to the table the conceptual and visual skill that they had shown in the Tide Point Office Campus and Waterfront Park on Baltimore's Inner Harbor, whose first phase had just been completed. In Baltimore, Wilks had managed to both renovate historic industrial buildings and use a minimal, industrial vocabulary to make a memorable waterfront park. She met the concerns of the local preservation commission, while still invoking a sense of play and waterfront romance through details like linear fog banks along the water's edge. This ability to articulate a thoroughly contemporary landscape while engaged in the review process of committees, commissions, and communities is an invaluable asset for the firm to bring to the Harlem project.

The waterfront concept developed by Wilks and her partners (now W Architecture, after Norten left the partnership later in 2001) includes an esplanade, defined as an "urban street" running the length of the site, and inland from the walkway, a narrow lawn that borders a slim, glass-enclosed waterfront structure—perhaps a restaurant to generate revenue for the maintenance of the park. At the water, the design includes an excursion boat pier at the end of 125th Street, and farther north, a long pier adjacent to the site for boating and fishing, with two smaller piers reached by narrow bridges farther out into the Hudson (fig. 13). The piers are skewed, not perpendicular to the shore but instead set at acute angles, both for pragmatic reasons (piers at an angle are easier for boats to dock at, given the Hudson's current and tides, and hold up better against ice) and for the visual relationships they set up with the complicated site behind them. As in Baltimore, Wilks demonstrates how simple moves can enhance the water's edge: here what the designer terms the "wharf/slope" softens the hard edge of the masonry seawall by building up a swale planted with tall grasses to absorb the walkway's runoff.

W Architecture evaluated the potential of the site in a profound way, understood its ribbons of north-south transportation, and used this connective tissue as a formal and programmatic reference. They have also been intimately involved in community discourse. The firm's ability to work with topography and existing infrastructure, the "ecology" of the EDC and the community, marks the promise of this design.

BRONX COMMUNITY PAPER PLANT: WHETHER AND WHERE TO REVIVE WATERFRONT INDUSTRY

Three miles due east, across Manhattan and the Harlem River, lie the Bronx Rail Yards, a few blocks north of the Triborough Bridge and extending along the ditch-sized Bronx Kill that runs between the Bronx and Randall's Island. It is where the best new waterfront project in the Bronx will never be built, after almost $3 million and eight years of work between 1992 and 2000 and untold expenditure of human, political, and emotional capital. For a city and a borough struggling with how to maintain a diverse base of jobs—not all service industry—and recognizing that the waterfront has intrinsic value to industry as well as to leisure, the Bronx Community Paper Plant, even at an estimated cost of $370 million, was a precious opportunity.

The project was driven by the National Resources Defense

14. BRONX COMMUNITY PAPER PLANT, RENDERING, BRONX, MAYA LIN AND HLW INTERNATIONAL

Council (NRDC) and was paradoxical from the start. The NRDC, an organization of environmental activists, wanted to build a paper plant, a seeming pact with the devil to anyone who has ever lived or inhaled within ten miles of a paper plant of the old school. Yet NRDC had seen recycling paper plants with very moderate emissions such as the de-inking plants that one of the project partners, Valmet Corporation, had built in Sweden. From the largest ecological equation, they argued that virgin forests would be saved, and at the city level, they explained how much the city's waste stream would be reduced, pointing to the benefits of 280,000 metric tons of wastepaper being recycled each year. By creating a local demand for wastepaper, they would radically increase the rate of recycling in New York, "consuming one half of the wastepaper collected by the City of New York," according to one of the project partners.[25]

On a waterfront full of industrial activity, NRDC planned to take advantage of proximity to the nearby sewage treatment plant to run the operation on its water rather than fresh water. At the local level, it partnered with the Banana Kelly Community Improvement Association, which had a stellar reputation for developing housing and services in what is a very poor, largely minority district, and worked with Banana Kelly on plans for job-training programs as well as strategies to ensure that local residents were able to get some of the plant's estimated six hundred new jobs.

The NRDC needed to build a plant that had symbolic as well as functional value. To achieve that, in 1993 they asked for the design insights of Maya Lin, who joined the team as facility designer a year after the architects, HLW International, where the design was led by Chris Choa (fig. 14). An artist and architect who won the Vietnam War Memorial competition as a student in 1980, Lin was a veteran of the struggle to sustain design integrity in the midst of public review. Working with Choa and a team of project partners and advisers, Lin brought her passion for public experience and expression to the project, envisioning a paper mill that was proud of itself, where even in the lunchroom employees, visitors, and tourists could watch the recycling process. In a National Public Radio interview, Lin described the design: "It's actually a series of very clean-line industrial metal buildings connected by glass passageways and skylights, and then a prominent feature will be a glass-encased smoke tower. Again, with the steam sort of misting up through it. But a lot of it is allowing the beauty of...the technological components to shine through. It's exposing a machine, in a way."[26]

There were community activists who did not want a machine, exposed or not, because they were unconvinced by arguments that the plant's emissions would be harmless, and they also questioned the value of increasing industrial activity in the Bronx. From another perspective, experts in the needs of rail freight feared that the project, which only occupied a section of the Bronx Rail Yards, would nonetheless shut the door on ever reactivating the disused transportation hub and thereby damage the potential for reviving rail freight in the region. In 2000, NRDC gave up, unable to get the combination of private and public financing it needed despite passing one major hurdle after another. The private developer who has a long-term lease on the site completed a large new waste transfer station on a different portion of the rail yards, but the recycling plant was dead.[27] In the evolving definition of what constitutes highest and best use, or just use of the waterfront from an environmental-justice perspective, no doubt too much of the Bronx has been relegated to industry. Yet this project, in its program, in its commitment to making use of the site, and in its faith that industry can be part of the future of New York, not just its past, is a missed opportunity for the city.

In the Bronx, there are also community-driven efforts to reclaim the waterfront not for industry but for recreation. With almost no resources beyond committed volunteers, the non-profit Cherry Tree Association is determined to renovate the Port Morris area just east of the proposed paper plant site, advocating the remaking of the 132nd Street pier out into the East River as well as marinas and other proposals. To the east, the banks of the Bronx River have been cleared of decades' worth of tires and rubbish, and the Cherry Tree Association has garnered public commitments for aid to establish the Bronx River Greenway, which would stretch from the zoo at 180th Street down to the East River between Hunts Point and Soundview Park. At the end of Castle Hill Avenue, only a few blocks east of the Bronx River's outlet, a renovation and expansion of a waterfront YMCA, by Donald Blair Architects, moved forward in 2001. These initiatives, some in the realm of ideas, others in new and renovated buildings and reclaimed public space, demonstrate how vital and effective it is for an urban waterfront to have local efforts. New York's transformation still needs investment at the scale of the paper plant, but it also needs to respect and understand the scope and impact of projects pushed forward by volunteer and local organizations. Ideally, there can be an ongoing dialogue between the two.

RANDALL'S ISLAND: SIMULTANEOUS ISLAND REALITIES: SPORTS, BRIDGES, HOSPITALS, CONCERTS, WATER TREATMENT, AND PARKS

In 2001, the Randall's Island Sports Foundation (RISF) announced a $200 million capital plan to build its vision of the island as the city's primary center for sport, with its shoreline partially restored to its ecological past and a few key commercial ventures installed to make the whole public-private enterprise solvent. The foundation sees the island, located where the East River bends out to the Long Island Sound to the east and breaks into the Harlem River to the west, as a place for playing fields and recreation, a green sports center beneath the spans and interchanges of the 1936 Triborough Bridge above. Robert Moses, mastermind of that bridge, conceived of this open knot between Manhattan, the Bronx, and Queens as part of an integrated system of highways, parks, and sports facilities, both on Randall's Island and out to the boroughs. RISF is a

return to that vision of infrastructure and sports and entertainment working in tandem.[28] In 2001, the plan gained new funding from the city and private sources, and in 2002, New York Mayor Michael Bloomberg, who served on RISF's board before his election, gave the project a pledge of city support in his "State of the City" address, in which he announced his unstinting belief in the plan, highlighted for creating 350 summer jobs for youth.[29]

Initiated in 1992, RISF partnered with the New York City Department of Parks and Recreation in developing the scheme as well as the ongoing management of what is officially New York City's 480-acre Randall's and Wards Island Park. (Since landfill joined the islands in the 1930s, there has been only one island, but the dual names persist.) Led by the indefatigable Karen Cohen, president of RISF, they have arrived at a plan that includes better access to the island, including anticipated ferry service and a better pedestrian path on the Triborough Bridge (there is an existing footbridge at 103rd Street), though still no guaranteed pedestrian access from the Bronx. The program includes a 19,500-seat amphitheater, opening in 2003; a track-and-field center; and a complex of soccer fields on a site made available by the razing of Downing Stadium, which was deemed irrecoverable despite its fame as the sports venue where Jesse Owens won the 100-yard dash at the qualifying trials for the 1936 Olympics.

Perhaps in reaching the final arrangements for revenue-producing parts of the plan, RISF appears to have lost some of the deft elegance of the layout in the master plan that Quennell Rothschild & Partners prepared in 1999, which put the stage tent on the peninsula at the southwestern edge of the northern part of the two-part island and kept the "themed family entertainment concession" hunkered down in the southern "Wards Island" section. By May 21, 2001, when Mayor Giuliani led the project's groundbreaking ceremony, the performance stage had floated north to become an amphitheater, and the family entertainment, now defined as a water park, had moved to the northwest corner, no doubt more comfortably located there now with the demise of the paper plant project across the kill. The political and financial strength of the project has soared, and a plan completed by Zurita Architects for RISF has competently addressed the revised program.[30]

On the one hand, it is an inspiring testament to the city's changed political and social landscape: In 1970 could anyone have conceived of a water park at the mouth of the Harlem River, set between Harlem and the Bronx, scheduled to open in 2004? If the city accepts a golf range at Chelsea Piers, there is little excuse for a Robert Moses–like diffidence about entertainment as popular as a water park, but the public should insist that whatever the norms of design set by water parks, the astonishing patience and success of RISF should be rewarded with design throughout the island that is at as high a level as their aspirations, from the shoreline to the amphitheater to the water park.

THE EAST RIVER: OPEN FOR IDEAS

Randall's Island sits at the bend of the East River, where the river turns from being a tidal strait off New York Harbor and becomes the mouth of Long Island Sound. In the eight-mile stretch south from Randall's to its end between the Battery and Governors Island, the East River embodies the complexity and opportunity of waterfront design for New York. As a primary site of the city's identity, even after September 11, and as a true interborough site, its ongoing transformation resonates for New York and its harbor as a whole. In addition to its central location, it is also one of the great spaces in New York that is easy to grasp. Despite its great length, it is narrower than the Hudson and more accessible than the harbor. It can be understood in theoretical language as a space of flows (transportation, tides, cultures), yet in the end it is visible as "ground," in the sense of a figure-ground drawing, in which a city's public spaces, even its water bodies, can be illustrated as open ground, and its private buildings are drawn as dark solids. In that balance, the "ground" of the East River is as clear and identifiable as Central Park or Times Square, a broad gap in the grid. The four-mile "reach" between the Williamsburg and the Queensboro Bridges is almost double Central Park, except that this park is in the middle of three boroughs, not at the heart of Manhattan. While it may be known mostly as a barrier to get over or go under by bridge or tunnel whose one great shared function is as the site for the Independence Day fireworks, the river is nonetheless a negotiable, comprehensible public space 365 days a year.

Its slaughterhouses long gone, the East River still has its menacing side, remaining the most likely place in the city for corpses to rise up from the bottom when the water warms up during the "floater" weeks in April. Less gruesomely, Roosevelt Island still has crumbling ruins at its southern end, despite countless unrealized proposals, including Louis I. Kahn's 1974 design for an FDR Memorial and Santiago Calatrava 's 1995 SOUTHpoint Pavilion. To stimulate design ideas and action along this liquid arterial, Van Alen Institute initiated an East River study that included a workshop, a Web site, a series of exhibitions, lectures, panels, and an international ideas competition in 1998. The city's commitment to public access and the "reach studies" by the planning department provided a point of departure for VAI's East River programs, enriched by questions about the role of the public realm and what could be achieved by the policy, planning, and design initiatives already under way.

Since the ideas competition, called Design Ideas for New York's Other River, the East River has moved forward with major projects, planning, designing, and building, yet much of it, especially on the Brooklyn waterfront, has not even been cleared of ruins, much less reached the planning stage. This long fallow period may give the city the opportunity to avoid the mistakes of other sites and at the same time to be inspired both by ideas, even the most theoretical, for its future, and by the ad hoc uses and experiences that the city and the local community have found for the river's edges since industry's decline, both of which were expressed in the project VAI sponsored.

Most entrants in the ideas competition for New York's "other river" focused on reclaiming the East River as a natural environment, however pointedly artificial they might make that nature. (The word *river* is itself inaccurate; the water body is a tidal strait between New York Harbor and Long Island Sound, though it has been called a river since the Dutch came.) Kevin Bone of Bone/Levine Architects and his team proposed "Transfiguration," a scheme that would "reintroduce...fragments of a more complex network of water-based natural systems." It offered a stunningly beautiful presentation of boards dense with information about the history, current use, and potential of aquatic landscapes for the

15. "FILTRATION BUOYS," VAN ALEN INSTI-
TUTE DESIGN COMPETITION: DESIGN
IDEAS FOR NEW YORK'S OTHER RIVER,
RENDERING, EAST RIVER, 1998, ERIK
ROGERS AND GREGORY WORLEY

drainages of Maspeth Creek, Bushwick Creek, and Hallets Cove in Brooklyn. By their names alone, the sites begin to speak of a far different East River, one fed by creeks as well as tides, and eddying into inlets. The Hunters Point Community Coalition's competition submission, produced by activist Eedie Cuminale and landscape architect Thomas Paino and their collaborators, advocated an integrated system of habitat restoration sites along both sides of the strait, with a special focus on a site north of Queens West. *Landscape Architecture* magazine commented on the "straightforward—if ambitious—designs for knitting humans to the waterfront," including landscape architect Alan Berger's "Landscape Strai(gh)ts" project, which buried the FDR drive, provided a complex natural habitat on the waterfront, and insisted that the shoreline become an earthworks-sized straight line along the length of Manhattan's East Side.[31] The project could be read as a man-made intervention at the scale of landscape. Berger's project, like much of Adriaan Geuze's work in the Netherlands and the larger landscape urbanism movement, makes the point that there is no necessary contradiction between an ecologically sound environment and the

straight lines, right angles, and geometric forms that cities continue to generate.

Architects Jens Brickmann and Fabien Gantois, with the freedom that an ideas competition allows, proposed "(this is not Manhattan)" in which the entire edge of Brooklyn and Queens becomes a beach to further intensify the divide between the towers of Manhattan on one side and the low profile of Brooklyn and Queens on the other. A graduate architecture student in 1998, Dirk Bertulant, in the Dagmar Richter Studio, proposed stone piers to slow down the speed of the river, "allowing the regeneration of marshland." The stone piers would replace the wood piling piers from the industrial era (decayed or gone, since the marine borers did their work). In the same studio, Sandra Topfer proposed an alternative to Queens West—a sewage treatment plant, elegantly rendered, bold in its siting and forms, and designed to declare that "the plant for water purification shall become the visible part of an interchange between the water and the city."[32]

Finalists Erik Rogers and Gregory Worley offered the most evocative vision of this interchange with filtration buoys that they demonstrated could actually serve to improve the strait's water quality, as they blended "imagery and function" with fragments of infrastructure floating as symbols of the ecological revival of the river (fig. 15). Garrison Siegel Architects pushed an urbanist agenda, calling for streets to terminate at the water and showing how relatively small programs could animate the edge. Aaron

16. "TILL," VAN ALEN INSTITUTE DESIGN COMPETITION: DESIGN IDEAS FOR NEW YORK'S OTHER RIVER, RENDERING, EAST RIVER, 1998, VICTORIA MARSHALL AND STEVEN TUPU

EAST RIVER: CORRIDOR FOR MANHATTAN: REISER+UMEMOTO

Neubert and Michael Jacobs stretched architecture out into the waterway; their "scattered public and abandoned spaces" along the Brooklyn waterfront would provide access to floating program vessels from libraries to markets.

For landscape architects Victoria Thompson and Steven Tupu, whose "Till" won first prize in the competition, the chief issue was creating a natural (though highly unnaturalistic) landscape (fig. 16). They identified the city's greatest physical problem as coping with waste and poisoned lands, and designed a new waterfront for Brooklyn and Queens with a vigorous topography of ramps and dales, coupled with an ambitious schedule of strategies for leaching out, growing out, and putting out the toxins in the waste and earth. At the same time, through their images, they indicated that the most valuable public space was space for recreation. Not that the ardor of work is absent: the images are of heart-bursting mountain biking and demanding play in "Rampland," which creates an "other" network of clean-fill megaslopes lined with garden terraces, storm water sinks, and orchards. Like all the strongest of the competition entries, "Till" took on a major issue—brownfields—and resolved it with an imaginative program that combined function with experience.

The Van Alen Institute's study of the East River also included the Van Alen Fellowship in Public Architecture. The fellowship supported Jesse Reiser and Nanako Umemoto of Reiser+Umemoto RUR Architecture and their team in developing the "East River Corridor" project.[33] Throughout their work, conventional notions of park, edge, waterfront, street, urban and ultimately public realm were put into question. For Reiser and Umemoto the challenge was to take what the architects termed the "destructive" entity of the FDR Drive and transform it into a generator of valid contemporary urban form and public space. Reviewing the community boards' wish lists for their waterfronts first compiled by the Department of City Planning's Plan for the Manhattan Waterfront study of 1994, supplemented by the Institute's East River study, Reiser and

17. "EAST RIVER CORRIDOR," RENDERING, EAST RIVER, VAN ALEN INSTITUTE FELLOWSHIP IN PUBLIC ARCHITECTURE, 1999, REISER+UMEMOTO RUR ARCHITECTURE

Umemoto construed a supple, self-regulating frame that integrated the FDR into multiple systems of slow and fast vehicular traffic, pedestrian territories, and millions of square feet of commercial, civic, and service space.

The Reiser+Umemoto proposal, agile in connecting the movement systems of its project to local streets, is not a Jane Jacobs–inspired celebration of the urban life of the street. Instead, it looks to the interaction among pedestrian, vehicular, and waterborne transportation systems, together with the programming of recreation and commercial space, to create an authentic contemporary public realm. Rather than romanticize a historic urban street as the generator of public experience, the architects find energy—some might even find it a kind of danger—in the scale, traffic, and complexity of the project's form. They deliberately oppose the grid: though thin in the east-west direction, the proposed area's length in the north-south direction coincides with the natural and artificial geography of the edge as opposed to the right-angled organization of the city's interior (fig. 17).

Like many architects, Reiser and Umemoto were drawn to where infrastructure and more traditional urban space seem to work together: "We began by looking at some very successful moments along the FDR corridor, such as at Sutton Place and Carl Schurz Park, where the city and park space deck out over the right-of-way providing direct contact with the river. These moments, however, remain only locally effective due to their isolation, their disconnec-

tion from the larger continuum."[34] Instead of burying the FDR, they have designed a "twisting, weaving system that would continuously negotiate the rises and falls of the FDR as well as incorporating public programming."[35] As they wrote: "Architecture must reengage the urban scale of the city, not simply to repeat existing patterns, but rather as a comprehensive project for the environment for coherent public space." Looking at the overall possibility, they see that "it becomes possible, then, to conceive of a public space at the waterfront which could function for the boroughs much like Central Park works for the various neighborhoods of Manhattan."

Charles Reiss, an architect and real estate professional who now works with the Trump Organization, argued at a 1999 forum devoted to Reiser and Umemoto's proposal that even as speculation this project was on the wrong side of the river, noting that if any place in the city needs a radical reinvention, it is the Brooklyn and Queens waterfront on the East River.[36] Yet for Reiser and Umemoto, beyond their fascination with the FDR Drive as an organizing system to play off of in their design, Manhattan and its iconic skyline were integral to the project of getting this important vision for the future of the public realm published, exhibited, and discussed, engaging a broad audience in New York and other major waterfront cities around the world. In the end, their project presented a powerful alternative to the esplanade as the primary urban design for the waterfront, whether or not it belongs along the Manhattan shore. They provided a full document of how it could work with existing community goals. Their vision for a major mixed-use development, which among other qualities shows a hand and eye for beautiful urban form, would yield an exhilarating waterfront experience through robustly different means than Battery Park City or Queens West. It is probably not a vision that New York needs to see built—Manhattan really does not need to thicken its edges with such a complex infrastructure—but the project has compelled New York to see its waterfront anew, recognizing that a bold design can keep major infrastructure at the waterfront and still provide a compelling future for public life.

THE EAST RIVER: OPEN FOR CHANGE

With the start of the new century, the transformation of the East River from a barrier into an amenity is well under way, beginning with projects set in motion in the 1990s. On the Manhattan side, the EDC was able to take advantage of the federal government's transportation enhancement program to push through improvements to the East River walkway: in the 1996 master plan by Carr, Lynch, Hack, and Sandell, the walkway was reconfigured and renamed as the East River Bikeway and Esplanade. The EDC progressed since then to open the esplanade in the late 1990s, complete the Wall Street Pier Ferry Terminal in 2001, and in the same year open Stuyvesant Cove Park, from 18th to 23rd Street, designed by landscape architects Johanssen & Walcavage. The park is still waiting to build the environmental center, developed by the

18. EAST RIVER FERRY TERMINAL, RENDERING, MANHATTAN, 2002, KENNEDY & VIOLICH

nonprofit Community Environmental Center and designed by Kiss+Cathcart Architects as a living demonstration of sustainable design in the city.

In 2001, the EDC, together with the New York City Department of Transportation and the New York City Parks Department, also engaged the Boston-based architectural partnership of Sheila Kennedy and J. Frano Violich to develop an overall concept and specific Manhattan ferry terminals along the East River and up to the Harlem River, where landings have been proposed at the ends of major crosstown streets. Kennedy & Violich Architecture invented an easily modified module for the waiting shelters, using perforated metal and incorporating photovoltaic panels, while Ken Smith Landscape Architecture took on the landscape design. The firm laid out a theoretical base to the design—representing the relationship between the physical infrastructure of transportation and the virtual infrastructure of an economy that even after the dot.com bust is still driven by information technologies. It expressed this condition in the "morphable" form of the ferry landing shelter itself, as well as in the digital community news and weather signage integrated into the proposal (fig. 18).

Not yet approved, the design has nonetheless already been recognized by the 2002 P/A awards from *Architecture* magazine, for which jury member architect Ming Fung said, "It's back to Hector Guimard's Métro stations in Paris," and architect and fellow juror Greg Pasquerelli added, "It's leaning towards the idea of mass customization. One would expect the city to throw standard bus shelters onto the piers. This is what we're hoping the government is going to support instead."[37] As Pasquerelli articulated, this is an example of the public sector taking a risk on an architecture of ideas, where the work of architecture on the waterfront is as cultural as it is functional.

QUEENS WEST: NEW SIGNS OF LIFE

While Queens West is most likely to hold to its original master plan—if it did not, the long and expensive preparation of a new environmental impact statement would delay its progress—but parts of it were reinvented, both before and after September 11. Gantry Plaza State Park showed the potential impact of new design on the site, with its ability to address ecological, historical, and programmatic complexity through hard and soft edges on the water, four inventively programmed and designed public piers, and restored gantries from the early twentieth century. The state and city partners in Queens West demonstrated their openness to a new approach to design for the project by taking part in a conference that the Port Authority—which is part of the Queens West public authority—the British Council, and VAI organized in October 2001,

Creative Cities: Renewing New York, a Conference on the Future of Long Island City South—Queens Plaza to Queens West. The thrust of the conference, held at P.S. 1 Contemporary Art Center a few blocks inland from the waterfront, was that Queens West had shifted from being a district intent on setting itself apart from Long Island City to one that recognized the value of its adjacency to an emerging arts community, and one that the arts community and cultural institutions could imagine as an opportunity rather than a threat. Given the project's evolving sense of itself, what could be modulated or more radically altered? How could Queens West be more culturally complex and more connected to its surroundings than, for example, Newport in Jersey City?

The conference explored possibilities of cultural programming at the waterfront, landscape and arts strategies to connect the arts corridor starting at P.S. 1 to the waterfront, and the imperative of waterfront transportation. Changes were already afoot for Queens West. In the commercial section of the development to the south of Gantry Park (Stage IV, the Commercial Core), Kohn Pedersen Fox Associates (KPF) was preparing preliminary designs for environmentally resourceful massing and materials for a complex of buildings with more than two million square feet of office space, sponsored by the LCOR development group and inspired by the goal of reducing dependence on overseas oil after September 11 by harnessing solar and wind energy at the waterfront. For KPF cofounder William Pedersen, the goal is to create buildings

19. QUEENS WEST, RENDERING, LONG ISLAND CITY, QUEENS, 2001, ARQUI-
TECTONICA NEW YORK

that produce and not just consume energy, and the massing, place-ment of turbines, and slimming-down of the floorplate to allow more natural light are all ways this can be achieved at Queens West.[38]

Before fall 2001, Rockrose Development Corporation had begun to push for building design that was more esthetically ambitious than any Queens West had yet seen, realizing that this district, not just Manhattan, would have a population that expected to be part of a culturally engaged built environment. The company hired Arquitec-tonica New York as the architects for a two-thousand-unit complex of new residential buildings adjacent to the existing waterfront esplanade, north of Gantry Park (Stage II, Northern Residential). Arquitectonica is an inspired choice for a project that needs to establish an identity through design. The firm originated in Florida, where its eighteen-story Atlantis apartment building, completed in 1982, became a symbol of Miami's stature as a city of enough style and cash to garner a primetime television series. With its blue *brise-soleil* panels cut open to the yellow inside of a hole with a pool and a palm tree, Atlantis gave Arquitectonica a reputation for cre-ating modern icons. For Queens West, it offers a less perfectly pitched symbol, but one that may work for the waterfront and is a welcome relief from the drab residential towers that have gone up

elsewhere on the harbor. Arquitectonica nods to the New York apartment building script—base, shaft, top, regular fenestration—yet it does manage to supplement the bland patterns of fenestra-tion with jumps to the scale of the apartment unit, rather than the window or the room. On the top floors, there are huge, glazed "tic-tac-toe boards" that operate at the scale of the waterfront: at night they will read as nine-square grids of light at the tops and sides of the buildings (fig. 19).

These iconic tops, designed without resorting to New York's default Art Deco pattern book, have to compete with a historic icon at their base: the Pepsi-Cola sign that has long held court just above the river wall on what is now the Queens West site. PepsiCo, which has owned the twenty-one-acre site for decades, made clear that if the sign did not stay in roughly the location where it has been since 1936, there would be no sales deal. Is the waterfront a place for signs, for advertising? Are signs qualitatively different than build-ings as icons? After a protracted back-and-forth (hardly give-and-take) between sign companies and community groups, the Depart-ment of City Planning amended New York's zoning code in 2000 to limit illuminated waterfront signs in their size and character. Yet a historic one, part of the lives of East Side Manhattanites for almost seventy years, is being kept for at least seventy more.

CON ED SITE: COMPETITION AND CONTROL

20. CON EDISON REDEVELOPMENT SITE CONCEPT MODEL, RENDERING, MANHATTAN, 2001, SKIDMORE, OWINGS & MERRILL

Queens West is controlled by a consortium of public entities, joined into a New York State–chartered public authority, and has followed a procedure for creating a master plan and then engaging the developers and designers to complete it through a request for proposals. Across the river, on the Manhattan side, a 2001 project led by a private company undertook a much different process, with potentially much different results. New York, founded as a trade outpost, and, at its best, still a formidably commercial city, has begun again, as it did in the middle of the last century, to understand that commercial instincts and those more often associated with patronage can be coordinated, if not joined at the hip.

There may be no better way to examine this coordination—or at least an attempt at it— than through the filter of the Con Edison site,

covering nine acres from 35th to 41st Street just south of the United Nations, a waterfront parcel where the image stakes (and potential leasing price per square foot) are high and the political and regulatory complexity intense. The property, containing the century-old Waterside Steam Plant that the utility company will close and demolish, was purchased from Con Edison for $680 million in November 2000 by a partnership of the Fisher Brothers and Sheldon H. Solow, now constituted as FSM East River Associates. Envisioned as a showcase, largely residential complex totaling more than five million square feet, the developers decided that rather than an interview or request for proposal process, they would hold a "sketchbook competition," a plan clearly influenced by the Museum of Modern Art's selection process for its expansion a few years earlier. FSM asked the executive director of the Pritzker Prize, Bill Lacy, to help invite the teams and supervise the process. Five teams were invited to participate: Henry Cobb and James Ingo Freed of Pei Cobb Freed & Partners and Machado and Silvetti Associates; Christian de Portzamparc and Gary Edward Handel & Associates; Skidmore, Owings & Merrill (SOM), Richard Meier, Peter Eisenman, and Hugh Hardy; Kohn Pedersen Fox Associates, Rem Koolhaas, Davis Brody Bond, and Toyo Ito; and HOK Architects and Schuman Lichtenstein Claman Efron. The range of participants, from the most celebrated Pritzker Prize caliber architects to firms less known for distinctive design, surprised some, as did the shotgun marriages of firms that had never worked together. In the final reckoning, however, none of the curious new partnerships would do. The developer chose not one sketchbook but tore pages out of this one and that. FSM selected Henry S. Cobb from one team and Marilyn Jordan Taylor from another to lead the teams for Pei Cobb Freed and SOM, respectively; Machado and Silvetti, originally with Cobb's team, and the Olin Partnership, a Philadelphia-based landscape architecture firm, which was not involved in the sketchbook process, join in as consultants.

It is not possible to comment on the winning design because there was not one, but the entry by the SOM-led team is notable for its unexpectedly slender high-rises, some sheared at angles and one torqued into digital anguish (fig. **20**). The towers would be distinctive, although the simpler ones may be too much like the banal eighty-eight-story rectangle that Donald Trump recently finished just north of the United Nations, while the twisted one offers a sculptural alternative to the discipline of the UN's slab. Like the neighboring UN, the huge project on the Con Edison site has a ground plane reaching out over the East River Drive.

Competitions are one way to get beyond standard expectations and practice, yet the Con Edison experience is a reminder of how difficult it is for a developer to accept the parameters of a competition. Very few competitions are run according to the standard that the American Institute of Architects published in the *Handbook of Architectural Design Competitions* in 1989, whether in the private or the public sector, because very few clients—art museum, hotelier, or urban development corporation—are happy with a process in which one is supposed to pick one horse and ride it. The Con Edison site competition was no exception, and its process was so hybridized, so lacking in the public dimension of a traditional design competition—no exhibition, no forum—that a standard interviewing process, raising fewer expectations and dashing fewer hopes, would probably have been preferable.

21. NEWTOWN CREEK WATER POLLUTION CONTROL PLANT, RENDERING, GREENPOINT, BROOKLYN, OPENING 2010, THE POLSHEK PARTNERSHIP

NEWTOWN CREEK: LEARNING TO CELEBRATE INEVITABLE INFRASTRUCTURE

Back on the east side of the East River and up Newtown Creek, a waterway that runs between Queens and Brooklyn, is a major infrastructural project. Con Edison may no longer need as many steam plants, but the city's Department of Environmental Protection has to continue to build more and better water treatment plants, and, fortunately, it has decided that architectural design and art should be an integral part of its endeavor. Sewage plants rely on a waterfront location as much, if not more, than luxury apartments. They are vital to the city's survival and to the continuing improvement of its water quality. As with the North River Treatment Plant, topped by Riverbank State Park on the Harlem waterfront, there is no way to absolutely eliminate the downside (or the windward side) of living by a water treatment plant, but the combination of techniques for abating smells and transforming the form and character of a treatment plant is being exercised in cities across the country.

The Newtown Creek Water Pollution Control Plant scheduled for completion in 2010, for which the Polshek Partnership is the lead architect, is a gratifyingly serious piece of design for what could have been relegated to an engineering diagram (fig. 21). The Brooklyn plant embodies the Department of Environmental Protection's respect for design. To meet the requirements of the Clean Water Act, the existing twenty-five-acre sewage treatment plant in Greenpoint, Brooklyn, is being upgraded and expanded to become a fifty-three-acre complex. Polshek's design combines the glistening steel, industrial-sized cylinders with an urbane orthogonal architecture, reflecting the firm's philosophy that it is not only cultural institutions, like the celebrated glass box of the Rose Center they designed at the American Museum of Natural History in 2000, that deserve design attention (and budgets) but also the facilities for dirty work such as sewage, printing, and power.

The scheme also incorporates a 735-foot waterfront walkway at the confluence of Newtown and Whale Creeks, where a decade before no one had expected people might want to stroll. Designed by artist George Trakas with the support of the Department of Cultural Affairs' Percent for Art Program, the walkway brings visitors down to the water, into an unexpectedly natural environment. Trakas, who paddled around Newtown Creek during its dirtiest decades, has a special affinity for difficult waterfront sites. As parks advocate and planner Marcia Reiss puts it, "Building a park on Newtown Creek is an act of faith."[39] For the city, the Greenpoint community, and Trakas to believe that the area next to a water treatment plant is a site for a park requires devout attention to design's potential to help regenerate the ecology of the harbor and the attitudes of the communities that border it.

BROOKLYN: THE RECEDING OF THE INDUSTRIAL GLACIER, EASTERN TERMINAL AND BROOKLYN BRIDGE PARK

South of Greenpoint, Williamsburg's waterfront has been a site of contention since its role as a port ended in the 1960s. The neighborhood, an area that runs from the Navy Yard to Bushwick Inlet where Greenpoint begins, was the subject of a Waterfront 197-A Plan (the official planning process in which communities prepare a document and submit it for review by the Department of City Planning, which, in turn assesses and recommends it to the Land Use Committee of the City Council) prepared by Brooklyn's Community Board 1. The 1998 plan is titled *A Matter of Balance: Housing, Industry, Open Space*. Robert Perris and Jocelyne Chait were the planning professionals engaged for the project, working with the support of the Municipal Art Society Planning Center and the Pratt Institute Center for Community and Environmental

22. SKATEBOARDERS, EASTERN DISTRICT TERMINAL SITE, WILLIAMSBURG, BROOKLYN, 2001

Development (a nonprofit founded in the heyday of community architecture centers in the 1970s, and one of the few in the country that has continued to play a valuable role). Spurred on by a community effort beginning in 1989, the Community Board plan was originally a combined initiative with Greenpoint, but in 1997, the northern, demographically distinct Greenpoint struck out on its own to produce an independent plan for its stretch of the Brooklyn waterfront.

For Williamsburg, there were three major waterfront sites to consider: the crumbling remnants of the Brooklyn Eastern District Terminal, where railcars were loaded with cargo deposited by ship and then freighted over to the railways on the New Jersey side of the Hudson; the Schaefer Brewery site, a remnant of Brooklyn's years as a center for beer production; and the Con Edison generating station site. The recommendations that came out of the Williamsburg process included "nonnegotiable industrial sanctuaries," maintaining density and the scale of existing buildings in new construction, restrictions on adult entertainment and "superstores," and rezoning several districts for residential use. The Community Board envisioned the plan being able to shape a "vibrant mixed-use urban waterfront."

Vibrancy is in the eye of the beholder, and one of the dangers of community design processes is that they can deaden expectations and increase resistance to change. Even in its current state of partial decline, Williamsburg has an actively occupied waterfront, where for years everyone from a new breed of local artists to longtime residents used the Eastern District Terminal site as their rakish front yard, rough garden, free-form art park, drinking parlor, and skateboard playground (fig. 22). For years, the film and advertising industry has shot at the terminal, despite a loose interpretation of permit requirements, because of the unparalleled combination of a green, half-wild foreground and the Manhattan skyline beyond. These are activities that ultimately cannot be permitted in a state or city park, and the occupation of the waterfront for legal and semilegal creative endeavors in Brooklyn, as in many national and international sites, is a dilemma for cities trying to genuinely recognize the value of unplanned, informal activities.

The community planning process in Williamsburg clarified what people did not want: they did not want the private USA Waste company to build a major waste transfer station on the terminal site, which they saw as deadly for a neighborhood with only a half acre of waterfront park, and they succeeded in their opposition. Yet some were afraid of losing the special vibrancy of the outlaw waterfront if they were to follow the park and esplanade model familiar from Manhattan and under way in Queens. One way to support a lively neighborhood without bowing to traditional edge making was conceived by the Brooklyn Architects

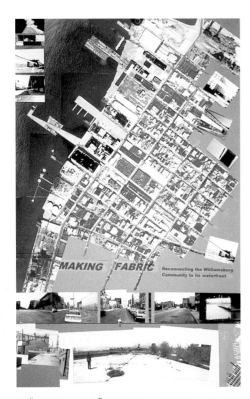

23. "MAKING FABRIC," RENDERING, EAST RIVER, VAN ALEN
INSTITUTE DESIGN COMPETITION: DESIGN IDEAS FOR NEW
YORK'S OTHER RIVER, 1998, BROOKLYN ARCHITECTS COL-
LECTIVE

Collective (BAC), which expressed its ideas for Williamsburg's renewal in "Making Fabric," a submission in VAI's East River competition, in which they strove to reflect the area's 197-A Plan (fig. 23). The main goal of the design was to reconnect the community to its waterfront through residential and light industrial development and by instigating small-scale public open space and waterfront access. Public space and streets would be extended to the waterfront. BAC opposed the concept of a waterfront promenade, suggesting instead a renaturalized edge. They were concerned not only about habitat preservation or renewal, but that an esplanade, even without a planned major development, would immediately increase the value of the properties—and the rents—next to the water, breaking up rather than enhancing Williamsburg's existing manufacturing- and arts-based community. Confronted by this proposal, City Planning Chairman Joseph Rose, who reviewed the competition entries in a session a few weeks after the jury, found the entry a destructive and untenable proposition. How can you reject improvement? he wondered. Yet for Ken Greenberg, an architect and urban designer who served on the East River jury and who fought to see this entry in the list of finalists, this was a

"real fight in the trenches to confront the formulaic and allow the real to evolve."[40]

At the terminal, a new formula that neither BAC nor Rose anticipated has emerged in a deal brokered by the Trust for Public Land (TPL), a national organization, to turn the northern portion of the site into a park and playing fields owned by New York State and managed by New York University. While not every community member was pleased with the outcome—the local/regional benefit dilemma is in bold relief here—it was a daring project for TPL, the university, and the state, given that the site, among other technical difficulties, is a brownfield that requires remediation. Martha Sutro, a Brooklyn writer long involved in the Williamsburg community, states that this public-private arrangement could be a "model for opening waterfronts from the Harlem River to the Hutchison River to the Bronx River."[41] It also shows that a brownfield waterfront site can be reclaimed, with private investment, albeit nonprofit, without requiring a huge return. There are more than three thousand waterfront brownfields in New York, and there has to be a middle ground between colossal commercial development (which will provide enough income to defray the expense of remediation), leaving them fallow, and making them all into public parks. The deal is original; perhaps the design by Sasaki Associates and URS Corporation will be as well.

Brooklyn Bridge Park has stimulated a very difficult debate on the appropriate reuse of industrial sites next to dense

24 HOTEL AND CINEMA, RENDERING, DUMBO, BROOKLYN, 1999, ARCHITECTURES JEAN NOUVEL

residential communities. Just south of the Brooklyn Bridge, after the thorough rout of a proposed multistory private development on Piers 1 through 5 in the 1980s, a publicly driven group is, once again, initiating a design process for the piers. In the DUMBO district between the Brooklyn and Manhattan bridges, David Walentas's twenty-year campaign, culminating in the late 1990s, to gain control of the Empire Stores, Civil War–era warehouses, has fallen through, perhaps for good, despite his success in garnering the zoning changes that allowed him to develop the loft buildings for residential units in the blocks surrounding the publicly owned, landmarked warehouses and waterfront green space officially known as the Empire Stores/Fulton Ferry State Park.

New York rarely entertains, much less builds, proposals for daring architecture, which makes it no surprise that another part of Walentas's vision, the eight-story, 350,000-square-foot hotel and movie theater by Jean Nouvel, north of the park, came to naught (fig. 24). Cantilevered out across the river just south of the Manhattan Bridge, Nouvel's design was dead on arrival for community activists. The French architect's bright stub of a bridge, which started but never finished its way across the water, was extraordinarily clever, featuring a cinema whose screen could fall away to reveal the live drama of New York. Yet it was politically and esthetically indolent in its indifference to the 1911 Manhattan Bridge to the north and its focus on the views it would allow of the Brooklyn Bridge and the Manhattan skyline to the south, creating breath-taking views for its occupants but interrupting the views around it. New icons need an element of aggression regarding existing landmarks, yet there is a necessary balance between old and new that Nouvel ignored.

Designs like Nouvel's are often wild cards in the planning process, images so compelling that they can make developers and community residents alike think about a site in a new way. They also assert that design is a visual art, not a management one, yet as evidenced by Nouvel's debacle, one will not work without the other. Architects and planners, in the throes of an all-American theory of management as unboundedly fungible, sometimes come to believe that a planning process can be as much a "design" as anything else and that this is a plausible and creative approach. As a whole the public meetings, the private meetings, the reviews, and the note taking can be embraced as a design challenge in and of itself. A significant leader in architecture, Thomas Fisher, dean of the College of Architecture and Landscape Architecture at the University of Minnesota, believes that for architecture, the "redesign of practice"—including new approaches to planning—is a necessary step toward keeping the discipline relevant and effective.[42]

An example of a "designed" planning process of great skill, and one that has set the ground for compelling urban design,

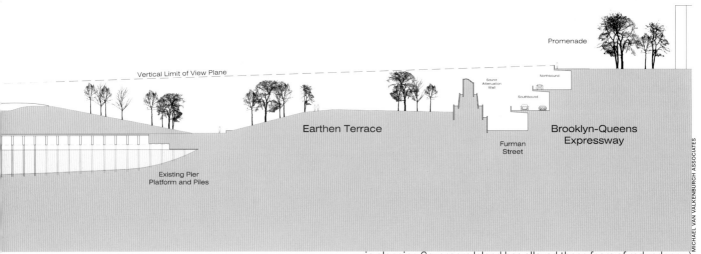

Promenade

Vertical Limit of View Plane

Earthen Terrace

Brooklyn-Queens
Expressway

Sound
Attenuation
Wall

Northbound

Southbound

Furman
Street

Existing Pier
Platform and Piles

MICHAEL VAN VALKENBURGH ASSOCIATES

25. BROOKLYN BRIDGE PARK, SECTION, BROOKLYN. PLANNING AND DESIGN TEAM: HR&A
ASSOCIATES, KEN GREENBERG, RAYMOND GINDROZ, AND MICHAEL VAN VALKENBURGH
ASSOCIATES, LANDSCAPE ARCHITECTS

landscape architecture, and architecture, is the Brooklyn Bridge Park process, stimulated in part, at least in its final phase, by the failure of the Two Trees Management proposal to go forward. The miracle of Brooklyn Bridge Park, like Hudson River Park on Manhattan's western edge, is that any progress was made at all, after the 1980s struggle with the Port Authority and with the generally heightened resistance to any change other than a passive park for the site, which includes not only the five piers below Brooklyn Heights but the land on up to the Empire Stores/Fulton Ferry State Park between the Brooklyn and Manhattan Bridges.

Alternative goals for the seventy-five-acre, 1.3-mile-long site were first set out by the Brooklyn Bridge Park Coalition, which was founded in 1989. The coalition developed a full proposal with landscape architect Terry Schnadelbach among others in the mid-1990s. It offered serious feasibility studies for a conference center with a public park that would pay for itself, an idea Schnadelbach had been seminal in developing. (Similar plans for Governors Island, which were discussed once the U.S. Coast Guard announced it was decommissioning its facilities on the island in 1996, led to concerns that there was not a market for two major self-supporting parks across a channel from one another, but the sluggish rate of progress in planning Governors Island has allayed those fears of redundancy.) Change had already begun in the area, just north of the piers, by the mid-1990s. The city's EDC had undertaken the $4 million Fulton Ferry Landing project (designed by landscape architect Signe Nielsen). Next to it, the unsinkable Bargemusic (a docked barge where concerts are performed, with the tide on bass) had begun its busy concert seasons. The area next to the Brooklyn Bridge Park site was changing, but the piers remained stagnant.

For nine years, the Brooklyn Bridge Park Coalition had been an extraordinary force in stopping plans it opposed (including the Two Trees Management project north of the Brooklyn Bridge) and creating its own proposals, but a public authority needed to step in if the project was to move forward. The Brooklyn Bridge Park Development Corporation was formed in 1998 by New York State, with a starting budget for planning of almost $2 million. HR&A, a consulting firm with planner John Alschuler in charge of the project, assembled a formidable team, including Ken Greenberg, landscape architect Michael Van Valkenburgh, and, as a consultant to the Brooklyn Bridge Park Coalition, which remained an intimate part of the process, architect Raymond Gindroz, cofounder of the Pittsburgh-based Urban Design Associates. HR&A, working with the Development Corporation, orchestrated more than sixty public participation meetings. In design, democracy takes time, money, and consultants.

Greenberg has a great gift for metaphor and referred to the

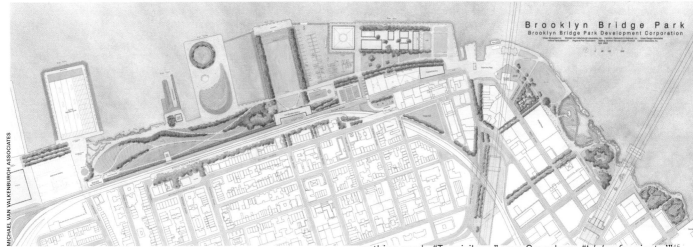

MICHAEL VAN VALKENBURGH ASSOCIATES

26. BROOKLYN BRIDGE PARK, PLAN, BROOKLYN. PLANNING AND DESIGN TEAM: HR&A
ASSOCIATES, KEN GREENBERG, RAYMOND GINDROZ, AND MICHAEL VAN VALKENBURGH
ASSOCIATES, LANDSCAPE ARCHITECTS

"receding of the industrial glacier" as a way to look at the piers as the team began design of the park in 1999.[43] Where did the planners and designers start? Greenberg says that he worked to find a "common language" for design and design potential and to "overcome skepticism," since people had been waiting for a viable plan to materialize for at least a decade. The team had to produce a visual, sited design but still intended it as a framework that would allow "creativity to be applied when people are actually selected to design parts of it."[44]

The team worked to establish a landscape typology. It started without a scheme, researching how the site had worked before the Brooklyn-Queens Expressway was built, and strove to "renew severed connections." In a sense, it was more backward-looking than Reiser+Umemoto's approach to the East River waterfront: the plan does not romanticize the value of the "thick," multilevel, infrastructural edge, although Greenberg insists that the team "did not want to make all of the twentieth-century infrastructure disappear" (fig. 25). If there was a bias, it was for the "great New York tradition of public parks with all kinds of people doing all kinds of things." The Brooklyn Bridge Park team wanted to provide a type of leisure that seems less and less familiar to New Yorkers, great tradition or not, of doing

nothing much. "To privilege," says Greenberg, "'dolce far niente.'"[45] He comments that this may not be the perfect way to design a park, and it is certainly a slow one, but to Greenberg it is far more effective than earlier approaches, and he does not see his role, much less Van Valkenburgh's, as that of a "recording secretary of community wants and dislikes." It works better, he notes, than the old scenario: get the job, do the design, present the proposal in a public hearing, then revise it (or, worst-case scenario, find the whole project abandoned in a firestorm of public protest). What distinguishes the design they arrived at? It is subtle in its barely visible architecture, forward in its landscape. In a deliberate opposition to the hyperprogrammed "destination" in front of the Empire Stores that Two Trees Management had dreamed of, the park offers a few grassy marshes and views of the preserved stores and the Manhattan Bridge. Van Valkenburgh proposes strategies of "natural," "boundless," "civic," and "urban" for the piers, including wetlands and coves.[46] Pier 1, just south of Bargemusic, is the only one crammed with activity: a hotel, cultural venues, and restaurants intended to generate income; Pier 2 is dedicated to general recreation; Pier 3 is topographically the most ambitious, with an earthen amphitheater and a fountain; Pier 4 is for fishing; and Pier 5 is for active sports and recreation (fig. 26).

Joshua Sirefman, a planner who played a key role for HR&A in the Brooklyn Bridge project and became chief operating officer of the city's EDC in 2002, notes that the goal for the park was not just a great plan or great design but a plan that would be a vehicle to convince the public sector to commit funds. From his perspective, the revenue-producing parts of the plan were essential to convincing the public sector to come forward, and, furthermore, are not necessary evils but rather parts of the program that will contribute to the well-being of the park as a "real place."[47] In 2000, the city committed $65 million, and in 2001 the Port Authority of New York and New Jersey and New York State committed an additional $85 million, an agreement reaffirmed in spring 2002.

OLYMPICS IN 2012: NOBLE DIAGRAM FOR THE TWENTY-FIRST CENTURY?

The plan to bring the Olympics to New York in 2012 is focused on the East River waterfront, because the water offers a crucial transportation route in the crowded city, and its undeveloped shore offers a development opportunity for sports venues and housing for athletes. The organization behind it, NYC2012, with a board of powerful New York players and the support of the mayor's office and the governor, is the microcosm of what could become a privately financed Olympics, on the model that Los Angeles followed in 1984, which resulted in a profit of $232.5 million.

NYC2012's research advised the avoidance of the Brooklyn Bridge Park's Piers 1 through 5 as a site for a sports venue—the site was simply the subject of too much contention—but the Olympics 2012 plan has provoked its share of dispute and enthusiasm

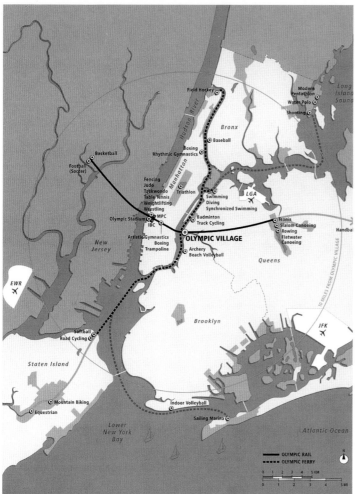

27. OLYMPIC X, 2001, NYC2012

anyway. It is, like any ambitious plan, highly vulnerable. Richard Kahan, who directed major New York waterfront projects including Battery Park City and Riverside South, and who is now dedicated to providing more playing fields throughout the city through private-public partnerships, stated at a public forum in 2001 that the proposal for the Olympics has "a million points of vulnerability" to lawsuits and specifically warned its organizers against counting on building a stadium on Manhattan's West Side, where the battle would be too hard and too long.[48]

Yet vulnerable or not, the Olympics represent a culmination of an intensifying aspect of New York's character. Artistic, money-mad, drug-taking New York has evolved an urban culture passionate about playing and watching sports, and the waterfront is already a paramount part of this transformation. When the waterfront esplanades broke ground, first in Battery Park City and slowly around the city, planners anticipated strolling families. The slow-moving families and lovers did come, but they were soon followed by torrents of bicyclists, in-line skaters, runners, and speed walkers, with more to come on vehicles not yet invented. Artist George Trakas used to be alone when he paddled around Newtown Creek; now there are kayak clubs. There are subway series and sold-out minor league games. Sports fit on the water. Personal sports like running and bicycling need less vehicular traffic and more distance

than the urban grid can provide. Field houses and stadiums, which need more space than the dense and tightly gridded city can spare, can make use of the large leftover spaces that waterfront industry abandoned long ago.

The six-hundred-page plan submitted by NYC2012 to the United States Olympic Committee in June 2001 relied heavily on the city's waterfront and waterways. (The next review is in late 2002, when the U.S. Committee reduces the list of potential sites to three or four American contenders, and the winner is chosen in 2005; many feel that after September 11, New York City's position is stronger, not weaker in this bid.) Alexander Garvin, director of planning for the NYC2012 effort through 2001, set out to give New York what the 1992 Olympics gave Barcelona, and what the Millennium projects gave London: an opportunity to stitch the city together, to reinvigorate its infrastructure, to renovate and build architecture including "dazzling" destinations, and to use the waterfront as the most important staging ground for the whole operation.

He has done so in a pragmatic, New York way, not razing neighborhoods and building hundreds of new structures as Barcelona did, and with the almost modest estimate—in an overall budget of $3.3 billion—of $1.182 billion for facilities, not including the cost of developing the area around the Javits Convention Center, where a new stadium is under consideration. This plan relies not just on a dollar figure, but a letter: after months of research and discussion in 2000 and 2001, Garvin and his collaborators arrived at the "Olympic X," a proposal in which moving athletes and spectators, the most critical part of the games' logistics, happens in the east-west stroke of subway trains between Brooklyn and Queens and Manhattan, and the north-south stroke of ferries running from the northern tip of Manhattan to St. George, Staten Island (fig. 27).

The "X" that Garvin and his partners arrived at is brilliant in it two-stroke clarity, and it is a legitimate heir to Burnham's alleged "noble logical diagram." New York's physical plan has lacked a noble diagram for too long, though the lesson from Robert Moses' highways is that, as with most noble diagrams, there are many ignoble decisions made. Even in the overcooked language of a press release, former Mayor Rudy Giuliani accurately captured the plan's visual energy when it was introduced just after Labor Day 2000: "It makes use of many of our city's greatest assets—its waterways, mass transit, wonderful parks, world-class facilities, and scenic vistas."[49] It is also politically astute in its incorporation of all five boroughs, from mountain biking and equestrian events on Staten Island to sailing off the Rockaways in Queens, water polo and shooting in the far Bronx (and, of course, baseball at Yankee Stadium), boxing in Harlem, and the triathlon in Central Park. And at the south end of Queens West (the point of Hunters Point, also known as Stage III, Southern Residential Area), the plan proposes an Olympic Village with 4,400 residential units.

The bid document explains why the plan is possible, given New York's crowded mass transit and roadways: For an Olympics you need to move 650,000 people a day, including the 15,000 athletes and coaches, and the at least 20,000 journalists (there were 21,000 at Sydney). For those who fear that these numbers would break the transit system, the document notes that in the summer, transit ridership falls off by 800,000 because the city's schools are closed. In short, there are 150,000 subway seats to spare. With the addition of intensified ferry service, with dedicated trains and boats for athletes, with a new stop for Metro-North and Amtrak, and with or without the proposed extension of the No. 7 subway line, which links Manhattan and Queens, Garvin believes the city can easily handle the transportation challenge.[50]

For the June 2001 report to the US Olympic Committee, the overwhelming goal of NYC2012 was to prove that the games could be played, either in new or adaptively reused facilities, according to the regulations that guide Olympic competition. Garvin hired a slew of talented architects to work up schemes including archery on the East River at the Eastern District Terminal site by Steven Harris & Associates, which uses its setting and the requirements of the sport to provide an intriguing sloping section (fig. 28), on what will most likely be NYU playing fields by then. Farther up the East River there is also a velodrome in Queens in the shadow of the Queensboro Bridge, by Deborah Berke Architects, and in deep Queens there is white-water kayaking and flat-water

canoeing in the middle of Flushing Meadows Park, a design by
Weiss/Manfredi Architects.

28. OLYMPIC ARCHERY FACILITY, NYC2012, RENDERING, EASTERN DISTRICT TERMINAL
SITE, WILLIAMSBURG, BROOKLYN, 2001, STEVEN HARRIS & ASSOCIATES

For an architectural audience, the projects commissioned by
Garvin were too fugitive to garner confidence in their outcome—it
was fine to explain that this was the steak (and some of it looked
like hamburger), and that the sizzle could wait, but many critics
could not wait and faulted the architecture for its lack of imagination, even when they admitted the skill and talent of the architects
in question.[51] The problem, Garvin explained, was not the caliber
of the design, but the phase of its development, because the time
for real design work begins late in 2002, after New York secures
its place in the next round.[52] Garvin knows the project, and knows
what his most important audience, the Olympic committees who
assess the bid, need to see, yet there may be reasons to sound the
alarm.

The siting of Olympic Village caused a great outcry. Annoyed at
not being consulted and concerned that the village would interfere
with Queens West's development plans, former Queens Borough
President Claire S. Shulman said "over my dead body" to its construction.[53] Perhaps more significantly in the long run, the repre-
sentation of the village does not send the message that the
Olympics—soaring expression of cultural, political, and physical
energy—should be able to communicate. Cooper, Robertson &
Partners have competently delivered a decorated massing diagram (which was all that they were asked to do) that would outline

Garvin's presiding design ethic, to give it the same character at
ground level as Brooklyn Heights.

He has a sound instinct: there is probably no more beautiful place
to live in New York than Brooklyn Heights, with its nineteenth-
century town houses and early twentieth-century apartment buildings and its century-old streets, trees, and gardens. A knee-jerk
reaction against the urban design and bones of the architecture
that chooses to emulate Brooklyn Heights is beside the point. The
issue is whether the Olympics, if they are to be harnessed as a tool
to rejuvenate the city's infrastructure and express an identity for
the next decades, can afford not to strive for ambitious architecture, even in trial designs before the final plan is set. The future of
public life may not look so different from its past—and public life in
Brooklyn Heights is pretty good—but it has so few built opportunities to present itself to the world as something more than the
asphalt and headphones that dominate the American public realm.
The controversy over the location of the Olympic Village (which is
perfectly sited in the crux of the x) may be melted away by the market and events: if Queens West finds the housing demand before
2005, its leadership is likely to accept the offer and put the Olympic
Village idea to rest. Yet the other, far more contentious part
of the plan—an Olympic Stadium that would also serve the

Jets football team and as an extension of the Javits Convention Center—may be the occasion for a much more inspiring architecture, one that engages the largest ideas of the future of urban life and the public realm. Talk of the stadium has provoked community and citywide opposition for years—if nothing else opponents dread the weekend traffic it would generate—yet it may be that design can offer a solution. Meaningful waterfront architecture works between the scales of the most local and the most regional, which is the ineluctable necessity of a great city's waterfront. It also works at multiple scales of ideas, as an icon and a destination, providing an experience no one expects, like a beautiful view where there was a brick wall. If the Olympics are going to fly in New York, they need projects as lucid and bold as the X itself. The city's greatest competitive edge is its cultural depth and sophistication, and the waterfront is the greatest stage to show that edge: the architecture of the Olympics needs to be visualized, proposed, apparent, rendered, built, and memorable.

NOTES

1. Barcelona Regional Agency, web site, www.bcnregional.com.

2. Alex Marshall, "Play Ball," *Metropolis,* Web site, www.metropolismag.com, August/September 2001.

3. Andy Newman, "A Rivalry across the Narrows," *New York Times*, 15 July 2001, B1.

4. Charles V. Bagli, "Campaigning for City Hall: Stadiums; Giuliani Races to Help Yankees and Mets; Others Want to Wait," *New York Times*, Web site, www.newyorktimes.com, 9 September 2001.

5. Peter Eisenman, interview by author, 16 July 2001.

6. Eisenman, interview.

7. Robert A. M. Stern, Thomas Mellins, and David Fishman, *New York 1960: Architecture and Urbanism Between the Second World War and the Bicentennial* (New York: The Monacelli Press, 1995), 860.

8. All quotations in this paragraph are from Eisenman, interview.

9. Marco Galofaro, "Notes on Staten Island," in Luca Galofaro, ed., *Digital Eisenman: An Office of the Electronic Age* (Basel: Birkhäuser, 1999), 78.

10. Eisenman, interview.

11. The Regional Plan Association of New York, New Jersey, and Connecticut, Plan for the Lower Hudson (1966).

12. Craig Whitaker, *Architecture and the American Dream* (New York: Clarkson N. Potter, 1996), 77.

13. The NewportCity.com web site, by its name, editorials, and reporting, is dedicated to changing the name of Jersey City's downtown waterfront, even beyond the boundaries of the Lefrak Organization's property, to Newport City, pointing to Battery Park City as an inspiration: see "Newport City is not a City," www.NewportCity.com, 2000. For opposition to overdevelopment, see "Newport Update: Will Skyscrapers be Built on 2 Piers?" www.NewportCity.com, November 2001.

14. Robert Hanley, "Jersey City's Mayor-Elect Seeks Wider Prosperity," *New York Times*, 7 June 2001, B4.

15. Marion Weiss and Michael A. Manfredi, *Site Specific: The Work of Weiss/Manfredi Architects* (New York: Princeton Architectural Press, 2000), 36.

16. Tom Topousis, "Commuters are Coming in Waves," *New York Post*, 15 April 2001, 16.

17. Arthur Imperatore, Jr., "Infrastructure and Urban Design: Stretching the Urban Design Envelope," in Daniel Patrick Moynihan, et al., *Fellows Program*, ed. Ann Ferebee (New York: Institute for Urban Design, transcript of the proceedings of 29 October 1998): 11.

18. Denny Lee, "They Don't Just Go to Staten Island Now," *New York Times*, 2 December 2001, City 4.

19. Michael Bloomberg, "State of the City" address, Web site, www.nyc.gov, 30 January 2002.

20. See Metropolitan Waterfront Alliance, "Harbor Loop Ferry," *Waterfront 21C* (Fall 2001); Andrew Jacobs, "A Ferry Loop Plan to Connect the Dots for New York Bay," *New York Times*, 10 February 2001, A1.

21. David P. Billington's publications on reinforced concrete include *Thin-Shell Concrete Structures* (1982; reprint, New York: McGraw-Hill, 1989) and *Robert Maillart and the Art of Reinforced Concrete* (Cambridge: MIT Press, 1990).

22. David Dunlap, "Going Downtown Downstream," *New York Times*, 10 December 2001, F1.

23. West Harlem Environmental Action, Inc. (WE ACT) and Community Board 9, Manhattan, Harlem on the River, draft planning document (November 8, 2000).

24. WE ACT and Community Board 9, Manhattan, Harlem on the River, postcard (1999).

25. The Affordable Housing Development Corp. served as a project development adviser; Bronx Community Paper Company project description, Jonathan Rose & Companies LLC, Web site, www.rose-network.com.

26. Maya Lin, "Living on Earth," interview by Jon Kalish, National Public Radio, 6 February 1998; transcript at www.explorecbd.org.

27. For a skeptical local opinion once the project collapsed, see *Inner City Press Bronx Reporter,* Web site, www.innercitypress.org, 27 March 2000 (January-March 2000), archive #1.

28. See Sharon Reier, *The Bridges of New York* (New York: Quadrant Press, 1977), 126–28. For background on the principles and themes of Randall's Island as a center for sports, see a report produced by the Center for Public Architecture (a program of the organization that became the Van Alen Institute in 1995),

Sports and the City, A Study for Randall's and Wards Island (1995), Andrea Woodner, Director; Deborah Berke, Senior Fellow; Ken Smith, Claire Weisz, design fellows.

29. Bloomberg, "State of the City" address.

30. For the change in the master plan in the Randall's Islands Sports Foundation Newsletter, compare material in *Island Views* 1 (Spring 1999) and *Island Views* 2 (Spring/Fall 2001).

31. "Manhattan Moment: Rethinking the East River," *Landscape Architecture* (September 1998): 20–21.

32. Design Ideas for New York's Other River, project statements submitted with competition entries to Van Alen Institute, 1998.

33. Publications of the "East River Corridor" project include "Riding on the Edge," *Daidalos* 72 (1999): 52–65, and "Reiser+Umemoto: East River Waterfront," *Architecture and Urbanism* 344 (May 1999).

34. Reiser+Umemoto, "East River Corridor: Manhattan Segment—An Interwoven System of Public and Private Infrastructure along the FDR Right-of-Way," project description, January 1999.

35. All quotations in this paragraph from Reiser+Umemoto, "East River Corridor."

36. Charles Reiss, Infrastructural Urbanism, forum at Van Alen Institute, speaker's comments, 9 February 1999.

37. "49th Annual P/A Awards," *Architecture* (January 2002): 83.

38. William Pedersen, "Queens West and Long Island City," *1=5: The Multi-Centered City*, Center for Architecture, American Institute of Architects New York Chapter, panelist's comments, 16 November 2001, author's notes.

39. Marcia Reiss, *Greenpoint Neighborhood History Guide* (Brooklyn: Brooklyn Historical Society, 2001), 38.

40. Ken Greenberg, "Design Ideas for New York's Other River," design competition jury comments, October, 1998.

41. Martha Sutro, "Taking Back the Waterfront," Trust for Public Land publications Web site, www.tpl.org, 22 April 2001.

42. Thomas R. Fisher, "The Redesign of Practice," *In the Scheme of Things: Alternative Thinking on the Practice of Architecture* (Minneapolis: University of Minneapolis Press, 2000), 91–102.

43. Ken Greenberg, interview by author, 16 February 2001.

44. All quotations in this paragraph from Greenberg, interview.

45. All quotations in this paragraph from Greenberg, interview.

46. Brooklyn Bridge Park Plan, Brooklyn Bridge Park Development Corporation, 2001

47. Joshua V. Sirefman, interview by author, 15 March 2001.

48. Richard Kahan, Sports in the City, presentation on the Olympics proposal organized by the Architectural League of New York and the Municipal Art Society, comments, 9 July 2001, author's notes.

49. Rudy Giuliani, "NYC2012 Announces Proposed Sites for Olympic Games," press release, 12 September 2000.

50. See *NYC2012: The Plan for a New York Olympic Games* (New York: NYC2012, 2001), as well as Alexander Garvin, interview by author, 6 March 2001.

51. Joseph Giovannini, "The X Men," *New York,* 15 January 2001, 52–53.

52. Garvin, interview.

53. Neil McFarquhar, "Plan to Put Olympics in New York Draws Fire," *New York Times*, 12 September 2000, B1.

EDGING TOWARD AN ECOLOGY

OF PUBLIC LIFE

I. GEORGE WASHINGTON BRIDGE, 1931, CONTEMPORARY LIGHTING, 2000

4

The Olympics proposal will never succeed unless it convinces New Yorkers that it is about more than redesigning a city for the transitory satisfactions of an international sporting event. Detractors of the games see them as little more than a distraction from the city's long-term needs, or more disingenuously, as little more than real estate speculation benefiting the few at the expense of the many. The sponsors of NYC2012 see the Olympics quite differently—as the driver for an urban transformation that will finally and fully unleash the city's awakened yet still somnolent identity as a dynamic waterfront metropolis. However New York fares in the national and international review of its suitability for the 2012 Games, it will only meet local expectations if its supporters can show that new projects (public parks and sports venues) and new infrastructure (land and waterborne transit) will be integrated into the life of the metropolis long after three hot weeks of summer in the city. In short, proponents of the Olympics have to prove their understanding of the ecology of public life—all those coexisting, interrelated systems of nature, infrastructure, and culture that together make urban experience possible.[1] The term "ecology," since it emerged in the mid-nineteenth century, has accumulated a complex set of meanings in both social and environmental science. While fraught with conflicting definitions, the word still has a powerful utility for defining the interconnectedness of the world: "the totality or pattern of relations between organisms and their environment."[2] The waterfront is the paradigmatic site for the term's complexity, as the place where a natural system, lapping up against what in cities is usually a hard, constructed edge, is busy with human organisms determined to make use of the water for work, leisure, or simple survival.

In its fullest definition, ecology encompasses so much that it is difficult to reconnect to its resonance for the design of cities. For too long, designers assumed that "ecological" design was a matter of mud bricks and soft edges, with the right angle banned and the history of Western architecture condemned and abandoned, whether by prelapsarians imagining an architecture before industry or by advocates of technologist efficiencies following in the footsteps of Buckminster Fuller. Assumptions that certain materials and forms were or were not "ecological" have receded, and there is an emerging practice of urban design, landscape design, and architecture that uses both the broadest definition of ecology and at the same time is able to focus on meeting high standards of environmental performance.

An important step in this regard is to reemphasize the value of infrastructure to cities. Infrastructure need not be hidden under a "natural" blanket but should be revealed, expressed, and even celebrated. Cities should romance their infrastructure; New York is beginning to learn how. It knows that its dense urban life—itself a model of ecological efficiency compared to most of the United States—demands intense infrastructural support, especially at the waterfront. The city's infrastructure offers an unrelenting lesson in the importance of how culture can support, or not, the necessary relationships between built and natural systems. Architects like UN Studio, F. O. Architects, and Stan Allen, and landscape architects like James Corner and Adriaan Geuze, integrate this approach into their work. Landscape architect and theorist Kathy Poole is among those who have articulated the importance of restoring infrastructure to the urban and architectural design imagination. She attests that an urban ecological approach must address natural and man-made systems in the same breath, "The city is never isolated from...natural biophysical resources," and she adds that "likewise, the city is also composed of essential built biophysical systems—

streets, sewers, water supply, waste disposal, and electricity—all of which provide the energy that enlivens and invigorates the city." She concludes by postulating that "by extending our contemporary understandings of infrastructure to include the city's natural ecology—and by reuniting the built and natural—we may find new and renewed understandings of the civic realm."[3]

New York has started this effort by looking back to its great era of infrastructure building, between the two world wars, and to its most overt constructions, its bridges. In particular, the new lighting of the George Washington Bridge, undertaken by the bistate Port Authority, which owns and operates the bridge, shows off the powerful steel structure of the 635-foot-high towers supporting the cables of the 3,500-foot-long span. The inaugural lighting on July 4, 2000, honored the first president and the coming millennium, but the Port Authority was also consciously celebrating the value of its work as more than merely functional. For New York City, it was a chance for the city to recognize not just the well-acknowledged value of its historic buildings, but also the whole system of services including transportation that have made it livable (fig. 1).

There is precedent for this. The bridge, designed by engineer Othmar Hermann Ammann, opened in 1931. Even before opening, it was heralded as an inspiring example of public investment.[4] Its form was celebrated, as when the steel towers, originally meant to be clad in stone according to the design of consulting architect Cass Gilbert, were praised in a "Bridge of Naked Steel," a *New York Times* editorial: "Ours is a utilitarian age, of course, and one afflicted at the moment with a disease called a Depression. But it is also an age with a powerful urge towards esthetic experiment."[5] Seven decades later, the original excitement of "esthetic experiment" was reborn when this colossal utilitarian structure was lit by eight hundred new fixtures in 2000. Turned on only a few times a year since then due to concerns about costs and conservation, the lighting of the George Washington Bridge is a formidable example of romancing the infrastructure. It is part of a desperately needed campaign to support infrastructure improvements, given the tens of billions of dollars of deferred maintenance and new construction that the city faces for bridges, tunnels, the water supply system, waste removal, and power. This is a campaign that the authorities and agencies that operate, plan, and construct infrastructure are eminently capable of undertaking, with enough political support, and one in which they are probably ahead, rather than behind, the city's cultural establishment. The Port Authority's director of tunnels, bridges, and terminals, Ken Philmus, who helped to lead the way to lighting the bridge, put it this way: "Sometimes, beauty is as important as function."[6]

Infrastructure, by its definition, connects to municipal and regional needs that go beyond individual programs and individual buildings or places. A bridge from the 1930s, however remote it may seem from twenty-first-century esthetics or ecological thinking, is nonetheless undeniably part of the analysis of "flow" that has per-meated the talk and action of design schools and practices in recent years, in which there is a perpetual struggle to incorporate the purposefulness and inevitability of infrastructure into the form and character of new buildings and sites. The wonderfully titled collection of visual and written essays, *Breathing Cities: The Architecture of Movement* (2000), opens with an essay that critiques a detailed computer model of a city as missing the whole stuff of life. Like most architecture designed to developers' specifications, the volume's editor, Nick Barley, argues, this sort of computer model fails to address the things that really matter: "the ceaseless flow of people"; the movement in and out of what those people consume and waste; the plants and animals that persist in the most urbanized environments; and the racing pace of "information" and "ideology."[7]

Amanda Sachs, a recent architecture school graduate who won the 2000 "Ecology of Public Life" Van Alen Dinkeloo Fellowship, brought the same ideas to bear on a single site, focused on a single piazza in Rome, where she would "chart the cycle of human use; the flows of water, both waste and supply...the locations of social interaction...the flow of product."[8] The dilemma for today's designers imbued in and producing this analytic approach is whether they must, after the "charting" is done, design infrastructure or structure to accommodate the "flow," as a bridge is designed to handle traffic, or whether they are able to produced designs that are some-how part of "flow" itself—designs that through their materials

2. PROTESTERS AT BROOKLYN BRIDGE,
BROOKLYN, 1998

and form change over time. Landscape architects have to see their designs as unfixed; growth, weather, and wear will transform their work no matter what they plan. Yet for architects, engineers, and urban designers, it is almost impossible not to fix the design at some point (as the engineer said about F. O. Architects' pier in Yokohama, at some point the "fish" had to stop moving). The struggle, however, to design buildings and places that try to work with the dimension of time is a productive one: it can be as preelectronic as reviewing how and when a copper roof turns green, or how a loft building can be reconfigured when a new tenant moves in, or how to phase in additional capacity for a water treatment plant; or it can be as information-era-inspired as an utterly "smart" building that transforms its surface and form in response to changing diurnal, seasonal, or even yearly demands for the flow of life it contains.

Could there be a design that could respond to community protest after it was completed, if not before? It is part of the give-and-take of the city, as much as moving goods and waste, and one with which most architects and landscape architects who work on the waterfront are very familiar. For planners and designers striving for unfixedness in their designs, trying to understand how their designs might perform over time, and trying to understand the ecology of how they can come to be, community protest has to be understood as part of the waterfront ecology as much as salt marshes and in-line skaters. An overview of the communities and property holders along the waterfront can help to explain why: a century of industrialization followed by a half century of decay coupled with expectations of great public benefit and profit does not build a gentle ecosystem. Architect and author Keller Easterling, looking over a diagram of East River waterfront site ownership prepared for a VAI workshop in 1998, commented that it looked like "a map of conflict."[9] Her prescience was revealed a year later when Brooklynites, prior to the Brooklyn Bridge Park agreement of 2000, rallied against what they considered a sellout of public property to a private developer, at the Empire Stores/Fulton Ferry State Park beside the Brooklyn Bridge (fig. 2). Protest is a part of the political process of urban development that, together with cultural systems like education, arts, entertainment, or even sports and the natural and built systems of the city, can add up to the diversity, balance, and potential for the evolution of a thriving ecosystem.

FLOW IN PLACE: THE WEST SIDE STADIUM

However evolutionary, even incorporating conflict, design has to come to resolution at some point. One of the two key proposals of the Olympics, the stadium on the West Side (the Olympic Village is the other), has moved from vague and general planning principles to a very definite design, one that will either deflect or generate an even greater volume of conflict. It is a design that is adamantly about its relationship to the ecology of the city, not only in the sense of flows of people and activity, but in terms of harnessing the energy of the sun and the wind. The members of Manhattan's Community Board 4, who have protested loud and long against the idea of a stadium of any kind in their west Midtown neighborhood, are unlikely to shift gears due to the apparent ecological sensibilities of the stadium proposal, having stated that

they are "unalterably opposed to the construction of a stadium over the West Side Rail Yards."[10]

In the NYC2012 proposal, released in June 2001, the design brief for the stadium was largely technical—85,000 seats and the transportation infrastructure to fill them—and political, incorporating the perceived urban planning needs of the city. Working together with the New York Jets, the professional football team that also wants a new stadium (with 75,000 seats), Cooper, Robertson & Partners prepared a scheme that fit into NYC2012's much larger vision for the city than what might come to pass on its assigned site at the end of the east-west bar of the "Olympic X," between 11th and 12th avenues and 30th and 34th streets. In the larger plan, New York's No. 7 subway line would run west and south from Times Square to reach the stadium. A new Metro-North commuter rail line would come in from the north, and the Long Island Railroad, too, would reach a platform on Manhattan's far West Side. The stadium would be connected to the waterfront by bridges over Route 9A at its southern and northern edges and from there on toward the ferry service a few blocks north. As urban design, it would feature a huge Olympic Square and a boulevard running north toward 42nd Street that would be a spine for new commercial development (which would, directly and indirectly, help to subsidize the momentous infrastructure improvements that would service it). The new development, in concept and in the renderings of the proposal, also allayed another concern that had been brought up during the years of stadium proposals for the site—that it would be hugely out of scale. Bordered by tall office buildings, and at the edge of the river, the Cooper, Robertson & Partners design fit in its context, albeit one of its own invention.[11]

The Olympics plan did not exist in a void. There had been decades of proposals for rebuilding over the West Side Rail Yards, always defeated by the hundreds of millions of dollars that decking over the site would cost, if not by more general fluctuations in the real estate climate. In 1999, the IFCCA ideas competition, the one for which UN Studio generated the "flow" diagram, had pushed the site into the realm of urban art, or at least the discourse on urban art. But the 2012 proposal was different, in part because, in addition to NYC2012, it comes with a vocal, well-heeled partner, the New York Jets football team. The Jets have never dropped "New York" from their name and have long bridled at playing in New Jersey (where since 1984 they have played home games in the New Jersey Meadowlands Sports Complex on another football team's field, Giants Stadium). Their lease runs out in 2008, and the Jets are ready to reconnect to their identity as a New York team. The other partner in the Olympic proposal, which has been more diffident, is the Javits Convention Center, which has focused on expansion to the north. Yet the Convention Center, too, is as pressed as the Jets for improving its facility, and the possibility of using the stadium to support events—in addition to still going ahead with expanding north—is in discussion. The convention center does need more

space: at 814,000 square feet, it is a bonsai compared with many big-city convention halls like Chicago's two-million-square-foot-plus McCormick Place.

By December 2001, NYC2012 and the Jets were acknowledged in the New York City Department of City Planning's Far West Midtown: Framework for Development, which called for thirty to forty million square feet of new development, as well as the extension of the No. 7 line—a position that Mayor Bloomberg has strongly supported in 2002.[12] To those who scoff at the scale and ambition of building an Olympic stadium and a new district over a railroad cut, Alexander Garvin counters that at the turn of the last century New York built what was, diagrammatically, exactly the same thing, Grand Central Terminal plus Park Avenue above its covered tracks. Today, he notes, there are few complaints about its impact on that neighborhood.[13] (From 2002 forward, Garvin faces an even greater challenge, having become vice president of planning, design, and development for the Lower Manhattan Development Corporation charged with planning at the World Trade Center site and its environs.)

Yet for all its official recognition, the stadium is far from a shoe-in. The Jets and NYC2012 know that they face firm opposition from the local community board and that their proposal is also at odds with the Vision for the West Side Rail Yards developed in 2000–2001 by the Manhattan borough president, Virginia Fields, with planners Buckhurst Fish & Jacquemart. The borough president's

3. JETS STADIUM PROPOSAL, RENDERING, WEST SIDE MAN-
HATTAN, 2002, KOHN PEDERSEN FOX ASSOCIATES

plan called for a fine-grained urbanism, with a high proportion of residential properties, including affordable ones, in the mix, and no stadium. (Fields's plan, like the Department of City Planning's Framework plan, is only advisory at this stage; there are years of hearings and review before the zoning law changes that either plan depends on could be put in place.) The Jets knew that to build their stadium, they would have to push very hard in the arena of public opinion, and they decided to pump up the architectural vision of the type of building their stadium would be—demanding an icon with high performance, political, cultural, and ecological.

In the original plan, the stadium had a north-south orientation that yielded little opportunity to open up to waterfront views or connections. In 2001, they brought in a major New York architecture firm best known for institutional and commercial buildings, Kohn Pedersen Fox (KPF), to try a new approach to the design that Cooper, Robertson & Partners had begun. In its design, which first tested public reaction at an architecture and urban design conference in late 2001, the firm was able to give the stadium a more compelling connection to its site (fig. 3). It is connected to the waterfront site in a surprising way: it ties into a 1.5-mile-long elevated freight railway, the 1934 High Line, which despite two decades of inactivity and the loss of its southern section and much of its purpose by

1960, has survived the postindustrial transformation of Manhattan. (The elevated highway on the waterfront came down, but the railway, one to two blocks back, held up.) The line's remaining section travels from Gansevoort Street just south of 14th Street up to 30th Street, where it turns west toward the waterfront and then heads back north along the stadium site. In the proposed design, the east-west 30th Street section of the High Line would be rebuilt and expanded, connecting to the new Penn Station between 8th and 9th Avenue to the east and, in a rebuilt form, moving around the perimeter of the stadium and flowing into the two bridges across to Hudson River Park.

While it is ironic that the stadium project has to knock down some of the High Line in order to give it a purpose, among the ideas for the reuse of this industrial-era relic, the idea of crowds traveling along the High Line on game day has an energy and purpose hard to find in most of the other proposals.[14] The project has the potential to be the same kind of urban fixture as the waterfront promenade from the transit hub at Harry Bridges Plaza in San Francisco, part of an urban ritual of getting from transit to the game, with an engaging view of the waterfront. Moving this many people is an operation at the scale and intensity of infrastructure, for which the High Line was built.

Yet it is not in its direct connection to its site but in its larger, ecological connection to the city and beyond that the KPF stadium design is most impressive, rendered in an exhilaratingly

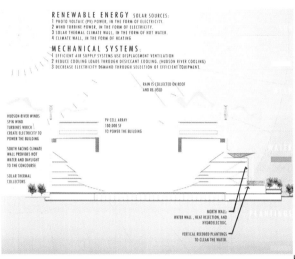

RENEWABLE ENERGY SOLAR SOURCES:
1 PHOTO VOLTAIC (PV) POWER, IN THE FORM OF ELECTRICITY.
2 WIND TURBINE POWER, IN THE FORM OF ELECTRICITY.
3 SOLAR THERMAL CLIMATE WALL, IN THE FORM OF HOT WATER.
4 CLIMATE WALL, IN THE FORM OF HEATING

MECHANICAL SYSTEMS:
1 EFFICIENT AIR SUPPLY SYSTEMS USE DISPLACEMENT VENTILATION.
2 REDUCE COOLING LOADS THROUGH DESICCANT COOLING. (HUDSON RIVER COOLING)
3 DECREASE ELECTRICITY DEMAND THROUGH SELECTION OF EFFICIENT EQUIPMENT.

4. JETS STADIUM PROPOSAL, ENVIRONMENTAL PLAN SECTION, WEST SIDE MANHATTAN, 2002, KOHN PEDERSEN FOX ASSOCIATES

new architecture for an American stadium. KPF designed a building with the thesis of stadium as energy-producing "power plant," turning on its head the notion of a huge sports facility as drain on the city's finances and infrastructure (fig. 4). Above the roof, there are double ranges of wind turbines (where the Baroque era would have put a row of statues), catching the energy of the winds off the Hudson. The south wall is a screen of solar thermal collectors that also allow natural light into the concourse. On the north side of the stadium, a "water wall" helps cast off heat gain and uses the runoff from the roof as a potential source of at least a modest amount of hydroelectric energy as it drops to the "woodland wedge" below.

The wedge is designed by Julie Bargmann, the landscape architect and University of Virginia professor whose D.I.R.T. studio has gained worldwide attention for designs to reclaim rural mining sites. Here, in the largest city in the United States, Bargmann has brought the same acumen for designing "natural" environments that do ecological work, like the "marsh" that will help filter water from the roof and services of the building. In sum, these elements are a "power plant," as KPF principal William Pedersen calls it, that adds, rather than detracts, from the city's energy needs. (The calculation of the building's energy-production-to-use ratio is based on the energy-use needs of the stadium's primary function, foot-ball, not the multiple other uses it might have, which would add up to greater energy use than that generated by the building, but it is still a significant advance in both literal and symbolic energy use for a major urban building.)

The design's impact, of course, also has to be measured for the performance of its primary function as a sports venue, not a power plant. It is full of inventive strategies in that regard: it is a huge machine masquerading as a building, engineered to expand out to the Hudson, perhaps only on a one-time basis, to accommodate the ten thousand extra seats needed for the Olympics and to contract down to arena size for basketball (if it manages to become the new Madison Square Garden as its planners hope). The roof opens and closes for different events, if it is needed in the end (neither the Olympics nor professional football needs a roof, but many other proposed uses do). If the city is to build a stadium for the Olympics, this is the level of architecture at which it would need to be: an iconic presence, a use of the waterfront site for access and experience, and a serious idea about the role of design in connecting the city to the world. Planner Ron Shiffman, long-time head of the Brooklyn-based Pratt Institute Center for Community and Environmental Development and a leading advocate of a "gray-to-green" transformation of New York's industrial waterfront sites, finds the KPF proposal a great step forward for New York architecture yet in the wrong place, not only due to the traffic it would generate but also because of the greater need for investment outside of Manhattan. In the end, the success of the project—be it for the Olympic Games or football or both—will depend on whether the Jets and their architects can convince the city that the West Side waterfront is the right place, because, after decades of waiting for an inspiring example of this building type, it is the right stadium.

SEATTLE WATERFRONT: URBAN ART AND ENVIRONMENTAL SCIENCE IN THE OLYMPIC SCULPTURE PARK

The Jets stadium proposal strives mightily to fit a huge, 320-foot-high building into an "environment" by building up a woodland wedge, bridging across to the waterfront, and treating the walls of the stadium almost as though they were natural features to be exploited to generate energy. It is a stadium that one might have expected, in, say, Seattle, where there is an intense civic culture of environmentalism, an ever burgeoning interest in design, and a spectacular waterfront. Seattle's old football stadium, the Kingdome, was so unloved that it was ceremoniously imploded in March 2000—a lesson in the limited value of building no-frills concrete boxes in the middle of cities, one that advocates of building a low-cost stadium in New York should review. The handsome new stadium, the Washington State Football/Soccer Stadium,

5. OLYMPIC SCULPTURE PARK, CONCEPT, RENDERING, SEAT-
TLE ART MUSEUM, SEATTLE, WASHINGTON, 2001, WEISS/
MANFREDI ARCHITECTS

scheduled to open in 2002 following a design by Ellerbe Becket, is focused not only on meeting the spectators' needs but also on being responsive to the city in its siting and form, without the "power plant" drive of KPF's West Side proposal. While it boasts views of Puget Sound from its upper concourses, it is a block back from the water and has had to contend with the 1953 double-decker, 2.2-mile-long Alaskan Way Viaduct between the city and water.

Seattle may find itself, like San Francisco after its 1989 earthquake, opening up to its harbor in a new way, because the February 28, 2001, Nisqually earthquake has unsettled the viaduct enough that it has been deemed unsafe.[15] The decision whether to rebuild it as it is, build a tunnel, or try to accommodate the traffic (which includes trucking) at street level is pending. Nonetheless, Seattle has to contemplate whether it can have the same long-awaited opening up of its waterfront as its California counterpart, which would not only allow Seahawks fans more of a waterfront connection but unleash a generation of new waterfront projects.

It may also impact another project, a few blocks above of the northern end of the viaduct, on a formerly industrial site that overlooks Elliott Bay and the Olympic Mountains. This eight-acre brownfield site, cut north-south by the major arterial of Elliot Avenue and, at the water, by the Burlington Northern Railroad tracks, is also in the path of one of the alternatives for rerouting the viaduct. Yet the Seattle Art Museum, which is planning the Olympic Sculpture Park here, never imagined it had a pristine site on its hands. The name, itself a testament to the self-effacing ways of Seattle's philanthropic community, at first seemed to verge on what *San Francisco Chronicle* urban design writer John King has warned about on his own city's waterfront, where planning "can be so defensive that the built environment offers nothing to rival the magnetism of the natural one."[16] Yet the art museum, which is highly sensitive to the need to balance agendas for art, architecture, and landscape design with Seattle's highly developed civic environmentalism and community-process culture, has no intention of building a plain vanilla park with a few sculptures in it.

After an invited competition for design approaches, in which it reached out to a boldly assembled short list of architects and landscape architects from around the world, the museum hired Weiss/Manfredi Architects in spring 2001 to develop a scheme that, while recognizing the significance of both the view and the sculpture, is also clearly a work of design art itself. Marion Weiss and Michael Manfredi, designers of the as-yet-unrealized proposal for Veterans Park in Jersey City on New York's harbor, will put their design philosophy to the test. They have written: "We reject the standard paradigms: neither the ideal of the untouched

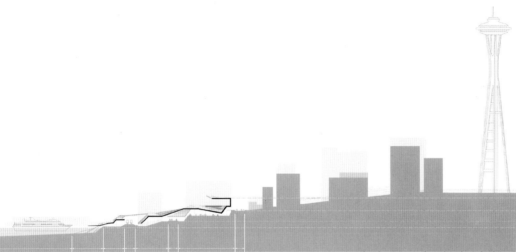

6. OLYMPIC SCULPTURE PARK, CONCEPT DESIGN, SECTION, SEATTLE ART MUSEUM, SEATTLE, WASHINGTON, 2001, WEISS/MANFREDI ARCHITECTS

site, awaiting the architect's free-standing monolith, nor its opposite, the privileged 'natural' or 'historical' site, to which any architectural intervention must defer, are legitimate for contemporary work. Instead, it is necessary to work from a definition of landscape that incorporates infrastructure (rail lines, highway off-ramps, utility lines), history (geologic, political, cultural), and natural systems (water, vegetation, toxicity)."[17]

They have all that and more in Seattle. The top of the site, at Western Avenue, is forty feet above grade at the waterfront two blocks below (fig. 5). The program requires a pavilion here, parking below, and then a route down to the waterfront, over Elliot Avenue and the railroad tracks. Weiss and Manfredi's key gesture was the path: starting from the roof of the pavilion, they designed a concrete path that works its way in a large zigzag to the north, then back across both the road and railway, then to the north into the existing Myrtle Edwards waterfront park. The proposal has evolved to incorporate "three ecologies": the "old" northwest conifer forest at the top, the largely deciduous "city" garden in the middle, and at the base, the "Sound" waterfront of shore pine and reed grass. This trifecta of ecosystems does not, however, overwhelm any sense of the design—in the midst of all this green, the thin concrete membrane of path and bridge is a visible part of the design.

At the upper levels, the site's relationship to the waterfront is largely visual, yet as it reaches the waterfront, the design intertwines more intensely with the infrastructure along the waterfront. First, its bridge across the tracks forms a canopy for the existing waterfront trolley, largely for tourists, which may in time be replaced by a light rail system. Most intriguingly, where the sculpture park meets the bay, the designers are striving to meet not the needs of urban transport or public recreation or art but of salmon. The Weiss/Manfredi–led team includes experts in habitat restoration, which is vital here, because Washington State is required by the federal Endangered Species Act to restore salmon habitat, after decades of fish runs depleted by industry, including seawalls at the edges of Puget Sound as well as locks and dams on streams and rivers. The seawall is in bad shape already, and may have to be rebuilt, but it will not be rebuilt to the same hard geometries as before. The team is exploring how to make a softer edge, with stepped layers and breakwater below the tide line that will engender, without resorting to naturalistic imagery, an attractive habitat for salmon (fig. 6).

It seems ludicrously Pacific Northwestern—only in Seattle would the public agencies, private firms, and community groups engaged in the built environment be so focused on how to restore salmon habitat, even with the motivation of federal law. Yet when New Yorkers recall that two decades ago Westway was stopped by court order to protect the breeding grounds of the striped bass, they may realize that Seattle is on to something. Westway was brought to a grinding halt by the bass: there was no way to design their way out of the court order. In Seattle, by contrast, the salmon has called forth the most sophisticated design intelligence—one in the service of a cultural enterprise, no less—to design the interface between land and water ecosystems.

FRESH KILLS: NEW YORK LIFESTYLE AND LANDSCAPE

Perhaps New York is ready, without sacrificing its cultural or industrial requirements, to apply the same design energy to its waterfront, recognizing that environmental concerns are not concerns alien to the gritty metropolis but part of it. New Yorkers have come to demand the kind of outdoor, waterfront recreation that used to be relegated to ecotopias like the Pacific Northwest, and the reality is that not only is Seattle becoming more like New York, but as any Hudson River kayaker knows, New York is becoming more like Seattle.

There are signs that New York is ready to look at itself in this new way, not only at the scale of the single building—even a huge one like the proposed Jets stadium—but also at the scale of the district, or even the borough. As in Seattle, this is not a call

7. FRESH KILLS LANDFILL, STATEN ISLAND, 1990S

for a back-to-nature movement, but rather one that recognizes how subtle and productive the design of relationships between human culture and natural environments can be. At what is perhaps New York's most "engineered" landscape, the 2,200-acre Fresh Kills Landfill, city agencies led by the Department of City Planning, with the Municipal Art Society, launched an international design competition in 2001 calling for ways to reuse the landfill after its 2001 closing (fig. 7).

History happened; just days after the finalist teams visited the landfill the twin towers came down, yet the Fresh Kills competition went forward, altered. The competition, called Landfill to Landscape, assumed that the last garbage scow to unload at the site on March 22, 2001, was indeed the last one, the last delivery of refuse, the last addition to the mounds that reach 225 feet. Set along the Arthur Kill between Staten Island and New Jersey, the landfill, even after fifty years of use, still has intact wetlands, and the Fresh Kills Estuary is hardly dead, holding its designation as a New York State Significant Coastal Fish and Wildlife Habitat. Yet it is hardly ready for a return to nature. After September 11, the southwestern portion of the site had to be reopened to handle World Trade Center debris, which arrived by barge, brought down from piers off Lower Manhattan.

The landfill's reopening brought up many questions about the rationale for its decommission. There is a long-running argument about whether it should have been closed, many contending that it had at least twenty good years left, that the alternatives bring more garbage through other boroughs, and that paying for shipping millions of tons of garbage around the country for the next century is an enormously expensive and possibly unsustainable operation.[18] This is a very serious issue for the city, yet the "equity" position of Staten Island regarding the landfill has been unshakable—after taking the four other boroughs' garbage for half a century, since 1948, Staten Island wants a new identity, so Fresh Kills' reopening is temporary: it will close by the end of 2002.

The Landfill to Landscape competition proceeded, its mission unchanged by the attack, although many submissions included or acknowledged a site for a memorial to those killed at the World Trade Center. The final teams' proposals were reviewed, presented to the public, and juried in December 2001, and three finalists were chosen to be interviewed for the master plan contract: the team led by Philadelphia and New York–based Field Operations; the team led by RIOS Associates of Los Angeles; and the London-based JPMP Landscape and John McAslan & Partners.

For city agencies, from planning to sanitation, cultural affairs, and parks and recreation, to undertake such a competition was extraordinarily bold, because it risked taking Fresh Kills out of the realm of purely technical and political solutions and into that of ideas and design, trying to wrest not only new uses but

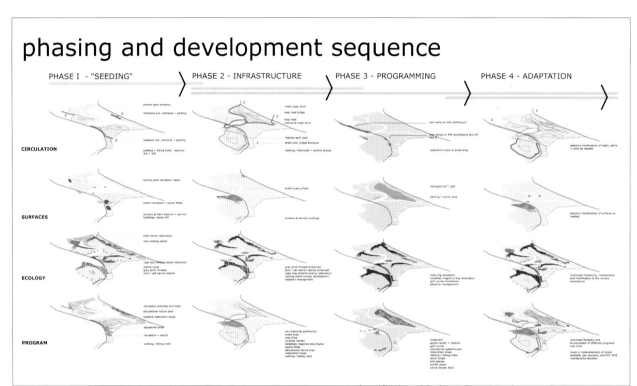

phasing and development sequence

PHASE I - "SEEDING"   PHASE 2 - INFRASTRUCTURE   PHASE 3 - PROGRAMMING   PHASE 4 - ADAPTATION

CIRCULATION

SURFACES

ECOLOGY

PROGRAM

8. FRESH KILLS LANDFILL TO LANDSCAPE DESIGN COMPETITION, PHASING AND DEVEL-
OPMENT SEQUENCE COMPETITION ENTRY, FRESH KILLS LANDFILL, STATEN ISLAND, 2001,
FIELD OPERATIONS

new meaning from the site. There were ongoing projects to renat-uralize the site, like that of Rutgers University professor of ecology Steve Handel, who has been steadily planting trees in thin layers of soil atop the hermetically sealed mounds since 1993, but the competition called for design of a different order of magnitude.[19] The participating agencies envision Fresh Kills as so important a site that, together with the revived waterfront of St. George, its rebirth may transform the entire notion of the borough. In 1999, *New York Times* reporter Jim O'Grady rhetorically asked, "Will Staten Island finally shed its image as New York's dumping ground and become, in the parlance of planners, a destination?"[20]

According to Field Operations, the first-ranked finalist who submitted Fresh Kills Reserve—Lifescape: A Reconstituted Matrix of Diverse Life-Forms and Evolving Ecologies, the answer to O'Grady's query is a definitive yes, the island will become a destination. "Staten Island will now be recast as an expansive network of greenways, recreational open spaces, and restored habitat reserves—a new nature-lifestyle island, both destination and envy of the surrounding urbanites."[21] The words are more than flattery for the local population; they express a real understanding of the deep well of resources Staten Island has: 40 percent of its land is open space now that the

landfill is added to the equation, and that percentage includes land along the Arthur Kill where Fresh Kills is located, some of the most important sites in the world for bird migration, as well as beaches, woods, and marshlands, bustling with animal and human activity.

James Corner and his partner Stan Allen, together with a sagely assembled team ranging from media to environmental experts, were adamant in expressing the philosophy of their approach; they were taking the opportunity to develop "a new form of public-ecological landscape, an alternative paradigm of human creativity, biologically informed, guided more by time and process than by space and form." Architect and writer Laurie Kerr, who focuses her research on ecologically oriented design, summed up the project by noting that "[r]egionally, it recasts Staten Island as the emerald jewel of the metropolis—showing how an ecologically reconstituted Fresh Kills could become the heart of an existing, though currently fragmented, system of parks and greenways on the island."[22] Or as *Time Out New York*'s Kevin Pratt put it: "The assertion that Staten Island's declining industrial base presents an opportunity to create a kind of twenty-first-century garden city is right on the mark."[23]

The team led by Corner and Allen did not change the basic engineering of the toxic mounds—the seals designed to prevent rainwater from working its way through the fill and coming out as toxic leachate and the methods for venting and harnessing the methane gas were already set. What it did do was suggest a

9. AERIAL OF FRESH KILLS PARK WITH MEMORIAL, REN-
DERING, FRESH KILLS LANDFILL, STATEN ISLAND, 2001,
FIELD OPERATIONS

series of phases, from seeding, getting going on restoring habitat and bringing in people to the site right away; to infrastructure, the building of new paths and services needed to occupy the site; to programming, when all the functions of, for example, extreme sports, bike, horse, and pedestrian trails, as well as the full range of open spaces are established; to adaptation, when new programs and connections are introduced (fig. 8). Throughout this process, Corner and his colleagues kept their focus on relatively modest interventions that could have enormous impact, with a design strategy of lines, surfaces, and clusters that will both stimulate the diversity of a hardy ecosystem and at the same time be legible as conscious design decisions.

They also presented a preliminary concept of a design for a memorial for the victims of the World Trade Center attack, a simple ramp to the top of the mound in the section of the landfill where the debris was brought (fig. 9). The perspective from that manmade hill offers a somber counterpoint to the almost giddy sense of a city that cannot stop looking at itself, a sense typified by the new waterfront along the Thames, for example. Yet the ramp is also more than a memorial. Oriented as it is to Lower Manhattan, it is a poignant reminder of the interrelationships of a dynamic water-front metropolis in which natural and human systems, as much as different political entities, have an inescapable dialogue. It will also be a vantage point from which to see the new Staten Island "emerald," if the plan unfolds as anticipated. The reinvention of Fresh Kills and the process by which it may well achieve its new life—from the competition through construction and habitat restoration—is of great import well beyond St. George, as New York, and especially Lower Manhattan, seeks to reconstitute its identity.

TOWARD A NEW APPROACH AT GROUND ZERO

In November 2001, New York's Governor Pataki announced the establishment of the Lower Manhattan Development Corporation (LMDC), with John C. Whitehead, the retired chairman of Goldman Sachs, the redoubtable downtown-based investment management company, appointed as chairman. Eleven members joined the board, appointed by the governor and the mayor, ranging from the private sector entrepreneur Roland Betts, one of the developers of Chelsea Piers, to Lew Eisenberg, the retiring chairman of the Port Authority of New York and New Jersey, to Madelyn Wils, the volunteer chair of Community Board 1, which includes Lower Manhattan in its purview. In 2002, five new members were added, including architect Billie Tsien. This is the type of state authority, with a combination of state and city appointments, that has been effective in the design and development of Hudson River Park, Queens West, and, right next to the World Trade Center site, Battery Park City.

The domain of the corporation is all of Lower Manhattan below Houston Street, from SoHo and the Lower East Side down to the Battery, but its focus is the World Trade Center site and its immediate surroundings. According to Chairman Whitehead, all decisions about what happens on the site will have to be approved by his board, which has $2 billion from the federal government assigned directly to its coffers. The LMDC can truly plan, although by April 2002 it was clear that the Port Authority intends to be a more than equal partner in the planning and development process. However, the bistate Port Authority, which owns the land, and Larry Silverstein, the private developer who leased the towers, as well as New York City's armature of economic development and planning corporations and agencies, will play a significant role in the reshaping of the sixteen-acre parcel, as may an array of civic groups that have been proactive in establishing design principles for the site.

In the first months after the attack, few expected the clean-up of the site to be done before 2003, yet through round-the-clock shifts and a sense of mission, it has taken less than half that time, and many expect construction, not only of the temporary solution for the PATH train from New Jersey, but of buildings, to begin even before the end of 2002. The time to ponder what would be the best solution, to find the program for the site, to envision it as a paradigm of public life or private enterprise, for charrettes, and for international competitions will be brief if it exists at all. So, whether the LMDC, the Port Authority, the city, and civic groups work together or apart, there will be a plan by the end of 2002, and it will have consequences for New York's identity as a waterfront metropolis.

The rush is driven by many things—in no small part because New York, having lost a hundred thousand jobs and facing a deficit of almost $5 billion in 2002 (and additional multibillion deficits in the years ahead), has an absolutely urgent need to declare that it is back, ready for a new surge of jobs, ready to reclaim downtown as one of the key capitals of the world economy. One of the ways it can do this is by rapidly realigning and reidentifying its connections to the waterfront and the rest of the city. The World Trade Center site, which is technically not on the waterfront, is nonetheless only a thousand feet from the Hudson. The site is intimately connected to the waterfront by the center's history—its fill now the ground for the Hudson-bound Battery Park City; its location straddling what had been the city's historic western shore at Greenwich Street before the nineteenth century; its builder, the Port Authority; its role as the harbor's skyline icon; and its now obliterated observation deck, where a vision of all the bays and rivers of the Hudson-Raritan Estuary opened up to a visitor.

Yet it is the literal connections to and beyond the waterfront that the site's multiple stewards are in a rush to revise. At the beginning of 2002, the connections had an aura of tragedy or at least inconven-

ience. There were the trucks rumbling to Pier 25 just north of Battery Park City, where the two-hundred-foot-tall cranes off-loaded their cargoes of twisted steel to barges that the tugs pulled and pushed to Fresh Kills. The Port Authority was the first to announce rebuilding plans, first for a half-billion-dollar plan to restore temporary transit service, balancing the expenditures between the PATH's Exchange Place stops in Jersey City and Ground Zero, and then, in early 2002, announcing its long-term plan for connecting the PATH far deeper into downtown Manhattan.[24] The Port Authority made clear that it had no intention of waiting—its long-term plan was, in fact, exactly about connecting the site to the waterfront. In the new configuration, the PATH trains would go all the way to Broadway, the extreme eastern edge of the World Trade Center site, to make their turn around back to New Jersey, allowing for platforms that connect on the east to Fulton Street and a newly configured transit hub there, halfway across the island. In the other direction, they would connect an underground concourse all the way to the Winter Garden at the heart of Battery Park City's waterfront. The 2,500-foot link would be a moving sidewalk, capitalizing on the Port Authority's expertise in airport design.

For urban designers, the Port Authority's proposal is both ingenious and frustrating. Ingenious, because it could work, both in the sense that it would move people from the waterfront to the heart of Lower Manhattan and back, and in the sense that—because of its commitment to being below grade—it could be

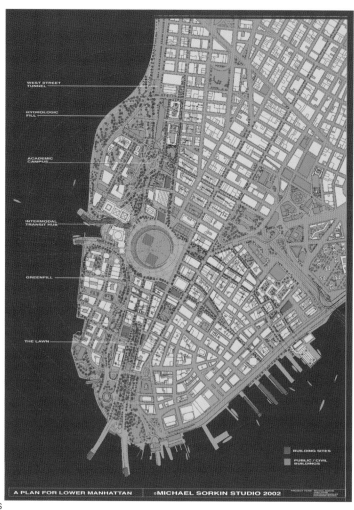

WEST STREET
TUNNEL

HYDROLOGIC
FILL

ACADEMIC
CAMPUS

INTERMODAL
TRANSIT HUB

GREENFILL

THE LAWN

BUILDING SITES

PUBLIC / CIVIL
BUILDINGS

A PLAN FOR LOWER MANHATTAN   ©MICHAEL SORKIN STUDIO 2002

10. A PLAN FOR LOWER MANHATTAN, FORMER WORLD TRADE CENTER SITE, MICHAEL SORKIN STUDIO, 2002

planned, designed, and built whatever the private and public plans for the ground above. It is frustrating, however, in that the idea of a 2,500-foot-long moving sidewalk could have a certain "infrastructural romance" to it, the greatest fear is that, like the drab shopping concourses that met the PATH's arrival beneath the twin towers, it could drain the city above of the kind of animation that even simple commuting brings and could be an excuse not to make the kinds of visual and physical connections that many believe need to be made aboveground.

For all the drama of the Winter Garden at the heart of Battery Park City's waterfront, it never realized its potential as an urban place because its approach from the World Trade Center across the West Side Highway through the North Bridge was too obtuse. The Winter Garden belongs at the end of a generous street or pedestrian way, not a sealed bridge with no clear connection to the plaza or buildings of whatever replaces the World Trade Center on the east side of the highway. There is no need to rebuild the entire grid of the streets that predated the building of the twin towers, yet opening up a few key axes that the 1960s superblock shut off would make the city's relationship to the waterfront far more open and experientially rewarding. In brief, the underground concourse needs to be matched by one aboveground, in which Fulton Street, which is the route to South Street Seaport on the East River, could also be the route to the Winter Garden and the Hudson River at its feet on the west.[25] It is not as elegant a diagram as it could be—Dey Street has

the better east-west axis with the Winter Garden, but it only runs one block from Broadway to Church Street, not east to the East River.

Most important, as is often the case with waterfronts, will be how the section is resolved—whether the high plinth of the World Trade Center is rebuilt, whether West Street is depressed into a tunnel or simply bridged over by large tubes as it was, how people will get up from Battery Park City to the reconstructed site, and how people will get down to the waterfront. The grade change will be there one way or another—Broadway is more than thirty feet up from the waterfront—yet how it is accommodated is the design challenge, one that has to be resolved with the full panoply of priorities for access and resources. The "great wall" of Battery Park City along West Street needs to be modulated, whether or not it is entered at the thirty-foot level. However it is worked out, and whatever the conceptual or fiscal pleasures of the superblock that was, cities need to breathe, and part of that respiration is letting their topographical identity—as a peninsula, in Lower Manhattan's case—be legible, an experience that even a resident or worker or tourist can have at the center, not just the edges, of the island. Unlike most massive urban design plans, proposals for the World Trade Center site have to envision a vital community while memorializing September 11. The resolutely visionary Michael Sorkin Studio produced a Plan for Lower Manhattan in early 2002, insisting that both extremes were possible (fig. 10). There could be an aggressively renewed city, with sweeping piers out to the harbor, a new more ecologically functional edge north of Battery Park City, and a new education center, while at the same time the design surrounded the sixteen-acre site with a berm, forever preserving it as a memorial. Sorkin's vision is unlikely to prevail, but it is a fierce reminder, not only for Lower Manhattan, of how far the design of a thriving waterfront metropolis can be from standard practice.

The specifics of what should be built on the World Trade Center site—be it all memorial, all commercial, a mixture, a significant cultural institution—belong to another narrative. Everyone wants an exceptional place, only no one is quite sure what that should mean. If the high-rises of the World Financial Center did not cut it off, one could argue that a strategy for keeping open views of the waterfront would be called for, but that is not an option, at least not below the twentieth floor of whatever is built here. All the talk of skyscrapers just as high as the twin towers (to show defiance) and a hole in the ground (to show profound loss) seems beside the point. What there needs to be is the constituent pieces of a vibrant city, either through formulas we already know, or new ones investigated by visionary politicians, designers, planners, engineers, ecologists, and others. In early 2002, the site was, as huge open expanses in the midst of the city often are, an awesome vision, six-teen acres that could be filled with nothing or almost anything. Downtown does need new icons, visible from the water and the waterfront, but there are many places to build and rebuild them— the World Trade Center will thrive or wither as a place in the city not based on exactly what transgresses there, but on that program's connections to the rest of downtown Manhattan, the harbor, and the city beyond.

CONNECTING TO THE WATERFRONT

Downtown's most vital connections, more often than not, are tied to its location near the waterfront. Battery Park City, of all the neighborhoods in New York, is probably closer to the spirit of the "lifescape" Field Operations proposes for Staten Island than any other. It has open space, art, native ecologies (albeit on constructed land), memorials, education centers (both schools and museums), boating, and even playing fields. The esplanade has proved a durable spine, and the district, often condemned for being cut off from the city, has, at a time when it truly was isolated by streets and transit thrown into confusion by the attack, shown its own astonishing durability as an integral part of Lower Manhattan.

The growth and densification of Battery Park City throughout the late 1990s and early 2000s has been characterized by a new gen-

eration of building: there is a tauter New York idiom, still in brick, still arduously contextual, yet now in the north end with a more industrial esthetic (with design guidelines drafted by Ralph Lerner Architect in 1994, updated by Hanrahan and Meyers in 2000), and in the south, there are new additions to its cultural and commercial district, including the crisp Ritz-Carlton Hotel and condominium tower designed by Gary Edward Handel and Associates and the Polshek Partnership, which opened at the end of 2001 (and which will have the Skyscraper Museum at its base designed by Skidmore, Owings & Merrill by 2003). The hexagonal Museum of the Jewish Experience, by Kevin Roche John Dinkeloo Architects, is expanding. At the North Cove, the Port Authority's own architects designed the handsome 160-by-200-foot floating pavilion for the expanding ferry service, with its 2003 scheduled opening pending.

Here at the edge of downtown New York—just west of the dense canyons of the financial district—New York had already begun to stake its claim as a twenty-first-century "garden city" in the early 1980s. It is a mistake to see Battery Park City's lifestyle as coming from an exclusively high-income mindset. From Harlem to Port Morris in the Bronx to Flushing, Queens, and the Gowanus Canal and Sunset Park in Brooklyn, populations across a full range of financial resources and heritages have come to expect at least the rudiments of the lifestyle that Battery Park City represents and that

Field Operations, with such unabashed marketing glossiness, proposes for Fresh Kills on Staten Island. It is up to

II. WHITEHALL FERRY TERMINAL AND PETER MINUIT PLAZA, SECTION, LOWER MANHATTAN, OPENING 2004, FREDERIC SCHWARTZ ARCHITECTS

Lower Manhattan, the iconic center of New York—a position for which it has paid a terrible price, but one that it cannot elide—to continue to be a leader in this transformation. Done right, it is not about prettifying and stultifying the edge, but about giving it back the complexity, both natural and cultural, it had more than a century ago when Melville took in the view, and doing it in a contemporary way.

Downtown has to take on major building initiatives, especially for essential public projects like the new Staten Island Ferry terminal. The most important waterborne transit system in America, its tens of thousands of daily passengers deserve a decent arrival, one that can also become part of the city's waterfront life. Frederic Schwartz has led a team that includes a full range of experts who are completing the design and realization of the Whitehall Ferry Terminal for the city's EDC and Department of Transportation (fig. II).[26] The unhappy process of rejecting the original design is long over, but every step of this enormously complicated project remains arduous. Schwartz has spoken of the "complex tangle of streets, traffic islands, buses, subways where sixty thousand people a day pass through. Underneath...there was almost no place to put a foundation."[27] Schwartz, at a panel on waterfront design, gave a dramatic reading of the more than forty agencies that had to approve the design for a bus turnaround on the terminal's plaza to underline the political and technical difficulty of the project.[28]

Nonetheless, he was able to imbue the plan with an "organic" energy and make a lucid and efficient section, orthogonal with the exception of the long sweep of diagonal roof rising toward the city; the challenge of the project is transparent yet resolutely resolved, in spite of the subway and roadway tunnels running below. The team has pulled off a lofty waiting room, as well as adding a viewing deck, five stories above water level, offering the best public views of the waterfront until the day that someone builds a higher observation deck downtown. Schwartz's team has designed what will be one of the most significant pieces of new architecture on the waterfront. It will not shout out media, or clock, or icon, but it will be a consummately modern building, completed in a process that requires two of the three slips of the existing terminal to remain running throughout construction and not interfering with the subway service a few feet away. Discretion may, in the end, be the better part of valor, and it may be that Schwartz, in an extremely difficult political and technical climate, will prove to be the terminal's Yoshio Taniguchi: New York wanted a well-designed ferry terminal, only subtly iconic, just as the Museum of Modern Art in Midtown chose the architect whose design would stay modern through decades of architectural fashion.

12. UPPER NEW YORK BAY FROM 2 WORLD TRADE CENTER, 2001

GOVERNORS ISLAND

The biggest waterfront opportunity for downtown Manhattan and the harbor, however, is Governors Island, which was connected to the ferry slips next door to the Whitehall terminal for decades (fig. 12). In 1996, soon after the U.S. Coast Guard announced that it was leaving the island it had taken over from the U.S. Army in 1966, Van Alen Institute sponsored an ideas competition, Public Property, prepared with urban designer and critic Andrea Kahn. The entries, before the official studies, before the Draft Environmental Impact Statements, were rich in ideas, including a finalist entry by Peter Hau, a graduate student in landscape architecture, who looked at the whole of New York and declared that this was the place for "Open Narratives," where a variety of environmental "cleansing" operations would enrich the island's natural ecology while creating

a compelling place for locals and tourists. Other entries proposed world's fairs, cemeteries, conference centers, sports centers for the Olympics, and, in fact, fully worked-out housing schemes that included an esplanade ringing the edge of the island, guaranteeing public access to the waterfront.

The official, yet still not executed or even finally approved, plan that emerged for the 172-acre island, a seven-minute ferry ride from Manhattan, came from a long process of public and private studies, charrettes, and planning efforts, spearheaded by the Regional Plan Association and a coalition of civic groups. It was announced in January 2000 by Governor Pataki and Mayor Giuliani. It called for $370 million in improvements for the island, with a hotel and conference center as its profit-making centerpiece as well as a fifty-acre park at its southern end, where most of the existing post–World War II structures would be demolished and replaced by a family entertainment center with a historical theme. Ferries would not come to the north end of the island as they had for generations, but to the middle of the island on its eastern shore, on Buttermilk Channel across from Brooklyn. New York University, which had been searching for playing fields for a decade, tentatively planned for sports facilities on the island. In the calculation of the time, a private investor was expected to put up $300 million, while the public sector put up $70 million, of which $40 million would be recouped in ground leases.

By the beginning of 2001, there had been less activity than anticipated. The structure for change, the Governors Island Redevelopment Corporation, a subsidiary of New York State's Empire State Development Corporation, was set up but could not move forward because the political agreement between the city and state, as well as the federal government, never gelled. Bill Clinton, in his last, pardon-crazed days as president, managed to get a National Monument designation for the twenty most historic acres (including Fort Jay and Castle Williams, both completed in the first two decades of the nineteenth century). Yet no one managed to confirm that the federal government, despite President Clinton's promise to Senator Daniel Moynihan five years earlier, would sell the island to the state for $1. Without the no-cost transfer, there was little hope of carrying out the plan.

By early 2002, the civic groups that had planned a "flotilla" in the harbor to take back Governors Island on September 16, 2001, had reorganized to consider their options. They recognized that while there was still hope for a no-cost transfer, especially if the city and state accepted some kind of binding restrictions to assure the federal government that they were not planning a bait-and-switch—promising a heritage-focused, low-intensity use for the island, then selling to the highest bidder—there was much less hope for a private investor coming forward with $300 million than before the creeping recession and the September catastrophe. Yet in its February 2002 letter to Mayor Bloomberg, the coalition held not only to planning principles but to design principles: there should be a public park of

no fewer than forty-six acres; a fifty-foot-wide perimeter esplanade; and no building higher than the fifty-foot-high cornice of Building 400, the colossal barracks that belt the island between its northern and southern halves. As for program, the coalition held to its position against housing, which it considers impossible without the construction of a bridge—one of the reasons that NYC2012 did not propose the island as the site for the Olympic Village.

The coalition's principles and guidelines for Governors Island are not radical in their conception of the future of public life, and they lack the fearlessness—even recklessness—of some suggestions made in the ideas competition and through the discussion of the island over the past seven years. They do, however, lay down the parameters of what could be incorporated in a "lifescape" vision as richly varied as the one proposed by Field Operations for Fresh Kills and Staten Island or as intense in design as Weiss/Manfredi's concept design for the waterfront sculpture park. Within the boundaries of the coalition's guidelines, an astonishing array of design and development proposals could be entertained, and will be, if the public sector can convince the federal government, the city, and the state to cooperate. In April 2002, Mayor Bloomberg announced his vision for the island: a new campus for the City University of New York, a use he declared incompatible with proposals for a 2,000-foot-high broadcast tower designed by Kohn Pedersen Fox, also suggested for the island. Whether either or both can succeed as strategies for public life remains to be seen.[29]

A NEW ETHIC FOR THE WATERFRONT

Evidence of the potential to join historic properties to contemporary design is embodied in a scheme by Thomas Phifer and Partners for a new performing arts center rising from the center of Castle Clinton in Battery Park, the round battery that matches Castle William on Governors Island. The proposal, developed well before September 11 for the Battery Conservancy and its president, Warrie Price, is a stroke of programming genius. Castle Clinton is among the least pure historic sites in the nation, given that it has gone through adaptive reuses over two centuries, including concert hall, immigration processing center, and aquarium, to its current, rather shabbily performed function as a place to buy tickets for the Liberty and Ellis Island ferries, with a poorly organized exhibition on the Battery itself. Lower Manhattan, which has been steadily moving

past its singular identity as the third largest central business district in America (after Midtown Manhattan and Chicago), has yet to have a major performance space.

Phifer and his collaborators—including the most experienced practitioners of adaptive reuse of waterfront buildings in New York, Beyer Blinder Belle, as well as the engineers of Arup—produced a design so lithe it does not touch the historic fabric (fig. 13). Slim columns reach down to bedrock to support a glass-and-steel platform, hovering above the center of the fort. Visitors would enter from the north and see a glazed elevator, which they could take to the performance level, rising slightly above the fort's thick walls. A balcony rings the project, offering a panorama of the harbor that is a significant improvement over the painted vistas in the current Battery visitors' center. The design offers a windscreen but no roof, allowing for performances with the inimitable experience of the harbor, yet with enough protection to make live events possible from late spring through summer and partway into the fall. The team has worked out a system of glazing and vents typical of the ingenuity of environmental engineering by Arup, with the talents of one of New York's most gifted designers of glass for architectural and art installations, James Carpenter.

It is exactly the type of project that needs to happen on the waterfront. Its programming, especially after September 11, is far more than a touristic distraction but rather part of a potential cultural rebirth of the harbor, in which historic properties are

13. PERFORMANCE SPACE AND VIEWING DECK, CASTLE CLINTON NATIONAL MONUMENT, RENDERING, THE BATTERY CONSERVANCY PROPOSAL, THOMAS PHIFER AND PARTNERS, BEYER BLINDER BELLE, ARUP, AND JAMES CARPENTER DESIGN

seen as generators of the new, not inhibitors of it. In its design and, hopefully, its realization, Phifer's scheme has the mixture of style and technological complexity that made the waterfront fascinating generations ago. In its responsiveness to its site and its ecological ramifications, in its connection to the hunger for the water view that has always been part of the best waterfront architecture, this is a project that deserves public support.

The National Park Service, which has jurisdiction over Castle Clinton National Monument, is moving with extreme, perhaps excessive, caution on the project, given its placement of a new building within the frame of a historical property. Yet there is evidence that the Park Service, and the initiating partner—now renamed the Battery Conservancy, without "historic"—and the whole range of partners including the Downtown Alliance and New York City's Economic Development Corporation and Department of Parks and Recreation, realize that this is an opportunity, especially at this moment in New York, to prove how history can be made, not just stabilized. Battery Park was thrown into service after September 11, dutifully absorbing the emergency construction of a large new temporary ferry terminal and accommodating security checks for the tourists boarding the Liberty and Ellis Island ferries, disrupting the path of the promenades so lovingly rebuilt by the Conservancy. Such contemporary history cannot be avoided, only given more impetus to ensure a more celebratory, constructive future, a future that would be symbolized by an iconic perform-

ance space and viewing platform at the most prominent waterfront site in Lower Manhattan.

Downtown New York should be the leader, not the follower, in moving past caution to action for the renewal of the city as a dynamic waterfront metropolis. As London architect Will Alsop said, "People are mad," they are ready for designs that challenge their expectations, they do not need to be protected by planners and institutions. If there was ever an opening for design that tested the waters of the public's appetite for innovation, it is now. Caution at the heart of New York's waterfront, at the tip of Manhattan, where the city began and its newest citizens once arrived, could inhibit the potential of the city's edge from Fresh Kills to the Bronx River to the Gowanus Canal to Sunset Park.

This is not an era for conservative design or programs. New York needs to embrace an ethic of waterfront design. It already has waterfront design guidelines, with sensible attitudes and subtle strategies toward height, bulk, and public access. The rules can be stretched without breaking the back of the plan: just as in the design principles for Governors Island, to reject guidelines outright misses the point. Even the most creative design is deeply anchored in restrictions, and at the waterfront they are legion.

Yet what is missing is an ethic shared, or shared enough, among designers, clients, and the public. There needs to be an ethic that respects the demands of civic infrastructure and the opportunity to create icons that work, whether that work involves art, power, waste, or sports. There needs to be an ethic that respects not only the flowing river of politics and debate but also the artifacts, the projects at the water's edge: new buildings, new parks, new public spaces are valuable and possible.

Every mile of the waterfront need not be the site for iconic buildings, or art, or even perfectly designed parks. The waterfront has traditionally provided an escape from the precious and the overdone, and there is a perpetual need to rediscover the uncharted elegance of architecture built to solve a problem as much as to express an idea, and in so doing, express the most interesting idea of all—that this life's material challenges can inspire our greatest art. An ethic for waterfront design has to recognize that the most important transformations of this constructed landscape have been enormous industrial undertakings, with enormous returns. Water treatment plants, parks, and iconic projects are equal in scope, and they need an ethic that can comprehend their large scale and their potential for public good. The city must encourage projects at this scale, because with the hundreds of brownfield sites, the hundreds of acres still nursing their long industrial hangover, the miles of still decayed waterfronts, it has to look for expansive projects even as it must value the incidental and the temporary.

Other cities move forward, roughed up and reconfigured by public debate though they may be. Amsterdam only built its icons of modernity on the harbor after years of debate, with struggles regarding the heritage of the harbor led by groups determined to preserve that city's magnificent stock of warehouses and other industrial buildings, and it benefited from the dynamic compromise that resulted. London is noisy with public debate on the merits of new designs, but the hue and cry does not stop inspiring new projects from going forward. In New York, too, passion for the fresh extends far beyond the boundaries of design-oriented galleries and studios, into the public agencies, into the private sector, and into communities. In New York's vivid culture of exchange, the demand for new design is louder, more diverse, and more aware of possibilities than it has ever been. With a new ethic, the city will meet the evolving demands for experience, transcendence, and service that Melville recognized at the Battery 150 years ago, and site New York's waterfront where it belongs, in the history of the future.

NOTES

1. Raymond W. Gastil, "Design and the Ecology of Public Life," program for the 2001 Van Alen Institute Dinkeloo Fellowship, Van Alen Institute with the American Academy in Rome, New York, December 2000.

2. *Webster's New Collegiate Dictionary* (Springfield, Mass.: G. & C. Merriam Company, 1973).

3. Kathy Poole, "*Civitas Oecologie*: Infrastructure in the Ecological City," *Harvard Architecture Review* (New York: Princeton Architectural Press, 1998): 127.

4. Robert A. M. Stern, Gregory Gilmartin, and Thomas Mellins, *New York 1930: Architecture and Urbanism Between the Two World Wars* (New York: Rizzoli, 1987), 676–81.

5. *New York Times*, 9 September 1931, cited in Stern et al., *New York 1930*, 26.

6. Ken Philmus, quoted in Hendrik Hertzberg, "Gorgeous George," *The New Yorker*, 26 March 2001, 77.

7. Nick Barley, ed., *Breathing Cities: The Architecture of Movement* (Basel: Birkhäuser, 2000), 5–6.

8. Amanda Sachs, proposal and portfolio, Van Alen Institute Dinkeloo Fellowship, 2001. Sachs ultimately focused her research on the Piazza di San Cosimato in the Trastevere district.

9. Keller Easterling, Waterfront Workshop, Van Alen Institute, and Miriam Gusevich, roundtable comments, July 1997.

10. Community Board 4 statement, quoted in Nathaniel H. Brooks, "NY Jets Stadium," *Architecture+Water: Van Alen Report* 9 (May 2001): 6.

11. "NYC2012: The Plan for a New York Olympic Games" (New York: NYC2012, 2001), 21, illustrates this relationship.

12. Michael Bloomberg, "State of the City" address, Web site, www.nyc.gov, 30 January 2002.

13. Alexander Garvin, interview by author, 6 March 2001.

14. See Casey Jones, Design Trust fellow, and Joshua David, writer, *Reclaiming the High Line* (New York: Design Trust for Public Space with Friends of the High Line, 2002), 28. The report envisions "interconnectivity" for the High Line on the 30th Street Rail Yards site.

15. Susan Gilmore, "Engineers to State: Viaduct Needs to Go," *Seattle Times*, Web site, www.seattletimes.com, 28 June 2001.

16. John King, *Renewing, Rebuilding, Remembering*, exhib. text (New York: Van Alen Institute, February–May 2002).

17. Weiss/Manfredi, partnership statement (2001).

18. Benjamin Miller, "The Folly of Closing Fresh Kills: City Is Loading Trash on a Big Barge to Nowhere," *New York Daily News*, 5 January 2001, 39.

19. Regarding Handel's work, see Jim Carlton, "Where Trash Reigned, Trees Sprout," *Wall Street Journal*, 23 January 2002, B1. This article was published only weeks after the announcement of the Landfill to Landscape competition finalists, yet it neglected to mention the competition.

20. Jim O'Grady, "From Dumping Ground to Destination: Staten Island Makes a Bid to Shed Its Outcast Image," *New York Times*, 16 May 1999, City 1.

21. Field Operations, "Landfill to Landscape" entry description, Web site, www.nyc.gov.

22. Laurie Kerr, "Tying Down Gulliver, The Fresh Kills Design Competition," *Oculus* (March/April 2002): 8–9.

23. Kevin Pratt, "Green Acres: The Finalists in the Fresh Kills Design Competition Envision an Urban Paradise atop an Old Dump," *Time Out New York*, 17 January 2002, 43.

24. Randy Kennedy, "Trans Plan Would Connect Dots Downtown," *New York Times*, 23 January 2002, A1.

25. This analysis is the author's, yet it is indebted to participation in the New York New Visions Coalition and to the coalition's "Initial Recommendations for the Rebuilding of Lower Manhattan," working draft (February 2002). See illustration "Connections at the World Trade Center Site," 34.

26. The Whitehall Ferry Terminal (Manhattan's Staten Island Ferry Terminal) and Peter Minuit Plaza (and park) reflects more than a decade of design work, including the first generation of effort by Venturi Scott Brown and Associates, and the parallel work from the start by Frederic Schwartz Architects, where project directors have included Paul Cali, Ronald Evitts, John Adams, and Felicity Beck. Principal consultants include TAMS (associated architects), Robert Silman Associates (structural engineers), and Flack+Kurtz (mechanical, electric, and plumbing).

27. Frederic Schwartz, "New York City on the Verge: New Design for the Waterfront," forum cosponsored by Van Alen Institute and Parsons School of Design Department of Architecture, 6 September 2001, quoted in Jayne Merkel, "At the Water's Edge," *Oculus* (November 2001): 10–11.

28. Schwartz, "New York City on the Verge," author's notes.

29. Michael Cooper and Karen W. Arenson, "CUNY Plans Visions High, Details Few," *New York Times*, 3 April 2002, B1; Jayson Blair, "Broadcast Tower Urged for Governors Island," *New York Times*, 1 May 2002, C18.

NORTH FROM THE MORRIS CANAL, JERSEY CITY, TO THE GEORGE WASHINGTON BRIDGE

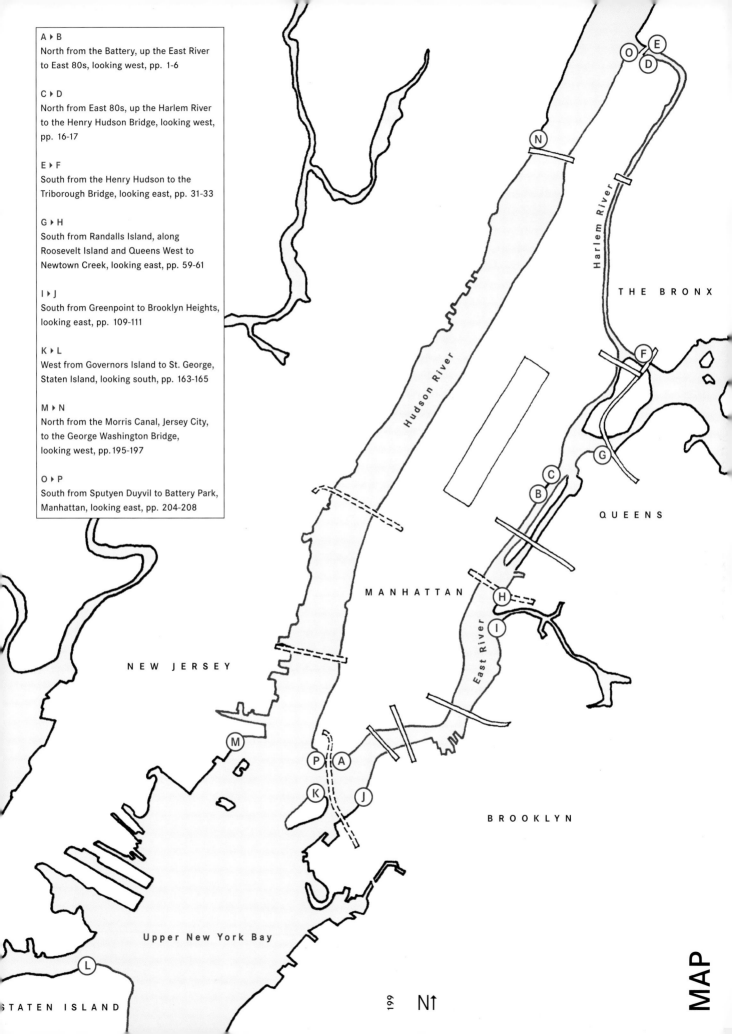

THE BRONX

Harlem River

QUEENS

Hudson River

MANHATTAN

East River

NEW JERSEY

BROOKLYN

Upper New York Bay

STATEN ISLAND

MAP

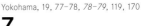

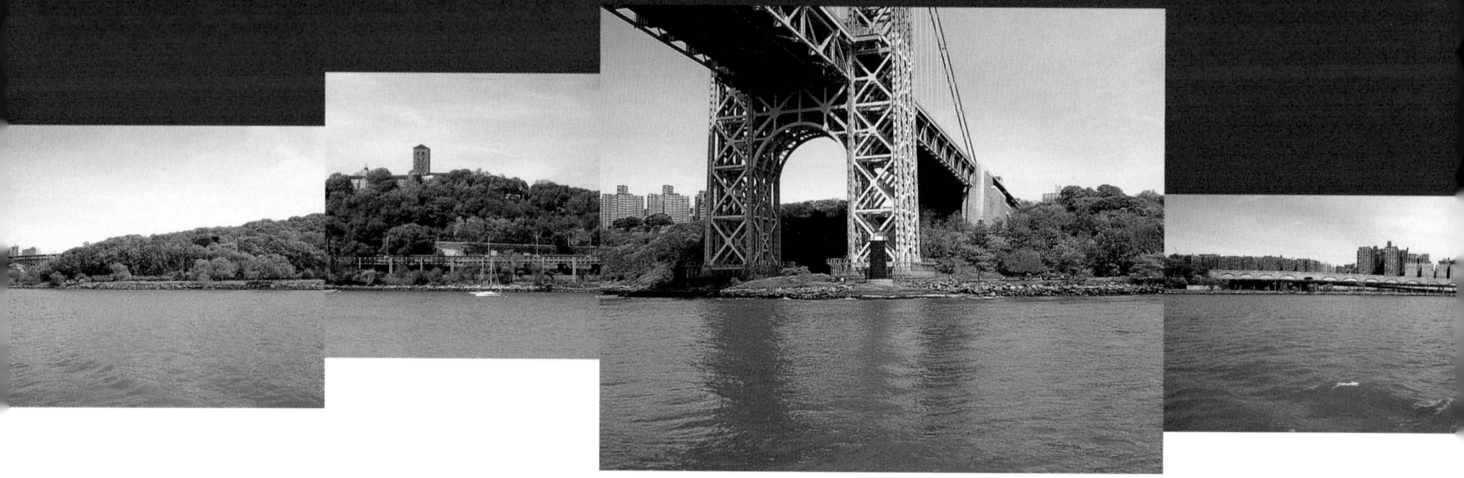